CHICANO NATIONS

CHICANO NATIONS

The Hemispheric Origins of Mexican American Literature

MARISSA K. LÓPEZ

New York University Press

NEW YORK AND LONDON

NEW YORK UNIVERSITY PRESS
New York and London
www.nyupress.org

LIBRARY OF CONGRESS CATALOGING-IN-PUBLICATION DATA
López, Marissa K.
  Chicano nations : the hemispheric origins of Mexican American literature /
Marissa K. López.
    p. cm.
  Includes bibliographical references and index.
  ISBN 978-0-8147-5261-6 (cloth : acid-free paper)
  ISBN 978-0-8147-5262-3 (pbk. : acid-free paper)
  ISBN 978-0-8147-5263-0 (e-book)
  ISBN 978-0-8147-5329-3 (e-book)
  1. American literature—Mexican American authors—History and criticism.
2. Mexican Americans—Intellectual life.   3. Mexican Americans in
literature.   I. Title.
  PS153.M4L66   2011
  810.9'86872073—dc22

                                                            2011015694

References to Internet websites (URLs) were accurate at the time of writing.
Neither the author nor New York University Press is responsible for URLs that
may have expired or changed since the manuscript was prepared.

New York University Press books are printed on acid-free paper, and their
binding materials are chosen for strength and durability. We strive to use
environmentally responsible suppliers and materials to the greatest extent
possible in publishing our books.

Manufactured in the United States of America

c 10 9 8 7 6 5 4 3 2 1
p 10 9 8 7 6 5 4 3 2 1

THE
AMERICAN
LITERATURES
INITIATIVE

A book in the American Literatures Initiative (ALI), a collaborative
publishing project of NYU Press, Fordham University Press, Rutgers
University Press, Temple University Press, and the University of Virginia
Press. The Initiative is supported by The Andrew W. Mellon Foundation.
For more information, please visit www.americanliteratures.org.

pa' mis hijos

Contents

Acknowledgments

In a 1976 interview, the poet Alurista, in a moment of uncharacteristic modesty, told Joe Torres that even though "we pose as authors, as writers, none of us is really the absolute, total creator of any of these pieces. I can't say that I wrote all this . . . these words and these images come from people . . . many of the words that we record as ours really come from other people." I must confess that although I understand what he was saying, Alurista's comments never *really* resonated with me until I wrote this book. Many people and institutions helped me on my way by inspiring me, feeding me, and shaping my thinking. Though words can never fully express my gratitude, I nevertheless give thanks here, first, to those who fed me. The research for this book was funded by fellowships from the Bancroft Library at the University of California, Berkeley; the University of California's Institute for Mexico and the United States; the Woodrow Wilson Foundation; the National Endowment for the Humanities; and the University of California, Los Angeles. Jacques Lezra taught me how to be a good reader, and Marcial González helped me become a responsible and committed analyzer of texts. José David Saldívar and Richard Candida Smith showed me how to bring Chicana/o studies methodologies to the nineteenth century and be gracious while doing so. I have had the good fortune to be surrounded by incredibly supportive colleagues at UCLA including, especially, Ali Behdad, Chris Chism, Liz DeLoughrey, Matthew Fisher, Alicia Gaspar de Alba, Jonathan Grossman, Sarah Kareem, Eleanor Kaufman, Rachel Lee, Chris

Looby, Mark McGurl, Kathleen McHugh, Sianne Ngai, Chon Noriega, Barbara Packer, Rafael Pérez-Torres, Karen Rowe, Mark Selzer, Jenny Sharpe, and Richard Yarborough. Their insights, challenges, generosity, and sense of humor have been invaluable. The members of the Southern California Americanist Group guided this book along more than they'll ever know, especially Sharon Oster, who made me see the life in Chapter 4's skeleton, and Mike Szalay, who forced me to figure out how to explain why I wasn't a cultural nationalist. Thank you, Caroline Levander and Rachel Adams, for inviting me to New York and showing me the hemispheric potential of my work. María Cotera has believed in this project since it was little more than a twinkle in my eye. Thanks also to Jesse Alemán and José Aranda for reading chapter drafts and offering ideas and encouragement at crucial, early moments, and to Mary Pat Brady, who has mentored me through the book's final stages with more love and support than I ever knew existed in our profession. I could not have completed my archival research without the help of Teresa Salazar at the Bancroft Library and Carol Dodge at the Sonoma Barracks, y mil gracias a Tanya Bunson y Daisy Salazar for helping me wade through miles of archaic Spanish and bad handwriting. Thanks to my students at UCLA for keeping me on my toes. Sheri Englund is a miracle worker and helped this book be all that it could be, as did Eric Zinner, Ciara McLaughlin, my anonymous readers, and everyone at NYU Press. And finally, thanks to Mitchum, without whom, it may truly be said, I could not have written this book.

Introduction: *Nuevas Fronteras* / New Frontiers

> *Technically, I don't qualify as a Chicano. I wasn't born in East L.A. I wasn't born in de southwest U.S.A. I wasn't even born in Méjico. Does dis make me Hispanic? . . . Dese terms, Latino and Hispanic, are inaccurate because dey lump a whole lot of different people into one category. For example, a Mayan from Guatemala, an eSpaniard from eSpain and a Chicana/o who speaks no Spanish might all be described, in some circles, as Hispanic. And de term Latino could include people as different as right-wing Cubans living in Miami, exiled Salvadoran leftists, Mexican speakers of Nahuatl, Brazilian speakers of Portuguese, lunfardo-speaking Koreans in Buenos Aires, Nuyoricans (dat's a Puerto Rican who lives in New York) and den dere's de Uruguayans—I mean dey're practically European. . . . As for me, let's just say . . . I'm a pachuco.*
>
> —WIDELOAD MCKENNAH, *FRONTERAS AMERICANAS* (27)

Guillermo Verdecchia's 1993 play *Fronteras Americanas* alternates between two characters, Verdecchia and his alter ego, Facundo Morales Segundo, who prefers the "more Saxonical" name Wideload McKennah (24). In the first act, Wideload interrupts Verdecchia's learned disquisitions on Latin American history with satirical monologues about Latino stereotypes and "de Saxonian community" (40). As Verdecchia ponders his conflicted relationships with Canada and Argentina, where he was born, Wideload plays ethnographer to the exotic Mr. and Mrs. Smith and their children, Cindy and John, while earning his "doctorate in Chicana/o estudies" (35). Having arrived in Argentina by the end of the first act, Verdecchia returns "home" to Canada in the second, finding himself increasingly depressed and confused about the nature of home until he realizes, "I'm not in Canada; I'm not in Argentina. I'm on the Border. I am home" (74). Wideload, meanwhile, has traded his jester's persona for commentary "en serio" about how "we are re-drawing the map of America because economics, [he's] told, knows no borders" (76).

The character Verdecchia embraces his own inner borders and divisions as a defensive counter to the dehumanizing forces of globalization Wideload describes. The surprising turn in these not-so-novel ideas comes in linking them with Argentine-Canadian figures who cross *pachuco* cool with literary lions of the Southern Cone. Domingo Sarmiento's

Facundo (1845) is a classic of Argentine and Latin American literature. In it, Sarmiento tells the story of the *caudillo* Juan Facundo Quiroga and rails against the regime of Juan Manuel de Rosas, while developing a theory of Latin American culture and strongman rule. The *pachuco* is the iconic figure of resistance embodied in Mexican American youth culture of the 1940s, popularized in Luis Valdez's play *Zoot Suit* (1972) about the 1943 race riots in Los Angeles between Mexican and Anglo-Americans.

Besides reminding readers that *pachucos* wore their hair in a style referred to as the "Argentine duck-tail" (Sherrow 146), what can Verdecchia's bringing together of Facundo and *pachuco* cool tell us about *latinidad*, the hemisphere, and the future of Chicana/o literary studies? How does Facundo get to Toronto and what does it mean for him to be there? *Chicano Nations: The Hemispheric Origins of Mexican American Literature* takes up a similar set of questions. Before crossing an indeterminate border in *Fronteras Americanas*, the character Verdecchia tells the audience to set their watches to "border time" where "it is now Zero hour" (22). At the end of the play he asks the audience to reset their watches, informing them that they "still have time [to] go forwards. Towards the centre, towards the border" (78). *Chicano Nations* charts that centering journey and resets the literary, historical watch by pushing the boundaries of Chicana/o time and remapping Chicana/o space.

Chicano Nations tells a story about spatial thinking in the Americas. Here, I explore the confluence of space, race, and nation, as well as how the geopolitical divisions of the period immediately following the disintegration of the Spanish empire, the early nineteenth century, helped codify racial thinking in the Americas and create a de facto Latino collectivity in the United States. It is not, I argue, nostalgia for the putatively lost land of Aztlán, the imaginary homeland of the Aztecs, that grounds Chicana/o imaginings of the nation but a deeper, older, transamerican vision.[1] *Chicano Nations* aims to reclaim and reinsert this vision into discussions of the Chicana/o cultural imaginary.

I turn to the nation in order to flesh out a Chicana/o literary genealogy grounded in hemispheric and transnational debates. Since Napoleon's 1808 invasion of Spain, which precipitated Mexican and Latin American independence, Mexican American writing has been grappling with what the nation means, searching for a way to work around its imperial underpinnings and racial logic, increasingly so after the Mexican-American War (1846–48). Chicana/o literature, I contend, is characterized by a deep ambivalence about the nation running through a diverse body of works. My central project is to situate that ambivalence in the history of spatial debate in the Americas. In the chapters that follow, I focus on how American space is imagined in the wake of empire. I look at how that space changes over time and through debates about nation formation and Pan-Americanism in the hemisphere, and finally, I show Chicana/o nationalism to be part of this long, transamerican conversation.

Fronteras Americanas assumes that something called "America" or "the Americas" exists, that we can know it, understand it, and trace its genealogy. *Chicano Nations* builds on this assumption by asserting the Americas less as bounded space and more as an idea, or network, whose contours, meanings, and participants are constantly in flux. In *Chicano Nations* I emphasize process over product; I do not document the literature of the Americas so much as ask why the Americas exist, what "America" means at different points in time, how its shifting meanings inform ethnic and cultural identities in the United States, and finally, how understanding the motile terrains of space, place, and subjectivity might ground a vision of humanity's future.

Like Verdecchia, the primarily Mexican and Mexican American writers and intellectuals I turn to in these explorations have written about the racial dimensions of space; also like Verdecchia, they have articulated a transamerican imaginary that undermines a precise cultural nationalism and troubles their inclusion in Chicana/o literary history. The scope of their visions, however, as I will show in the following chapters, strengthens, bolsters, and expands *chicanismo* at the same time it poses serious challenges. While *Chicano Nations*' concerns are rooted in a particular, material, and geopolitical place, this project is also concerned with spatial imaginings and philosophies more abstractly. After all, if we ask, "What is America?" we have also to ask, "What is a nation? How does it create national space?" Even further: "What is space? How is it represented? How do we see and imagine ourselves in it?" These questions are at *Chicano Nations*' conceptual center.

Spatial Thinking

These spatial queries also have a very long, rich intellectual history in geography and the social sciences, with physical geographers searching for ever more precise means of measuring space and human geographers pondering its metaphysics. Both approaches have their limitations, of course. While they presuppose objective, spatial truths, empirical methods actually offer their own murky, subjective knowledge. Anne Godlewska has described the map, for example, as "part of an arsenal of coercive tools designed to reinforce particular aspects of the social structure" that reflect domestic and international conflict (21). Further, the impulse to define space precisely leads to spatial distortions like those resulting from the Mercator projection, which enlarges objects as their distance from the equator increases, making northern spaces such as Europe and the United States appear larger than they actually are (27). The drive toward spatial knowledge thus pushes us further from spatial truths, as Michael Goodchild admits in a discussion of recent developments in geographical information systems, which make representations of aggregate data possible. It is, however, increasingly difficult, says Goodchild, to represent data's complexity and uncertainty (80).

Human geographers, by contrast, eschew empiricism in favor of human experiences of place and space. In the late 1970s, geography experienced an urban, sociological turn during which the idea of space as relative and relational began to take hold (Hubbard, Kitchen, and Valentine 5). In *Social Justice and the City* (1973), for instance, David Harvey argues that a city's built infrastructure codifies class inequality, and Immanuel Wallerstein's work on the world system illuminates how geopolitical divisions enforce the global division of labor. The 1991 translation from French into English of Henri Lefebvre's *The Production of Space* brought his ideas squarely to the fore of Anglo-American criticism. There, Lefebvre argues that absolute space cannot exist since the instant of human-spatial interaction renders space relative and historical.

Modernity, Lefebvre writes, produces spaces with "specific characteristics: homogeneity-fragmentation-hierarchy" (*Key Writings* 210). Homogeneity facilitates surveillance and social control, but it produces a false unity because this homogeneous space is actually quite fragmented and parceled out among various owner-interests. These fragmented spaces—ghettos, commercial and residential zones, and so forth—are then arranged in a hierarchy of relationships to centers of production and civic life. "This space," Lefebvre observes, "exerts a curious logic . . . which hides real relationships and conflicts behind its homogeneity" while achieving a level of general abstraction affecting learning, culture, and social life (210).

Against these abstracting moves Lefebvre posits what Edward Soja refers to as a spatial "trialectics" in which space can be understood as perceived (through unreflective daily life), conceived (with maps and other tools of spatial abstraction), and lived (*Thirdspace* 61). Lived space enacts the emergence of *place* as a kind of space defined by conscious, social engagement. Yi Fu Tuan, whose work I take up explicitly in Chapter 6, builds on Lefebvre's spatial trialectics to further theorize *place* as made space, emphasizing that people live not within geometric planes but in a rich world of mutable meanings constructed from their daily, spatial engagements. Lefebvre sees place-making as a counter to the homogenizing forces of capital, though the precise relationship between the two processes remains under-theorized in his work, as he himself admits. "Could there not emerge," he asks, nevertheless, "through and against hierarchization, here and there, in architectural and planning terms, some thing that comes out of the existing mode of production, that is born from its contradictions by exposing them and not by covering them with a veil?" (212). Lived space, in other words, has the potential to work through capital's spatial contradictions and oppressions.

The idea of this potential informs my reading, in *Chicano Nations*, of the transamerican places imagined by the authors included herein as grounds for progressive social change. Their American imaginaries, I argue, offer the possibility of transcending the racial inconsistencies of the empirical nation-state. In this attention to space, place, and identity I follow in Mary Pat Brady's and Raúl Villa's footsteps who, in *Extinct Lands, Temporal Geographies* and *Barrio-Logos*, respectively, address human geography's lack of attention to race and sexuality by applying Lefebvre's and Soja's theories to Chicana/o negotiations of U.S. space and place. My contribution to this discussion is to use the long history of Chicana/o literature to move beyond the local spaces of *chicanismo* documented by Brady and Villa to show how the desire to create and contain Chicana/o spaces is part of a larger story about the partitioning of hemispheric space.

Beyond documenting a Chicana/o national imaginary, then, a fundamental task *Chicano Nations* takes up is constructing its genealogy, excavating its etymology, and exploring its meanings and contradictions. I ask how the contradictions of a Chicana/o national imaginary—like the spatial contradictions of capitalism Lefebvre notes—resonate with a larger network of geopolitical tensions glossed over by *el movimiento* (the Chicana/o civil rights movement of the 1960s and 1970s). My readings of relatively iconoclastic Chicana/o authors demonstrate the enduring globality of local consciousness and reveal the contradictions that emerge from a nation's desire to obfuscate the political, cultural, and historical reality of its global interconnection.

The Space of Chicana/o Nationalism

My decision to ground *chicanismo* in that larger, spatial story by looking at representations of the nation in Chicana/o literature from 1834 to 2008 is perhaps counterintuitive since Chicana/o nationalism is quite narrowly defined in Chicana/o cultural studies and "Chicana/o" is understood in historically specific terms. Chicana/o nationalism is often conceived as coalescing around the imagined space of Aztlán; it is also typically thought, following Américo Paredes in *With His Pistol in His Hand* (1958), to have its roots in the mid-nineteenth century, during the Southwest's violent transition from Mexican to U.S. rule. The following chapters will redraw that map, however, expand the historical and geographic scope of *chicanismo*, and make imaginary spaces real. Aztlán is part of a broad geographic and historical continuum, a vast network of transnational *latinidad*, within which, I argue, Chicana/o nationalism must be understood.

In the Chicana/o cultural imaginary, however, nationalism is difficult to separate from the homophobia and sexism of 1960s and 1970s Chicana/o politics, and it is further complicated when considering the feminist critique of nationalism, as well as immigration into the United States from Central and South America during the 1980s. Chicana/o nationalism is often understood as an ethnic nationalism that makes specious claims to Aztlán, grounding Chicana/o identity in an embrace of indigeneity, working-class roots, the myth of an Aztec heritage, and the patriarchal family. Political rhetoric surrounding Aztlán and Chicana/o nationalism in the 1960s and 1970s, such as "El Plan de Aztlán" formulated at the 1969 First National Chicana/o Youth Conference in Denver, was galvanizing.[2] The militant, masculine, and heteronormative identity it set forth, however, fractured under the pressure of internal feminist and queer critiques, diminishing its capacity as an organizing tool.[3]

Chicana/o nationalism of the 1960s and 1970s sought to reify Chicana/o identity in ways similar to the workings of most ethnic nationalist movements, as Étienne Balibar describes them in his essay "Racism and Nationalism." In Balibar's analysis, the objectification of such identities ignores the fact that they emerge over time. Ethnic and racial categories are neither monolithic nor objective, and their very subjectivity undermines an ethnic nationalist project, he argues. Chicana/o studies has made similar arguments, the most well-known appearing in Gloria Anzaldúa's groundbreaking work *Borderlands/La Frontera* (1987). Since the queer, feminist theoretical moment crystallized in Anzaldúa's work, invocations of the nation in Chicana/o literature are seen as reflecting one of two things: a militant, separatist politics or a disavowal of ethnic solidarity in favor of assimilation into U.S. culture. The productive and galvanizing force of the national idea has since, however, been dismissed, as Miguel López notes in *Chicano Timespace* (2001).[4]

Thus, the story of nationalism in Chicana/o cultural studies works as a progress narrative in which we move from patriarchal nationalism to an enlightened inter- or transnationalism in which Chicana/o subjectivities correlate to hybrid Chicana/o spaces, or border zones. *Chicano Nations* asks what happens to this story when we shift perspective and see Chicana/o nationalism developing in other times and other spaces. What happens when the space we want to identify as "Chicana/o" or "Mexican" or "Aztlán" emerges as transnational and multivalent, not newly so but historically and constitutively?

Thinking of globalization as a process beginning long before the 1947 international conference in Bretton Woods, New Hampshire, which established the World Bank and the International Monetary Fund, forces us to think about earlier periods of Chicana/o history much differently and to see their relationship to our contemporary moment in increasingly complex terms. The nineteenth century appears much more inter-American and transnational when we understand the southwestern United States as part of a hemispheric, even global, network of market forces. We also see, in this period, Mexico and Latin America resisting U.S. continental and hemispheric rhetoric in ways that closely resemble Chicana/o responses to U.S. racial realities post-9/11. This dual embrace and resistance of hemispherism is evident throughout the long history of Chicana/o literature and culture. The transnation has always held power and promise, the threat of imperial dominance and the possibility of transcendence; and the ambivalence about the nation so characteristic of Chicana/o literature must be understood in terms of a hemispheric and global resistance to the racializing and excluding work of nations.

Negotiating *Movimiento* Nuance

Such a reading of Chicana/o nationalism as grounded in a hemispheric history of ambivalence and uncertainty is difficult to negotiate, however, in Chicana/o literary studies, and in many ways my hemispheric approach takes issue with the geographic parochialism of Chicana/o studies, which has its roots in *movimiento* ideological conflict. José Limón's impassioned defense of "critical regionalism" as an alternative strategy to José Saldívar's "critical globalization" ("Border Literary Histories" 166) reflects longstanding intellectual and organizational fissures within Chicana/o scholarship and activism clearly evident in Chicana/o cultural production of *el movimiento*. *El movimiento* and its writers have been mythologized and vilified in such a way as to obscure the very real debates concerning political philosophy and cultural production that preoccupied movement activists. These are the same tensions between the global and the national grounding the long history of Chicana/o literature, a history that begins long before Gregorio Cortez ever picked up a pistol or Zachary Taylor crossed the Nueces,[5] tensions beautifully exemplified by Buffalo Zeta Brown, the charismatic lawyer-activist who is Oscar Acosta's literary alter ego.

In *The Revolt of the Cockroach People* (1973) Brown connects the Chicana/o struggle in Los Angeles to the conflict in Vietnam and develops a global vision of "the Cockroach people" as "the little beasts that everyone steps on" (135). Yet, at a student rally at UCLA, he berates the mostly white crowd for the attention it pays, from a position of unthreatened privilege, to a distant Vietnam at the expense of local inequities right down the road. "When the fires start up," he asks the crowd angrily, "when the pigs come to take us all, what will you do? Will you hide behind your skin? . . . Will you join up with the Chicanos and blacks? Or will you run back to the homes of your fathers in Beverly Hills, in Westwood, in Canoga Park?" (180). Limón's criticisms of Saldívar's very influential book *Border Matters* (1997), with its "hurried globalizing reading of this complex regional experience [of life in south Texas]" (Limón, "Border Literary Histories" 164), finds its antecedent in Brown's critique of the UCLA protestors and the Chicana/o Militants' anger at Brown, later in the novel, for disappearing to Mexico at a crucial time in their organizing (Acosta 196–97). Throughout Chicana/o scholarship and culture runs the suspicion that a shift in focus from the immediacy of Chicana/o experiences in the United States, or on the border, signals a shift away from "real" Chicana/o concerns.

Brown's desire to connect the local with the global is not usually addressed in scholarship on the novel. A similar critical myopia has informed the reception of *movimiento* poet Alurista (the pen name of Alberto Baltazar Urista Heredia), who began publishing his poems in the 1960s, is still publishing in the twenty-first century, and is referred to by some as the Chicana/o poet laureate. Alurista's work epitomizes the central conflicts in Chicana/o literary studies, as well as the tension between locality and globality expressed in the critical dispute between Limón and Saldívar. His early poetry gives voice to Chicana/o experience, yet as his writing develops he begins to critique and problematize the nature of the individual, experience, history, and culture, even the existence of a discrete speaking subject, the very terms upon which affirmations of *chicanismo* were built. The nation, both real and imagined, is a primary metaphor through which this shift in Alurista's poetics is evident. It surfaces again and again in his work as a paradoxical signifier of colonial capitalist enterprise and grassroots international unity. Alurista exploits this paradox in order to put forth a global perspective that privileges national differences. This paradox is manifest in the concept of Aztlán, which, through the preamble to "El Plan," Alurista is widely credited with introducing into the Chicana/o lexicon.[6] "El Plan," which has been roundly criticized for its silencing of Chicana and queer concerns with specious claims to communal homogeneity, actually puts forward experiential notions of Aztlán that argue for the national imaginary as a global humanizing force, a nuance that, like Brown's internationalism, is often lost on Alurista's detractors.

Alurista's unpublished poem "History of Aztlán" illuminates his political and poetic aims for Aztlán.[7] The poem offers visions of mestiza nations, independence on a bronze continent, and the connections between blood, labor, nation, and North America to which "El Plan" alludes but does not elaborate. "History of Aztlán" describes the historical progression of Aztlán from that which unified pre-Columbian, artistic Toltecs with the warlike Chichimecs to that which will unify contemporary Latin American nations in their fight against multinational capital.

While Alurista may have intended Aztlán to serve as an abstract concept, other activists understood Aztlán materially, as the Aztec homeland. Alurista's transformative, unifying metaphor is lost in the struggle between the two positions. But a lexical shift in "History of Aztlán" gives powerful voice to Alurista's unifying metaphor and shows how separate nations can come together as a collective, humanizing force. Toward the end of the poem, Aztlán becomes Amerindia, a term Alurista also uses freely in interviews. This slippage from Aztlán to Amerindia (indigenous America) in the poem and Alurista's colloquial use of Amerindia are significant, often overlooked elements of how Alurista understands Aztlán. If Aztlán is the Chicana/o homeland, then it is also something more; it is the idea of unification in the face of divisive, colonialist control.

Aztlán, as Alurista theorized it, is local and global, yet Chicana/o studies has a difficult time reconciling this complexity, as evidenced in the debate between Limón and Saldívar, as well as the field's critical turn away from nationalism. Recent work in Chicana/o studies has placed much emphasis on the global or transnational dimensions of Chicana/o culture. Ellie Hernández's *Postnationalism in Chicana/o Literature and*

Culture (2009), for example, correlates the global to a series of flexible, novel identities unavailable within a rigid, patriarchal, national structure. Hernández's work exemplifies the attraction of Limón's "critical globalization" for Chicana/o studies scholars who have embraced the transnation as a way to work around the conceptual difficulties posed by the nation, both real and imaginary. In *Chicano Nations* I seek to restore the critical multivalence of Alurista's Aztlán, of the nation, to the study of Chicana/o literature. Aztlán and the Chicana/o national imaginary it has come to reference are part of the interactional space of the transnational *latinidad* traced in this book.

One might reasonably ask, then, why I argue so strenuously for a flexible *chicanismo* rather than abandoning a moniker whose inconsistencies and philosophical limitations I have taken pains to enumerate. It is vitally important to think of the authors in this study as Chicana/o because they are of Mexican descent and that *mexicanidad* engenders a unique relationship to the United States that is very similar to that of Latin America but historically very different as well. The United States absorbed nearly half of Mexico in 1848, and the essence of *chicanismo* lies in negotiating that engulfment. I intend "Chicana/o" as the lexical equivalent of the serpent eating its own tail or of the two-headed serpent's confrontation with its own other as it emerges from Coatlique's neck.[8] Insisting on "Chicana/o" illuminates the theoretical problem this book takes on: the local's imbrication with the global. The Chicana/o struggle in the United States is intimately connected with the global struggle against oppression, as Buffalo Brown passionately argues, and Chicana/o studies must understand that globality in order to parse the ever-changing dimensions of *chicanismo*. We must also understand that a global, Chicana/o consciousness is not simply a function of a putative post-NAFTA, postmodern enlightenment but very much a part of a hemispheric, Latina/o sensibility and a function of the transnational *latinidad* that lies at the heart of this study.

As the Hemisphere Turns?

My hemispheric approach to the study of Chicana/o literature has its dangers, however. Just as Chicana/o studies scholars embraced the transnation as a way to work around patriarchal nationalism, so too have U.S.-based American studies scholars embraced a hemispheric framework as a critical evasion of U.S. hegemony. But, just as Chicana/o studies has a tendency to repress its own troubling prehistory, so too does the hemispheric turn in U.S.-based American studies scholarship, of which *Chicano Nations* can be considered a part, run the risk of falling into an intellectual solipsism that mirrors U.S. geopolitical dominance.

Amy Kaplan and Donald Pease heralded the beginning of American studies' hemispheric turn with their anthology *Cultures of United States Imperialism* (1993), which examined U.S. culture through the lens of U.S. imperial conflict abroad. A range of provocative studies of U.S. literature followed in Kaplan and Pease's wake.[9] As Ralph Bauer cogently reminds us, however, this hemispheric turn, while new to U.S.-based American studies, is hardly novel. Its critical tradition stems from the moment Herbert Bolton, in his 1932 presidential address to the American Histori-cal Association, challenged that organization to consider whether or not the Americas had a common history (Bauer, "Hemispheric Studies" 234). Since then, inter-American scholarship that considers the hemisphere from across the disciplines has flourished with, as Bauer notes, a sharp increase in the late 1990s when U.S.-based American studies shifted its perspective from "a United States centered multiculturalism toward a trans- and postnationalism" ("Hemispheric Studies" 235).

The new hemispheric American studies that followed from Janice Radway's exhortation, in her 1998 presidential address to the American Studies Association, to cease conflating "America" with the United States, was based largely in English and American studies departments, had its methodological roots in U.S. multiculturalism, and, as Bauer recounts, irked Latin Americanists and others who had been engaged in inter-American scholarship for many years, with its pretensions to novelty and its focus on the United States in a hemispheric context ("Hemispheric Studies" 236–37). This focus foregrounds the hegemony of the U.S. nation-state and the artificiality of borders, coalescing around postcolonial readings of race. Hemispheric American studies thus differs substantially from inter-American or Latin American scholarship in that the former seeks to leave behind an imperial nationalism while the latter has tended to see the nation as a protective counter to U.S. dominance.

Conceptions of the Americas thus can differ subtly yet substantially, as the Mexican philosopher José Vasconcelos argues in his essay "Bolivarismo y monroísmo" (1934). "Bolivarism is the Hispanic American idea of creating a Spanish cultural federation," he writes. "Monroism is the Anglo Saxon idea of incorporating the twenty Hispanic nations into a Nordic empire by means of a panamerican politics" (1305).[10] Vasconce-los emphasizes the political histories of critical language, a point Walter Mignolo also makes in *The Idea of Latin America*, where he describes *latinidad* as a nineteenth-century French ideological project designed to assert control in the region and identifies "Latin America" less as a material space and more abstractly as a political tool of elite *criollos* (colonists born in the "new" world) as they established a postcolonial identity (58–59). Similarly, Arturo Ardao traces the term "latinoamericanismo" to France and, like Vasconcelos, describes "panamericanismo" and "Pan-America" as part of U.S. efforts to dominate the Americas (157). Ardao sees "interamericanismo" as a variant of Pan-Americanism (170) and extends his list of problematic terms to include "Panamericana" (158), "americanismo" (166), and "hispanoamericano" (166), each of which connotes, to some extent, the region's continuing subordination to Western powers.

Ardao's lexical stringency leaves scholars little room to maneuver, but in this study I have chosen to use "transamerica" to refer to the vision I see my authors developing of hemispheric connection and progressive social change. "Transamerica" adumbrates the physical spaces my writers move within while remaining attentive to the fraught narrative history of the region. Though a transamerican ideal does originate with white-identified elites, it does so in conjunction with their growing awareness of their own racialization in U.S.-dominated American space, as I argue in Chapter 1. Thus, imbricated in the hemispheric, at times global, vision of the nineteenth-century writers I discuss are the theoretical foundations for a progressive politics of global humanism, which is, in my final analysis, the value and potential of Chicana/o literature.

In broadening "Chicana/o" in this way, in reading Chicana/o nationalism as an unsuccessful attempt to resolve contradictions in Mexican American identity, in situating the literal and metaphorical nation hemispherically and focusing on nationalism as a function of a narrative relation to the past, *Chicano Nations* seeks to define "Chicana/o" and *chicanismo* as something other than oppositional and anti-Anglo. Such an approach undercuts traditional notions of "identity" by understanding "Chicana/o" to be less experiential and reactionary and more of an historical process. Chicana/o consciousness, in the analyses that follow, exists as an evolving project to think through the nation in philosophically productive ways that transcend the oppositions of identity politics.

Consequently, *Chicano Nations* makes three significant interventions in the study of Chicana/o literature and U.S. literature more broadly: first, it dislodges the United States as the cultural center to which Chicana/o literature responds; second, it puts Chicana/o literature in the context of political and cultural debates in Latin America, a move that shifts the focus of U.S. ethnic studies from an exercise in U.S. exceptionalism toward a global theory of race; and third, it develops a model for reading earlier Chicana/o texts as a meaningful part of Chicana/o literary history, something that has heretofore eluded scholars.

Thus, while *Chicano Nations* explores a global and hemispheric context for Chicana/o literature, the readings that follow remain invested in the nation as both political reality and abstract imaginary. In the same way that some scholars maintain a healthy suspicion of a potentially colonizing hemispherism, *Chicano Nations* seeks a balance between transamerican potential and national realities.[11] Other recent studies have moved in a similar direction, and while they have broadened readings of *chicanismo*, *Chicano Nations* seeks to extend the historical and geographic horizons of these representative studies.[12] Following Manuel Martín-Rodríguez's claims in *Life in Search of Readers* (2003), however, I argue that we cannot draw a direct representational line from the nineteenth century to the twenty-first. Martín-Rodríguez calls for an approach to Chicana/o literary history that realizes the fundamental contradiction between the heterogeneity of a Mexican American past and historiographic tendencies toward homogenization. *Chicano Nations* makes just this sort of intervention.

The Adventures of Ali, Ali, and the Writers Included in *Chicano Nations*

> I wish to remind you, at this crucial juncture in our shared geographies, dat under dose funny voices and under dose funny images of de Frito Bandito and under all this talk of Money and Markets there are living, breathing, dreaming men, women and children. . . . Consider those here first. Consider those I have not considered. Consider your parents, consider your grandparents. Consider the country. Consider the continent. Consider the border. —WIDELOAD, FRONTERAS AMERICANAS (76)

> OK, it's OK if you don't want to stop jihad because, from what we can tell, here in the postmodern, post-industrial West, it is not your actions that count so much as your image. —ALI ABABWA TO OSAMA BIN LADEN IN THE ADVENTURES OF ALI AND ALI AND THE AXES OF EVIL (115)

Chicano Nations explores the transformations of national space and national imaginaries in Chicana/o literature. It traces a broad, historical arc from the deconstruction of the Spanish empire's borders and the construction of national borders in the Americas, the multiple Latina/o identities and racial epistemologies those borders engender, to border morphology post-9/11 and the continual transformation of Americans and the Americas. I am interested here in the ebbs and flows of space and place, people, borders, and the possibility of transnational *latinidad* to profoundly reorient our understanding of the racialized logic of the nation-state.

Chicano Nations comprises three parts: "Imagining the Americas," "Inhabiting America," and "American Diasporas," each of which explores the grounding, evolution, contemporary manifestation, and future possibility of a hemispheric vision for Chicana/o literature. "Chicana/o" is itself as fraught a term as the transamerican networks of influence it aims to suture. "Chicana/o" resonates hemispherically and is tightly connected to longstanding debates in Latin American literature and culture about the nation's relationship to the hemisphere. This book is therefore organized around three moments of *international* pressure on what it means to be Mexican and what it means to be Mexican in the United States. These three moments—Latin American independence and U.S. expansion, the Mexican Revolution, and September 11, 2001—chart the emergence of race in inter-American mappings, both cartographic and narrative, and demonstrate the containment and expression of racial ideologies. These historical markers are key flashpoints in Chicana/o history tracing at the outset the creation of new national boundaries and subsequent articulation of new racial identities; then, the first major challenge to the north-south divide of the U.S.-Mexico border and the spatial identities it engenders as immigration north from Mexico increases dramatically before and during the revolution; and finally, 9/11, which marks a radical shift in the shape and feel of national borders that fundamentally redefines the space of *chicanismo* and the meaning of transnational *latinidad*.

The book charts several different journeys, one of which is captured in the distance between Verdecchia's *Fronteras Americanas*, with which this introduction opens, and a later play, *The Adventures of Ali and Ali and the Axes of Evil* (2005), cowritten with Caymar Chai and Marcus Youssef. *Fronteras Americanas* describes a Latina/o subject split between an imaginary homeland and the reality of living as an Argentine in Canada, a story fleshed out in the first two parts of *Chicano Nations*. "Imagining the Americas" describes the emergence of a Chicana/o national imaginary in the nineteenth century while "Inhabiting America" focuses on the racialized subjects living in the United States in the early twentieth century. *Ali and Ali*, which is about traveling performers from

Agraba, a fictitious Middle Eastern country, examines the impact of both the War on Terror and liberal hypocrisy on Western ethnic identities and stereotypes.[13] "American Diasporas," the final part of *Chicano Nations*, enacts this explicitly global turn in examining the meaning and historicity of post-9/11 *chicanismo*.

In Part 1 of *Chicano Nations*, "Imagining the Americas," I stake my central claim that Chicana/o literature has always had a hemispheric, even global, vision. The two chapters included in this part—"*Latinidad* Abroad" and "*Mexicanidad* at Home"—trace the emergence and evolution of a transamerican ideal in Latina/o arts and letters. My goal here is to show how Mexican and Mexican American writers participated in that dialogue, and in my analyses I place particular emphasis on putting them in conversation with political and cultural debates in Mexico and Latin America. These two chapters illuminate the hemispheric network out of which concepts like the global and transnational emerge, as well as the long, intellectual histories of the principles of anti-racism and anti-colonial struggle, which are primarily associated with twentieth-century *chicanismo*.

Chapter 1, "*Latinidad* Abroad," examines three narratives written by Mexican and Latin American travelers in the United States in the early nineteenth century. Mexican politician Lorenzo de Zavala's *Viaje a los Estados Unidos del Norte de América* (1834), along with the Argentine Domingo Sarmiento's *Viajes por . . . América 1845–1847* and the Chilean Vicente Pérez Rosales's "Algo Sobre California" (1850), illustrate a hemispheric racial ideology wherein the United States constructs Latin America as an infantile other to be drawn under the cloak of U.S. protection. In producing a vision of the United States for Mexican and Latin American consumption, these writers must mediate the internal contradictions of their own burgeoning nationalisms while grappling with increasing U.S. hemispheric dominance. Zavala, Sarmiento, and Pérez Rosales begin, each in his own way, to reconcile their national ambitions with a hemispheric ideal that potentially transcends the liberal state.

Their hemispherism works in productive tension with the galvanizing nationalisms of nineteenth-century Latin America. Taken together, they demonstrate how writing, particularly travel writing, becomes a core function of state making and how it parses public concerns about the state, citizenship, and the racial composition of the body politic. From Zavala to Sarmiento to Pérez Rosales we note the increasing racialization of Mexicans and Latin Americans in the United States. Twentieth- and twenty-first-century Chicana/o cultural production hinges on the links forged between race and nation that we see emerging here in each writer's attempts to narrate a transnational space. Reading Zavala in conjunction with his Latin American contemporaries establishes a broader referential context for his *Viaje* and consequently for the formation of Chicana/o literature.

Chapter 2, "*Mexicanidad* at Home," builds on this context in its explorations of the literary connection between the historian and publisher Hubert Bancroft and Mariano Vallejo in late nineteenth-century San Francisco. In *Literary Industries*, his 1890 memoir, Bancroft describes his relationship with Vallejo, the former Mexican military commander of Alta California. Bancroft convinced Vallejo to contribute his own recollections to Bancroft's historical project, recollections that eventually became Vallejo's five-volume *Recuerdos Historicos y Personales Tocante a la Alta California* (Historical and Personal Recollections Touching upon Alta California). In this chapter I consider Vallejo's *Recuerdos* in relation to Bancroft's *Works*, investigating the intersections of historical narrative with nationalist sentiment. The two men's respective histories of California reveal complex processes of national identification at work, processes that suggest new ways of thinking through both the role that wealthy rancheros play in Chicana/o literary history and the applicability of terms like "transnationalism" and "globalization" to the nineteenth century.

Critics have read *testimonios* like Vallejo's as textual evidence of the consolidation of *californio* identity as a racialized, proletarianized community collectively oppressed by Anglo-American dominance.[14] The *testimonios* are generally seen as regional in scope and, though they point to broader national trends in racism and class struggle, they are rarely seen as speaking to transnational or global concerns. Here I ask how we can understand Vallejo's place in Chicana/o literary history as something other than a narrative of loss, conquest, racialization, and woe. While *testimonios* such as Vallejo's do reflect the rise of Anglo-American power in California, that rise adumbrates a number of other social, political, and economic factors as well. Mexican Californians were both subjects and objects of these forces, and a full reading of texts such as Vallejo's must understand them as such. Teasing out processes of Mexican American racialization in California through an analysis of Bancroft's and Vallejo's histories reveals how philosophies of history and economics manifest themselves in narrations of the nation, offering more nuanced ways to understand interracial and international relations and texts.

While "Imagining the Americas" puts the emergence of Chicana/o literature in the wider context of nineteenth-century Pan-American debates, Part 2, "Inhabiting America," tracks the development of those national imaginaries in the early twentieth century. This part focuses on how literature represents the reality of living as a Mexican in the United States. As the transamerican dream shared by the writers of Part 1 fades, Part 2 pays attention to the intertwining of space and race at the turn of the century. As national spaces codify so does the idea of a national race, and the two chapters in this part ask how notions of race, ethnicity, and nation evolve during this period, taking on the oppositional cast of later twentieth-century activism. At the same time, in fleshing out the roots of this oppositional subjectivity, Part 2 examines the nuances and complexities of early twentieth-century *chicanismo*, tracing the fault lines of intracommunal class and race tensions, which contribute to the diversity of Chicana/o communities but regularly go unnoted in scholarly studies. These two chapters work to integrate that diversity and tension into Chicana/o literary history while rooting them in the transnational debates of the nineteenth century.

"Racialized Bodies and the Limits of the Abstract," Chapter 3, discusses María Mena and Daniel Venegas as two authors whose writings straddle the Mexican Revolution. Their writing reflects two disparate, diasporic Mexican communities who eventually do become part of a Chicana/o collectivity in the United States. The tensions of class, race, gender, and nation evident in their works are exacerbated in comparison with each other and are foundational to intracommunal Chicana/o conflicts. The political alliances reflected in their writings mark the inception of the fissures and camps characteristic of later twentieth-century Chicana/o political and cultural production.

Mena and Venegas inhabit "America" at the same time that the United States is trying to inhabit Latin America. Their writings embrace and refute otherness; they try to both define and embody an idealized Mexico while simultaneously critiquing the essentializing logic of an idealized nationality. In short, Mena's and Venegas's writing is a window into the moment when Chicana/o literature incorporates the idea of its own race. That incorporation results in myriad contradictions and inconsistencies evident in Mena's and Venegas's disparate approaches to the question of what Mexico means. The political conflict evident in reading them against each other is one of the constitutive political tensions of Chicana/o literature: between the materiality and the abstraction of race.

Chapter 4, "More Life in the Skeleton," dwells on the distinction between the lived experience of race and the political expediency of racial abstraction. The chapter opens with an analysis of two different artistic renderings of a skeleton, by Mexican and Anglo artists, encountered by the reader early in Jovita González and Eve Raleigh's novel *Caballero* (written in 1937 but not published until 1996). The artistic differences the narrators describe articulate the ineffable significance of race, a project taken up also by José Vasconcelos in his essay "La raza cósmica" (1925). Vasconcelos is concerned with the future possibility of race, not the lived present. He sees *mestizaje* (racial mixing) as the key to human uplift and is not concerned in his writing with what it means to actually live as a mestizo in either Mexico or the United States.

Caballero bridges the divide between these two poles. Like "La raza cósmica," the novel seeks a new racial epistemology that moves beyond the capitalist logic of nations, and, like both Mena's and Venegas's works, the novel must contend with the lived experience of racial oppression. Like "La raza cósmica," *Caballero* postulates a new model of racial thinking that is about neither assimilation nor Anglo supremacy but total spiritual uplift, and like Vasconcelos's essay *Caballero* posits a complex and contradictory theory of historical time that undermines nationalist logic. Because *Caballero* critiques Mexican nationalism and does not reflect an easily recognizable, oppositional Chicana/o politics, it, like "La raza cósmica," is most often read as making conservative, elitist, and assimilationist arguments about race and nation. In this chapter I read *Caballero* in the context of Vasconcelos's essay in order to bring forth both texts' internationalist arguments. Shedding light on them helps situate both in the rich tradition of nationalist debate that *Chicano Nations* traces.

The long history of this debate is occluded, in Chicana/o studies scholarship, by *el movimiento*. This was a remarkable and galvanizing time, but its lionization in the critical canon has severely limited our ability to appreciate what came before and after. The critical work of articulating Chicana/o identity and experience, performed by political and cultural activists of *el movimiento*, was crucial, if anomalous in its hermeticism and militancy. The fluid geopolitical and personal borders characteristic of feminist and queer work of the 1980s and 1990s, while often seen as a response to *movimiento* patriarchy and homophobia, are actually better understood as part of the long history of hemispheric exchange outlined in this study.

From the early twentieth century, therefore, I move to its close and the dawn of the twenty-first, during which time Chicana/o literature is dealing with the same internal identity crises occasioned by the waves of Mexican immigration during the 1920s. Part 3, "American Diasporas," looks at how Chicana/o literature incorporates the tectonic shifts occasioned by the Central American migrations of this period and how assertions of U.S. power abroad shape domestic, ethnic tensions. The two chapters in "American Diasporas" explore how borders change, the impact of immigration on Chicana/o communities, and the effect of September 11, 2001, on literary representations of space, place, belonging, and ethnicity in the United States. The political conflicts of the early twenty-first century are novel, and yet they return Chicana/o literature to its intellectual heritage of transamerican and global perspectives.

Chapter 5, "Ana Castillo's 'distinct place in the Americas,'" examines two novels by Castillo, who was herself a *movimiento* activist in Chicago but whose writing challenges *movimiento* theorizations of history, identity, and narrative, as well as their critical descendents. Scholars have read Castillo as part of the queer, feminist critique of *movimiento* nationalism. That is indeed an undeniable aspect of Castillo's work. However, in juxtaposing *Sapogonia* (1990), an early novel, with her more recent *The Guardians* (2007), this chapter aims to connect this critique to a long history of Chicana/o nationalist debate extending far back into the nineteenth century.

Sapogonia's invocation of an imaginary, South American country rent asunder by civil war is a clear allegory of U.S. involvement in Central America, as well as a commentary on Latina/o political organizing in the United States in the 1980s. The abstract theorizations of identity, history, and art the novel puts forth are grounded in the material lives of the characters in *The Guardians*, a family drama about Mexican immigrants on the Texas-New Mexico-Mexico border in the early 2000s. The novels differ significantly in form and content—*Sapogonia* experiments with non-linear narrative and shifting focalization in its tale of world-traveling artists and lovers, while *The Guardians* is a linear story about a family grappling with the geopolitical realities of a post-9/11 border—but both make similar claims about a capacious *chicanismo* and human connections forged through literature.

Castillo's novels depict the new networks of affiliation engendered by cross-border flows of capital and people that rapidly accelerated after World War II. She situates them within a Chicana/o national community that looks very different from those of nineteenth-century Latino and Mexican travelers or the early twentieth-century Mexican American working and middle classes. Though their historical situations differ greatly, each of the writers treated thus far takes up the similar task of constructing national narratives rooted not in rigid isolationism but in an international perspective. Castillo's contribution is to recognize the connections between nativism and imperial capital, connections toward which the writers in the previous chapters could only gesture.

The four novels discussed in Chapter 6, "Border Patrol as Global Surveillance," explore these connections through the figure of the Chicana/o detective. Detective fiction thematizes surveillance and paranoia, both of which emerge in this chapter as products of the War on Terror, represented in the novels in three domains: the 2003 U.S. invasion of Iraq, technologies of surveillance, and discourses of international trade in people and commodities. The novels chart a progression through the shifting spaces of Chicana/o literature and provide a discursive map of its global engagement. Alicia Gaspar de Alba's *Desert Blood* (2005) focuses on the rapidly changing environment of the U.S.-Mexico border. In this book, as in so many others, the border is amorphous, despite clearly demarcated points of entry between the two countries. Moreover, Ivon, the novel's protagonist, is often disoriented in Mexican spaces, and the specific place she is trying to locate is, unbeknownst to her, mobile rather than fixed. Gaspar de Alba's porous border is manifest, in Martín Limón's *The Door to Bitterness* (2005), as the international resonance of U.S. concerns. Limón, like Gaspar de Alba, trades in global capital's flexible shape, and his novel traces U.S. influence in postwar Korea, using Korea's evolving racial identities, and their U.S. correlates, as indices of U.S. power.

Both *Desert Blood* and *The Door to Bitterness* comment on the culture of paranoia and surveillance that has emerged in the United States in the wake of 9/11, though neither novel mentions the War on Terror directly and *The Door to Bitterness* is set well before. Mario Acevedo's *The Nymphos of Rocky Flats* (2006) and *The Undead Kama Sutra* (2008) take up the policies of the Bush administration directly, featuring Felix Gomez, a Chicano detective who was turned into a vampire while serving in the U.S. Army during Operation Iraqi Freedom. Acevedo's novels, like Limón's, depict race as a geopolitical product fashioned, in part, in response to U.S. force abroad. Acevedo, however, reigns in Limón's international scope to focus more precisely on U.S. concerns, introducing the sublimely ridiculous—in the shapes of vampires, extraterrestrial beings, and sensual wood nymphs—into discussions of contemporary immigration policy and ethnic identities. Taken together these novels map a journey—from the U.S.-Mexico border to Korea and the exercise of U.S. power abroad and finally to outer space—as the funhouse mirror to U.S. xenophobia and paranoia. This spatial progression charts an expanding arena for Chicana/o racial and ethnic identity, showing no one place as epicenter, arguing instead for a definition of *chicanismo* as a critical mode of engaging with U.S. power.

In many ways, the characters encountered in Chapter 6 do not differ much from the travelers of Chapter 1. They all try to make sense out of foreign spaces and grapple with their own foreignness. In many other ways, however, these travelers differ, most notably in how race conditions their perceptions of themselves and their relations to state power. All, however, understand the power, promise, and problems of the state: how it both protects and threatens, conditions identity while placing those identities in hierarchal relation to each other, includes and excludes. All are caught between the desire to either harness state power for themselves or transcend the state in search of more ethical, alternative social organizations.

This tension forms the core of the long history of national, hemispheric, and racial imaginaries in Chicana/o literature that *Chicano Nations* excavates. This is also an excavation of the idea that race lies at the heart of social organization and demonstrates that Chicana/o literature has always been actively engaged in undermining philosophies of race and nation through its gestures toward hemispheric alliance. These are the same alliances presented in Verdecchia's Argentine Canadian plays. At the end of *The Adventures of Ali and Ali*, Ali Ababwa has a dream about Agraba but is confused because "the whole world was Agraba" (124). In the dream, dead friends and family are alive, children run through streets overgrown with grass and trees, all are employed, and "our words had grown taller than our swords" (125). He thinks it must have been some mystical vision of heaven. "No, Ali," says Ali Hakim. "I think perhaps it was the future" (126).

PART ONE

IMAGINING THE AMERICAS

1 / *Latinidad* Abroad: The Narrative Maps of Sarmiento, Zavala, and Pérez Rosales

Fearing for his own life after the assassination of many of his political allies, the Mexican politician Lorenzo de Zavala fled Mexico City for the United States late in 1829. Arriving in New Orleans, he traveled northeast through Mississippi, Kentucky, Ohio, Pennsylvania, New York, and eventually Canada, recording his observations along the way. A decade later, the Argentine writer, soldier, and provocateur Domingo Sarmiento, also fleeing political unrest, traced a similar path across the United States and Canada. Just three years after Sarmiento, Vicente Pérez Rosales, a Chilean journalist, businessman, and admiring critic of Sarmiento's, left along with thousands of other Chileans to seek his fortunes in the golden hills of California. Each published an account of his travels in which, while simultaneously producing a vision of the United States for Mexican and Latin American consumption, they negotiated their own countries' burgeoning nationalisms against the increasing hemispheric dominance of the United States.

Sarmiento, Zavala, and Pérez Rosales document their adventures, but their narratives also reflect the appearance of racial thinking in the Americas. Race emerges in the nineteenth century, as Ralph Bauer has argued, "as a transnational discourse of identity and difference based on biological factors, such as skin color" ("Hemispheric Genealogies" 36). These modern ideas of race, however, do not necessarily correspond to colonial discourses of difference, Bauer continues, contending that to speak of race in the modern sense before the nineteenth century is anachronistic. In the writings of Sarmiento, Zavala, and Pérez Rosales we see the shift to modern racial thinking as the United States moves inexorably toward constructing Mexico and Latin America as political and ultimately racial others.

Against the threat of U.S. hegemony, Latin American countries, in the early nineteenth-century wake of independence, asserted their unique, national identities. As Zavala, Sarmiento, and Pérez Rosales parse the meanings of Mexico, Argentina, and Chile against an ideal of hemispheric cooperation, U.S. market dominance continues to grow, consequently determining the meaning of American space and its inhabitants. This moment, when the various countries of the Americas begin to understand the potential and the danger of inter-American cooperation, is the ideal place to begin a study of Chicana/o literature. The moment when Latin America emerges as a potential other in the U.S. imagination also marks the inception of a Chicana/o national imaginary.

The limitations and contradictions of cultural nationalism also become apparent in this historical moment. As the writers under consideration in this chapter struggle to distinguish themselves and their home countries, they slowly come to understand the ways in which the United States is, in fact, all too willing to consider them as others. Political hierarchies in the Americas are codified concomitant with racial hierarchies into whose vortex Sarmiento, Zavala, and Pérez Rosales are unceremoniously swept. They are aware of this process to varying degrees, as the emerging language of race is unevenly available to them, evident in the differing roles race plays in each traveler's narrative. When they do speak in recognizably racial terms, their intended subjects are difficult to correlate to twenty-first-century understandings of race. Sarmiento, Zavala, and Pérez Rosales are, therefore, not direct, philosophical ancestors to contemporary Chicanas/os. Considering the shifting conceptions of the Americas in their travel narratives does, however, reveal how racial thinking evolves with national thinking and how both are imbricated in a nascent Chicana/o national imaginary.

The advent of a Chicana/o and Latina/o racial identity in the United States shuts down the transamerican possibility with which the century begins, and to which Sarmiento, at least, clings so hopefully in his narrative. The story of Sarmiento's, Zavala's, and Pérez Rosales's travels is also, then, the story of how race becomes available as an organizing principle of Chicana/o identity. In telling this story I have two aims: one, to make the hemispherism of these early nineteenth-century writers available to contemporary Chicana/o cultural workers as the grounds for a progressive politics; and two, to illuminate the historicity of race. Chicanas/os have a complicated racial history—grounded in the interconnected histories of Mexico, the United States, Argentina, and Chile—that involves its own fair share of oppressive colonial moves.

Setting the Historical Scene

Independence movements across the former Spanish empire were connected but uneven, and nation building in each of the four countries considered here involved the simultaneous, symbiotic development of national and transnational hierarchies of race and class. Though intimately related, independence movements took root more quickly in loosely populated regions like Argentina, located far from colonial centers in Mexico City and Lima. The structure of Spain's colonial governance, however, ensured that independence unfolded along similar lines, developing similar factions, in each newly sovereign nation. Across the empire the chain of command was the same: the *cabildo* (town council) reported to the *intendencia* (middle management intended to limit *cabildo* power), which reported to the *audencia* (regional political center), which reported to the viceroy, who answered to the crown (Shumway 10). *Criollos* (Spaniards born in the colonies) were not allowed to hold positions of significant political power, but they were allowed a fair amount of leeway in their fealty to imperial decree. Tolerating occasional disobedience allowed Spain to keep *criollo* power in check and maintain a loyal class of civil servants. The *criollo* population in the colonies was largely content until Napoleon's 1808 invasion of Spain created warring factions of loyalists and patriots who came to dominate politics in the post-independence era (Shumway 18–20).

Partisans of the crown in Mexico, Chile, Argentina, and elsewhere evolved into Centralists favoring a strong central authority, while patriots, or supporters of independence, became Federalists, favoring cooperative leagues of states within each new nation. These intranational conflicts informed emerging international relations in Latin America, as Simón Bolívar explained in "The Jamaica Letter."[1] There he expressed hopes for a Latin American federation, organized loosely along the lines of the old viceroyalties, which would work together for the liberty and progress of the continent, a plan that met with much resistance from ardent nationalists.

Despite resistance to federation, Latin American countries took an active interest in their neighbors' political development, with, for example, Argentina's famed general José de San Martín aiding in the independence of Peru and Chile. Cultural production was similarly interdependent. Most of Argentina's "May Association" of politically progressive writers opposed to the Argentine dictator Juan Manuel de Rosas operated from exile in Chile and Uruguay (Katra 10). Sarmiento, who was not a member but an avid observer of the May Association, also fled to Chile. There he worked as a journalist and editor, eventually publishing his *Facundo, or Civilization and Barbarism* (1845), an anti-Rosas manifesto and classic theory of both *caudillismo* (strongman rule) and Latin American development.

Such international cultural connections as existed between Chile and Argentina fell prey to the same political tensions Bolívar faced, however, with Vicente Pérez Rosales calling Chile a "refugium peccatorum for Peruvians and Argentineans" (173)[2] and harboring antipathy for Sarmiento in particular whose "rude and shameless arrogance" prompts him to, "in a corrupt Spanish, [print] whatever bit of nonsense tickled [his] pen" (174).[3] Sarmiento, for his part, editorialized that it "was folly to study Spanish, because Spanish was a language dead to civilization," viewed Chileans as "dim-witted," and claimed that "while the muses happily caressed [Argentine writers], in Chile they did nothing but sleep like a log" (Pérez Rosales 175).[4] Even so, Pérez Rosales found Sarmiento impressive and interesting, as did the Chilean government, which tolerated his presence in their country and funded his trip to the United States ostensibly to evaluate foreign education systems but also to deflect extradition pressure from Rosas's government.

Pérez Rosales's and the Chilean government's reluctant tolerance of Sarmiento is a lens through which to focus cultural and political hemispherism in nineteenth-century Latin America. Bolívar's desire for a Latin American federation became the crux of debates about nationhood in post-independence Latin America, a debate fueled and exacerbated by U.S. observers in the region, among whom Joel Poinsett, whose diplomatic career emphasizes the deep connections between the four countries discussed in this chapter, truly distinguishes himself.

In 1810 Poinsett served as a special agent for the United States in Buenos Aires and Chile, quixotically supporting both the Spanish crown and nascent revolutionary forces. During 1822–23 Poinsett was special agent to Mexico, where he fomented civil strife by supporting competing Masonic factions. In 1825, not long after Monroe delivered his 1823 doctrine, Poinsett was appointed U.S. minister to Mexico, from which position he worked, until 1829, to secure trade and diplomatic concessions from Mexico. Poinsett's behavior—so strikingly intrusive as to lead Mexicans to coin the term *poinsettismo* to refer to meddle-some actions—characterizes the emerging diplomatic persona of the United States in the early nineteenth century. His actions generated such mistrust that Bolívar famously did not want to include the United States in the 1826 Congress of Panama, which sought to establish a Latin American league of nations (Bushnell xxxv). Though unsuccess-ful, the congress attendees grappled with fundamental questions about the meaning of the Americas and what role the United States would play in the American imagination.

A genealogy of Chicana/o literature can be traced from this moment of the Congress of Panama's failure, from this same nexus of race, na-tion, and global capital emerging in Latin America's post-independence period. An exploration of this genealogy begins with the travel narrative as emblematic of hemispheric possibility, similarity, and contradiction. It was, after all, the travel narrative that created the idea of the Ameri-cas in the European and American imaginations. Alvar Nuñez Cabeza de Vaca's account of his wandering across Texas in the early sixteenth century, in *La relación* (1542), presented Europe with one of the first an-thropologic accounts of the "new" world intended for a broad audience. In addition to imagining the native as a lesser form of humanity, Euro-pean natural historians tended to imagine American space as degenera-tive and inconsequential as well. Thomas Jefferson did much to refute these notions in *Notes on the State of Virginia* (1784), but perhaps the greatest proselytizer of American grandeur was the Prussian natural sci-entist Alexander von Humboldt. His multivolume *Personal Narrative of Travels to the Equinoctial Regions of America*, which Mary Louise Pratt describes as a "print epic" (119), documents his early nineteenth-century trips across South America and the Spanish Caribbean. Humboldt's breathlessly romantic drawings and descriptions of the Andes, the Cor-dilleras, the Amazon basin, and other natural wonders of the continent did much to create a sense of South America's natural largesse.

As Pratt argues, Humboldt marks a transition from travel writing as an instrument of empire to travel writing as a genre South American writers embrace as a means of asserting American particularity in the post-independence age. For nineteenth-century Latin American writ-ers like Andrés Bello, Esteban Echevarría, Sarmiento, and even Bolívar, Humboldt emerges "as a point *from which* Americanist consciousness set out, and *beyond which* it sought to go" (181, emphasis in original). The in-tersection of natural history and travel writing embodied by Humboldt becomes the means by which *americanismo literario* (the movement to create an autochthonous literature of the Americas) could reclaim the Spanish empire and describe it as uniquely American.

In my readings of Sarmiento, Zavala, and Pérez Rosales, I explore how travel writing simultaneously articulates and deconstructs transamerican space and culture. I am particularly interested in how each discursively maps the Americas, arguing either for or against hemispheric unity. How, in the midst of establishing their own nations, do these writers grapple with the idea of the Americas, how do they write the United States into that vision, and how does race emerge as a way of organizing problems of nation and citizenship? Humboldt's landscapes were instrumental in narrating American particularity, and Latin American writers deployed Humboldtian convention, as Pratt shows; here I wish to push travel and its accoutrements—writing, transportation, maps, and hospitality—to account not just for a post-independence pride grounded in natural history but also for the geopolitical realities and shifting power dynamics in the hemisphere.

Traveling Through Racial Histories with Sarmiento

Sarmiento certainly works from a Humboldtian ideal in *Facundo*. Locating the gaucho's "barbarism" in the desolate geography of the pampas defined *caudillismo* as a uniquely American phenomenon rooted in the land's specificity. Positing the "natural" gaucho against "civilized" Buenos Aires constructed the city as a denaturalized, European space toward which the country was progressing.[5] But famously, Sarmiento had never seen the pampas he wrote about in *Facundo*. Though he had traveled quite a bit by 1845, he had never traveled through the Argentine spaces his narrative attempts to contain. I turn here, therefore, to Sarmiento's *Viajes por Europa, Africa, i América, 1845–1847*[6] to see what Sarmiento makes of the other spaces within which he actually moves, and I look specifically at his journey through the United States in order to lay the groundwork for the transamerican ideal emerging in these early Latin American, post-independence pilgrimages north.

Whereas *Facundo* posits the Argentine landscape as an irreducible difference, in *Viajes por . . . América* Sarmiento represents nature as absorbing differences of race and class, relegating them to the past. The United States is constituted as a nation, incorporating difference as the Yankee moves across and transforms natural space. But even as Sarmiento celebrates this spatial transfiguration, he balks at Yankee utilitarianism. He also expresses an uneasy sympathy with those relegated to the natural past (indigenous Americans) and domestic space (American women). *Viajes por . . . América* should be read, then, in terms of its praise for Yankee progress but also for its moments of discontent, the ways in which Sarmiento's hemispheric vision collides with U.S. political realities.

Sarmiento begins on a resoundingly positive note, describing the United States to his friend Valentín Alsina, to whom *Viajes por . . . América* is structured as a long letter, as the perfect country (118, 336).[7] Land is freely available and it is resource rich, but even these qualities do not fully explain the success and uniqueness of the United States, a project Sarmiento intends to take up in his narrative. He tells Alsina not to expect "an orderly description of the United States" for Sarmiento has "another purpose" (117):[8] to explain its success and difference from other American countries. The differences between Argentina and the United States, Sarmiento explains to Alsina, are racial, economic, and geographic, but he sees these things as subsets of something larger, which emerges in the narrative as travel: the ability to move freely through and transform national space.

Travel is particularly noteworthy for Sarmiento because it was, for him, a relatively novel liberty. Before the Spanish constitution of 1812, movement within the Americas was severely restricted, requiring significant paperwork and passage through numerous checkpoints (Mexal 83). Indeed, this was the case throughout much of Europe. John Torpey, in *The Invention of the Passport*, draws a clear connection between freedom of movement and freedom of thought in European countries, a point with which Sarmiento would have wholeheartedly agreed. "The word 'passport' is unknown in the states," he tells Alsina (158),[9] asserting further that "if France had abolished the passport liberty would have been advanced more than it has been in half a century of revolutions and advanced social theories, and the proof is in the United States" (161).[10] Travel, then, comes to serve three functions for Sarmiento: it furthers a public morality grounded in the romantic optimism of the United States; it produces the material traces of the nation with roads, maps, and a hospitality industry; and, in so doing, it drives expansion, increasing the space under national control.

Sarmiento comes to these observations about travel elliptically, however, and spends a good deal of his narrative working through seemingly tautologous relations between public institutions and public sentiments. He initially settles on an ambiguously defined "political conscience" (171)[11] or public "morality" (172)[12] to explain the political difference reflected in U.S. institutions, but even in so doing he admits his inability to name that which he has observed. "There is something going on in the United States [that] has not until now been precisely defined," he writes, while at the same time admitting his own inability to write it (172).[13] He speaks of individual morality, but he is also trying to get at something larger, a morality of "association, the larger morality which applies to millions of men and exists among families, cities, states, nations, and humanity in its entirety" (174).[14] Sarmiento wants to explain this public morality, but he can only describe it through local reports of well-trod territory including trial by jury, freedom of religion, public education, universal literacy, and free elections. But these phenomena are merely the material signs of democracy, and Sarmiento seeks explanations. Analyzing legislation such as Oregon's Organic Laws, Sarmiento argues for a theory of politics as the organic emanation of public feeling but then reads public feeling as a finely crafted political product (171, 380).[15] Examining the institutions might explain the desires, Sarmiento allows, and here he appears to give up his goal of explaining the emergence of the legislative body, the public morality of association. He cannot really let this question go, however, because for him this phenomenal association is what makes the United States truly unique. Interspersed, then, with his entertaining and informative descriptions of the land, people, and institutions of the United States, Sarmiento returns repeatedly to dance around this question of why these institutions appear in the first place.

Sarmiento's realization that travel grounds the public morality he observes occurs almost by accident when he visits Montreal, the residents of which do not travel and hence have, to his mind, an exceedingly parochial take on politics and culture. While Sarmiento finds the center of French Canadian life very beautiful, he criticizes the city for its self-isolation, its hatred of all things English—he describes several instances of people pretending not even to hear, let alone understand, him when he speaks the language (234, 440)—and its maintained allegiance to an idealized France. Sarmiento notes flows of neither people nor ideas into or out of Montreal, a physical and philosophical rigidity that results in political boundaries that hermetically seal the people from the future. By contrast, the English Canadians lead "flexible and active" lives (238).[16] Sarmiento measures English success in terms of motion and interaction, immigration and commerce, and also by the desire to associate with the United States (238, 440), a flexibility closely linked, in Sarmiento's reading, with travel.

Sarmiento sees travel as the root of a cosmopolitan idealism closely linked to the public morality supporting the political institutions and freedoms he so admires and understands as furthered by U.S. romantic optimism. "Romantic" here indicates heterosexual, romantic love, which Sarmiento situates at the center of a complex nexus. He spends a great deal of time describing the "young couples of twenty years of age embracing, reposing each in the bosom of the other" (136)[17] who honeymoon throughout upstate New York and Niagara Falls on the Hudson River steamboats, taking in the sights before settling down to produce a family. These newlyweds are both a traveling cause and an effect. Their public displays of affection convince others to travel—"I attribute to these ambulant amours . . . the mania for travel which distinguishes the Yankee," Sarmiento writes (138)[18]—and their affection ultimately produces future citizens who will, in their turn, continue to travel.

These honeymooners make the nation, in the abstract and material senses of the word. They produce the romantic optimism pushing people onto the road, water, and railways, consequently generating the public morality Sarmiento seeks to understand; and they generate the means to control the space they explore, engaging in an activity fueling an entire industry that Sarmiento describes in great detail: how the desire to travel drives rates down so that it is affordable, how hotels take over religious buildings in communal importance, and how map production increases as more space is gathered into tourism's fold. Sarmiento links this leisure-inspired cartographic proliferation to the flooding of the United States "with millions of maps of Mexico" during the Mexican-American War. He describes the joy taken by U.S. citizens in plotting and following troop positions on these maps as news comes over the telegraph wire (138).[19] The reader learns of the "Yankee's" proleptic positioning of the U.S. Army in Mexico and his obsession with knowing where the troops are "at this very moment," locating them "with his finger on the map," rearranging his pretend army accordingly, and learning more about the "topography, products, and resources of the country" than any Mexican resident (139).[20]

Technologies of travel become, then, for Sarmiento, part of his ideological justification for U.S. expansion, which relies on a cartographic temporality. Sarmiento's Yankee inhabits an eternal now in relation to maps that capture the past in such a way as to drive representation toward the future, the space to come. The maps collectively unfurled by Sarmiento's fellow passengers as towns come into view describe the present state of the terrain, but that present is already past in its moment of capture because Sarmiento's Yankee is always pushing forward, dominating and historicizing nature. Sarmiento admires this ambitious ingenuity, as is evident in his descriptions of New York's Croton Aqueduct (229, 436), but it troubles him as well. Sarmiento is a conflicted romantic at heart, as struck by the sublimity of a revenue-generating aqueduct as he is by Niagara Falls' awe-inspiring natural power. When, at Niagara, a Yankee concurs with Sarmiento that the falls are beautiful, Sarmiento balks at his realization that the Yankee sees only profit in them. "I believe the Yankees are jealous of the falls and will occupy them in the same way they occupy and populate the forests," thinks Sarmiento, apparently refuting his earlier admiration of Yankee ingenuity (229).[21] At the same time he praises the Yankee's taming of natural space, on some level it gives him pause.

Sarmiento experiences his offense at the man's utilitarianism as culture's antagonism toward capital and turns his own appreciation of Niagara's sublimity toward manufacture. "For two days," he writes, "I was enraptured by the contemplation of nature and at times discovered in the depths of my heart a strange feeling which I had never before experienced" (230).[22] The feeling is an acute desire to open a factory and move permanently to the United States. Realizing he has nothing to make, Sarmiento falls into a deep depression wherein he wonders what use he and Spanish culture, by extension, are in this world: "To teach or write what with this language that no one needs to know?" he wallows (231).[23] The Spanish can make nothing from nature, Sarmiento contends, while Yankees make beauty and public good, a productive trait he links directly to the historicization of nature. Sarmiento, in his description of his travels, reacts sentimentally to nature but treats it as a thing of the past, the containment of which grounds cultural progress.

Sarmiento describes several natural spaces as "primitive" throughout his narrative, setting them against scenes of travel and motion. "As the steamboats and trains pass through primitive forests" (133),[24] Sarmiento roots nature in the past in relation to the Yankees, those forward-thinking wanderers deploying their traveling and viewing technologies. Even though Sarmiento praises Yankee pragmatism, he never becomes a manufacturer, and his ambivalence here, the offense he takes at the Yankee observer at Niagara Falls, is notable. Though he supported the United States and modeled many of his own decisions as Argentine president on U.S. political practice, Sarmiento was a critic as well.[25] He calls Yankees "the most uncivil little animals under the sun" (150),[26] which in *Viajes por . . . América* grounds a professed egalitarianism but inspires, later in

Sarmiento's career, pointed political critique of U.S. perversion of the Monroe Doctrine.[27]

Though he eventually comes to critique the United States in practice, Sarmiento continues to believe in its ideals, offering his own transamerican vision with *Ambas Americas* (Both Americas), an educational journal he began publishing during his time as Argentine ambassador to the United States (1865–68). *Ambas Americas* published letters from educators across the Americas and covered pedagogical and institutional philosophy. Sarmiento's most transamerican policy initiatives were educational as well, as he understood himself primarily as a teacher. Though he had a long political career, his most lasting innovations in Argentina were his efforts, such as importing sixty-five New England schoolteachers, to develop Argentine schools (Dorn 83).

In his work as Argentine ambassador to the United States and later as president of Argentina (1868–74), Sarmiento envisioned a truly American partnership between the two countries, reflected in his literary and educational activities, which he saw as only sporadically reciprocated at the level of U.S. foreign policy. We can read his celebrations of Yankee ingenuity and travel in *Viajes por . . . América*, then, not as a concession to manifest destiny (despite his suggestions that Yankee knowledge of Mexico denoted them as its rightful owners) but as a celebration and initial narrative cartography of a transamerican space and a desire to harness the traveling power of North America for his southern compatriots.

"The liberty which has emigrated to the North gives to him who goes there wings to fly!" he writes, suggesting that travel is a direct function of liberty. The "venerable spirit of investigation" reflected in the Yankee drive to travel then transforms the space traversed, preparing the "soil" for "man's occupation." As "human torrents" move into the "primitive forests," news of this travel passes "silently overhead on iron strings to spread" the word far and wide (124).[28] Sarmiento analogizes a traveling liberty's transformation of space to Benjamin Franklin's harnessing of electricity, thereby reading North American settlement as the embodiment of transnational forces of freedom and curiosity, and imagining the transformation of the Americas as a natural and manifest destiny.

Sarmiento's ability to imagine himself as a traveler in this space keeps this from being a celebration of U.S. dominance, however. Juxtaposing his own travels across and between the Americas, with admiring treatises on Yankee travel, ingenuity, and the transformation of natural space, situates Sarmiento as a fellow traveler who can harness the abstract spirit of travel for deployment in the Americas. Travel becomes not just the explanation for North American success but the embodiment of a transnational desire for mobility and the unity of the Americas. Sarmiento's travels trace the transamerican ideal narrated later in *Ambas Americas*, embodied in the traveling teachers, and thwarted by an aggressive U.S. imperialism.

That trajectory is, however, almost too easy to trace. Just as he experiences a tension between culture and capital, or natural sublimity and manufacture, Sarmiento recognizes that only certain people have the freedom to travel. The mobility of women and African Americans is severely limited, an irresolvable contradiction in Sarmiento's theory of public morality and the transformation of the Americas of which he seems at least partially aware. The reader sees, in Sarmiento's discussion of the honeymooners, the connection between romance, travel, and the production of the body politic. Women are idealized figures for Sarmiento, who cannot quite resolve a contradiction in terms of the freedom that they both embody and represent: women produce a free people and yet they themselves are not free. The happy couples Sarmiento describes return from their honeymoon "to the blessed boredom of the domestic hearth." The wife says "good-bye forever to the world, whose pleasures she had enjoyed for so long in complete liberty. . . . From now on, the closed domestic asylum will be her perpetual prison, ROASTBEEF her eternal confessor, a swarm of blond and frolicsome little ones her constant torment" (137).[29] If travel makes the free citizen, then what to make of Sarmiento's description of said citizens' producer as a prisoner tormented by the very citizens she brings forth?

In Sarmiento's transamerican ideal, freedom rests on the subordination of the other—of barbarism, of nature, of women, of Africans, of Indians—but he seems genuinely troubled by these contradictions, if only because he spends so much time rationalizing them. "American women belong to the same class, and their good looks honor the human race," he opines (140).[30] Women stand for the absence of class and race, yet their ability to stand as such is rendered in starkly physical terms, as objects of nature subject—like blacks, natives, and landscape—to dominance and control.

In his discussion of women Sarmiento seems to recognize the contradiction in a transamerican ideal that relies on the absorption and elimination of otherness from the body politic. Here he rationalizes it with humor, but his discussions of slavery and native populations are riddled with philosophical inconsistencies and sloppiness. Slavery is justifiable in the South because the slave is an enemy of the state, he argues

(175, 382), while later recognizing slavery as "the deep ulcer and incurable fistula which threatens to corrupt the robust body of the Union" (304).[31] He understands the slave as a potentially civilized subject but recognizes the impossibility of their existing as such in the United States (305, 490). Similarly, Native Americans are consistently described as beyond the pale of civilization, hiding in the shadows of the "primitive forests" (133).[32] Excised from the body politic and relegated to natural nostalgia, neither the African slave nor the Native American can occupy Sarmiento's utopian transamerica. They cannot stay but neither can they go for, as Sarmiento writes, slavery is "the soul of the society which supports it" (304).[33] It animates the body just as Yankee energy transforms nature, just as the word is carried by the telegraph.

If the body politic already contains slavery as its soul, this suggests the impossibility of relegating the other to the natural past, as Sarmiento does when he claims that the landscape of North America renders difference obsolete. Like "water, by rubbing the uneven surfaces of different stones together, produces pebbles which look like brothers," so does the landscape form this homogeneous new civilization (124).[34] Niagara Falls, for instance, literally absorbs the irreconcilable other. Sarmiento tells of Indians, prisoners, and children who have all fallen prey to this cataract that "does not even deliver up the bodies of its victims" (223).[35] In stark contrast to the abstract freedom of physical sovereignty, the raced and gendered others of Sarmiento's transamerican space are literally, violently, and irrevocably subsumed into the natural past and its transformation into civilized space.

Sarmiento's narrative sublates racial and gender difference into a homogeneous social body through which he projects the imagined space of his transamerican ideal. He rationalizes the sublimity of Niagara's "white violence" (223)[36] with stories of its suppressing bodily difference and frames his entire discussion with detailed descriptions of travel, thus deploying the same containment strategies as the opportunistic Yankee he critiques at Niagara. Writing nearly twenty years previously, on the other hand, the Mexican political exile Lorenzo de Zavala—a much less passionate admirer of North America—finds Niagara an apt metaphor for civil war in Mexico and the dangers of U.S. expansion.

The Political Sublime and Mexico's Body Politic

Niagara Falls has a long and loaded history as an American signifier for U.S. and Latin American writers, as Kirsten Gruesz describes in *Ambassadors of Culture,* where her reading of the Cuban poet José María Heredia and his Anglo-American translator William Cullen Bryant hinges on the geographic and political dimensions of each poet's narration of American sublimity. Gruesz sees Bryant as a conflicted prophet of expansion and Heredia as an anti-colonial subject whose critique in the poem "Niágara" portrays sublimity as political terror, rendered simply as picturesque, poetic sorrow in Bryant's translation. Similarly, what Sarmiento reads as a natural tool for eradicating difference in the service of a transamerican ideal is, for Zavala, a powerful symbol of political treachery and economic hegemony.

Mexico's national debt and political intrigue dominated Zavala's personal and professional lives. Born in Mérida in 1788, Zavala was a third-generation Yucatecan, *criollo* not *gachupine,* born in the colony rather than Spain, hence forbidden by Spanish colonial law from holding significant political or clerical positions. An educated and voracious reader, steeped in the philosophies of Locke, Voltaire, and Rousseau, Zavala founded and edited the first newspapers on the peninsula, work that eventually led to his arrest in 1814.[37] Zavala studied medicine and English during his three-year imprisonment; upon his release he worked as a physician and politician, serving as Yucatecan representative in the Spanish parliament and, after independence in 1821, as a member of Mexico's constitutional congress where he became embroiled in the country's civic struggles.

The conservative elite and progressive *criollo* factions that defined colonial governance came also to define political life in the post-independence period with Centralists favoring a strong, authoritative center of political power and a greater role for the Catholic Church, while Federalists advocated a secular, republican state. Violent conflict between the parties was a core feature of Mexican politics in the 1820s and 1830s. When Federalist president Vicente Guerrero was overthrown in 1829, Zavala, an ardent member of the same party, fearing bodily harm and possible death, fled Mexico for the United States, whose natural grandeur provided a context in which to air his political distress. "Oh Niagara!" Zavala writes, meditating on Mexico's woes, "I was seeing in you the most melancholy representation of our disastrous revolutions. I was reading in the succession of your waves the generations that hasten on to eternity, and in the cataracts that proceed to your abyss the strength of some men that impels others to succeed them in their places" (57).[38] In stark contrast to Sarmiento's joyful celebration of the falls, Zavala crumbles before them in despair.

Their wildly different reactions to Niagara reflect broader differences in their strategies of mapping the Americas and in their views of transamerican possibility. Sarmiento celebrates nature's absorption of difference and sees technologies of travel reflecting a liberal state that contains difference within itself, an ideology that grounds his belief in hemispheric cooperation. Zavala is much less optimistic. For him, Niagara signals the production of political difference that the state cannot absorb. The mechanisms of the liberal state suggesting possibility for Sarmiento suggest only political division to Zavala, producing a kind of remainder that lies beyond state rhetoric, marking a boundary that transamerican idealism cannot traverse.

Zavala's *Viaje a Los Estados Unidos del Norte de America* (1834) attempts to explain Mexico by charting that remainder, by identifying what lies beyond the state's pale and offering real solutions for its incorporation. Over the course of the narrative race emerges as that which the state cannot contain, as the materialization of an abstract philosophical problem that coalesces in the physical body and its relation to the body politic. Zavala sees Texas as a racial utopia where *mestizaje* results in true liberty: a space that both produces and incorporates natural difference. This utopian, American hope ultimately fades as events unfold, history that Zavala dies too soon to witness but which other moments in his travels indicate he could have predicted. Zavala's meditations at Niagara Falls, for example, make clear that transamerican rhetoric relies on the existence of discrete states that remain in hierarchical relation to each other. This political impression is couched in observations of physical and mental health, which coalesce around questions of race and citizenship.

Niagara gives Zavala occasion to gloss Mexico's civil conflicts, from which he ventures several opinions about international relations that ultimately slide into a discussion of human psychology. "The Niagara River and the lakes form a very weak barrier to prevent Canada from one day being a part of the United States of the North," he muses (56).[39] He also notes that though the Canadians appear happy with their English colonial status, certain trade restrictions might make them less so, which links Canada to Mexico, whose trade had been similarly restricted by the Spanish. Rather than independence, Canada might opt for annexation by the United States, a realization that gives Zavala pause as he connects Canada to Alta California. Mexico's strict trade regulations in that territory caused much discontent, of which Zavala would have been aware as a member of both the Colonization and Finance committees in the

Mexican congress (Henson 22). Zavala's recognition of Canada's tenuous separation from the United States provokes a moment of clarity wherein he understands that Mexico is also intimately connected to its northern neighbor. The Monroe Doctrine offered one Pan-American vision; Zavala has a much darker view of hemispheric connection, invoked in his discussion of waterfalls.

Zavala materializes his recognition of Canada's and Mexico's similar political position with images of people jumping to their deaths. Noting the many waterfalls on the way from Albany to Lake Erie, Zavala tells his reader, "At the first one a maniac named Sam Patch died; he amused himself jumping from waterfalls." In the same paragraph Zavala moves immediately south to Mexico: "I remember hearing of a certain Rodriguez, also crazy, from Merida, Yucatan, who was continually climbing on church steeples and the highest buildings, jumping with great agility, and he died in one of his undertakings" (145).[40] Whereas Sarmiento imagined the telegraph connecting the Americas, Zavala offers suicidal tendencies as a transamerican sign. The waterfalls symbolize internationalism, or national expansion, mediated by powerful, uncontained nature. The shifting border is an untamable, truly wild frontier where the logic and rationality of the nation break down, where instead of citizens we find broken people. The insanity of the suicidal jumpers suggests that the other cannot be incorporated into an expanding body politic, as Sarmiento would have it. Rather, this idea of the traveler transforming space, the nation flattening racial and gendered difference, is illusory: the state cannot transform space, and the transnation cannot erase or subsume its other.

Mexico, despite its position as the national other to a hemispherism centered on the United States, can learn quite a bit from the example of its northern neighbor, as Zavala argues throughout *Viaje*. His descriptions of the United States are very clear and direct critiques of Mexico, including, for example, his energetic praise for the free press. "In no country in the world is there as great a number of newspapers in proportion to the population as in the United States of the North," he writes, only to use that observation to trace the ideological distance between the United States and Mexico "in which those who try to direct public affairs . . . put obstacles in the way of the intellectual progress of their fellow citizens" (72).[41] Not only are ideas allowed to circulate freely, but U.S. citizens are also trained to appreciate and develop them. Zavala, like Sarmiento, marvels at the high rates of literacy in the United States. He connects the ability to read with the willingness to engage in public debate and notes a direct correlation between the number of newspapers in circulation and progressive racial laws. The more reading in which citizens engage the less likely they will be to pass crushing legislation such as he finds in Louisiana, which prohibits "disturbing the peace" of the white population by inciting slaves, through the press, to think of liberty (22).[42] As abhorrent as he may find these laws, Louisiana's ability to pass them signals something far more significant to Zavala.

He spends considerable time describing the intricacies of states' rights. Tariff controversies along with state constitutions and governance are presented in loving detail by this self-proclaimed "legislator-philosopher" (139)[43] who seeks to help Mexico develop a similarly beneficial mode of governance. A passionate Federalist, Zavala never directly declares Federalism the best mode of governance, but his detailed descriptions make the case clearly enough. *Viaje* illuminates Zavala's belief that power should be distributed equally between a central authority and states united in a loose federation, as it was, in theory at least, in Mexico. His opinion that a central authority should maintain limited control over citizens' public lives grounds his support of church and state separation. Zavala approvingly cites the claim of New York's Episcopalian bishop John Henry Hobart that "the prostitution of religion in the service of secular politics has produced much prejudice."[44] Zavala views state influence on religious authority as anathema to both Federalist and liberal principles, and his attention here to the separation of church and state in the United States is a direct critique of Mexico's 1824 constitution, which established Roman Catholicism as Mexico's national religion.

Separation of church and state, states' rights in conjunction with a federal authority, a literate citizenry, and freedom of the press are all laudable institutions, according to Zavala. They evolve, however, from a specific body politic and so Mexico's direct emulation of them would be an error.[45] "The model was sublime, but not to be imitated," writes Zavala, referring to U.S. political influence on Mexico. He analogizes this to visual art, claiming that while painters might be able to copy a masterpiece in detail, "they never manage to equal those sublime concepts" that underlie the art itself. "Original artists do not copy . . . they invent," Zavala concludes, asserting that Mexico must identify and develop its own political sublimity (193).[46]

Zavala's narrative map of U.S. institutions attempts to identify that difference, the Mexican political sublime, and to make sense of contradictions in liberal discourse that advocates for both the natural self and its deferral to state authority.[47] Zavala wonders, that is, about the possibility of a self that lies beyond the state and a Mexico that exists beyond the shadow of the United States. Zavala's travels become a cartography of the body politic, the physical bodies that make up the United States and the racial and religious minorities that are left outside its institutional discourses. Zavala speaks of their incorporation in terms of physical health and renders public policy as medical metaphor. Race emerges in *Viaje* as a way to articulate this liberal impasse; though Zavala offers a forceful critique of slavery, only very slowly and imperfectly does he come to recognize race as signifying larger, epistemic problems for the Americas.

Slavery, Zavala dryly remarks, is "not very natural in a country where they profess the principles of widest liberty" (90),[48] and he brings this contradiction to bear on hemispheric nationalist debates. The impossibility of transamerica emerges for Zavala at the nexus of race, the state, and citizenship. *Viaje* is primarily concerned with the making of Mexican citizens and a liberal Mexican state, though Zavala later joined the fight for Texan independence and abandoned the Mexican Federalist cause. Where Bolívar argued that a shared Spanish colonial history bound Latin America in such a way as to isolate the United States from the Panama conference, Zavala found American commonality in the very thing that rendered Mexico so unique.

Zavala finds Mexican sublimity in the racialized bodies of indigenous Mexico; this corporeal sublimity both unites and divides the Americas but escapes representation. "And what shall we say of the Indians at Chalma, in Guadalupe, and in other shrines," he asks rhetorically. "Ah! The pen falls from the hand in order not to expose to the civilized world a horde of idolaters." The Indians are impossible to write because Zavala does not want to make them visible, though he cannot ignore the naked, homeless acolytes coming "to deliver into the hands of the lazy friars the fruits of their year's work" (35).[49] The Mexican Constitution of 1824 attempts a similar erasure, as Martha Menchaca has shown, in that the liberal state constituted therein did not allow for race, eliminating it as a category of social identification (161). As Menchaca argues, these liberal humanist gestures, such as mission secularization, do not rectify racial inequality; they just render it less visible (166). Zavala makes this same argument in his discussion of the Indians at Chalma and reveals social inequity as largely conditioned by race.

Zavala's example of race relations in the Church highlights the state's inability to eliminate race in its constitutive documents. Race still exists, still inhabits a materiality around which no amount of politicking can maneuver. For example, in describing the efforts of Robert Finley's

American Colonization Society (ACS), Zavala notes that establishing a nation of free blacks in Africa will not address the putative "natural stigma" of race that he astutely observes is much more a function of class than of color (143).[50] The Hurons in upstate New York further exemplify the materiality of race conditioned by class. The circumstances of this once "noble and warlike" tribe, decimated by "brandy and gunpowder," greatly depress Zavala. "Christianity is the only benefit that the Indian has received from the whites." But even this "sublime" gift is suspect, Zavala concludes, considering the fact that, in exchange, Anglos have "cheated, robbed, corrupted and ruined" indigenous populations. Salvation may be "sublime," Zavala grants, but natives "must mistrust a gift that comes from such people" (62).[51] The Indians at Chalma and the Hurons exist in subservient relation to Anglo models of religiosity that justify extreme inequality with the promise of otherworldly salvation. Calling that salvation sublime connects the hypocrisy of that relation to the sublimity of U.S. democracy, which is offered to Mexico but at what cost?

Religious salvation and liberal democracy both come at the expense of populations whose subordinate class position becomes articulated as racial difference, a difference that remains beyond the pale of citizenship. For indigenous populations this means a continuing struggle for sovereignty and definition within the state; for Latin America this results in ongoing debates about transamerican geopolitics. The transamerican ideal fails, in Zavala's narrative, because of the liberal state's necessary construction of a racial other that it is unable to incorporate. I do mean "incorporate" here in the most material sense of the term as relating to a physical body grounding the abstract notion of a body politic. Zavala is able to track and parse race's changing meaning in the Americas of the 1830s through a discourse of public health that posits the materiality of the body against the abstractness of a transamerica grounded in liberal democracy.

Zavala's narrative turn to public health should be read, given his earlier, direct attention to slavery and indigenous Americans, as a metaphor through which he explores the racial meaning of the Americas. On the one hand, his deployments of physicality do mirror the Enlightenment impasse of a theoretical equality that cannot reconcile the raced and gendered other. He marvels at the beauty of North American women, dwelling on their "very good color, large bright eyes, [and] well-shaped hands and feet" (81).[52] Likewise, Zavala's descriptions of indigenous Americans are grounded in materiality, in contrast with his descriptions of white men's personalities and emotional states. The Indians at Chalma are naked and destitute (35) while Martin Van Buren has a "spiritual face" (112),[53] Andrew Jackson is an "honorable old man" (33),[54] and John Adams, a "strange man," is "cold and circumspect" (153).[55] Zavala's descriptions of women and natives contrast markedly with his descriptions of white men and, to a certain extent, illustrate the paradox of citizenship in the liberal, nineteenth-century state: rational citizens manage irrational bodies, a human rights agenda that relies on hierarchies of the human.

Zavala, however, for whom the connection between physicality and morality remains under-theorized, is troubled by the liberal state's distinction between body and mind. Mind is body, according to Zavala, which is evident in his descriptions of women and natives. The women are mainly physical objects, but they have ineffable qualities that distinguish them nationally: the North American women cannot quite compare to Mexican women (81, 278).[56] Moreover, natives may be objects of study for Zavala, but he empathizes with their plight and analogizes their social position to that of Mexicans vis-à-vis the United States. Far from remaining outside the state, raced and gendered bodies enjoy a symbiotic relationship with it, in Zavala's analyses, simultaneously constituting and being constituted by the political institutions they inhabit. Zavala claims that the difference in political organization does not explain the different ways Mexico and the United States handle their affairs. The difference can be traced, rather, to the "enormous distance existing between the material and mental capacities of both countries" (139).[57] Mexico's physical difference from the United States, in other words, explains its political difference.

On the one hand this assertion appears to contradict Zavala's view of Mexican political troubles as functions of its colonial past (89, 286); but this colonial past is not enough, he later argues, to explain Mexico's political differences from the United States, which he understands as physical and mental, as rooted in the body. The body becomes, for Zavala, the basis for the distribution of political power, meaning that political institutions manifest the physical constitution of the body politic. Race emerges, in Zavala's reading of political difference as both colonial legacy and material difference, as a material reality as well as a social construct, located in all bodies, not simply those that are "other" to the liberal state.

This view leads Zavala to dwell on deployments of the body in his descriptions of the United States. While Sarmiento's travel narrative metaphorized maps as signs of industrial progress, Zavala's travel writing turns the body into a metaphorical map of how such progress produces American political conflict. His travels coincide with the height of what Ruth Engs terms the "first Clean Living Movement," a period of intense health, religious, and political reform in the United States from 1830 to 1860 (21). Zavala witnessed a wave of health reform that followed closely on the heels of the second Great Awakening, a groundswell of Protestant revivalism rolling across the United States during the first part of the nineteenth century. Zavala admiringly describes the energy and excitement of the "Camp Meetings" (32)[58] forming the center of this religious activity but is quick to condemn what he sees as the religious extremism of the Shakers (149, 344) and the Puritans (165, 362). He carries his critique of religious extremes over into his analyses of the health movements they inspire, focusing on the medical merits of mineral springs, temperance, and chastity.

Zavala approves of ingesting water from the mineral springs in and around Saratoga, New York, commenting on the benefits of their particular combination of "sodium chloride, sodium carbonate, calcium carbonate, magnesium carbonate, and iron carbonate" (64).[59] He even takes the time to stop in Ballston on his way to Albany to visit the springs there. Zavala takes a similarly moderate, proactive stance on temperance. It can do no harm to ingest mineral water, and it certainly does a body well to moderate one's alcohol intake. "What," he asks, "is apparently more reasonable than" setting sober example (143)?[60] However, he feels it is unhealthy to take sobriety to the extreme, citing the "frequent sudden deaths" of those who drink cold water straight from the well in the heat of summer after exercising. "All doctors are agreed that if this were mixed with a little brandy it would not cause such dire effect," he admonishes (144).[61] Likewise, though Zavala admires the Shakers' asceticism as a mode of drawing closer to God, he sees their extremism as physically detrimental. "Generally they are pale, and do not appear to be in very robust health," he writes. "It seems that they must be going contrary to the strongest inclination of human nature" (149).[62]

Positioning these analyses of religious and physical extremism immediately after his critique of the ACS suggests that the idea of a healthy body provides a space in which Zavala can work through the unknowable and unspeakable contours of race. Though he describes the society's colony favorably, Zavala cannot bring himself to admit that exiling blacks to Africa is a solution to racial conflict. He takes issue with the argument that Africans are physically and mentally different from Anglos, suggesting, "It is not certain that mixing the castes would ever erase their natural stigmas."[63] The original Spanish juxtaposes natural stigma with social construction in a convoluted double negative implying that racial mixing will dispel racial prejudice. Positing "casta," a term used mainly to describe the social value of race, against "estigmas naturales," instead of "raza" or "genero," more biological terms for race, emphasizes the body's social construction. A social shift might engender a shift in how U.S. citizens conceive of putative bodily facts, such as African inferiority, he argues. This becomes clear in his commentary on the healthy human body, immediately following, which renders legible his vision of a multiracial body politic.

Zavala's understanding of health and disease as systemic stakes a position in the debate between the nineteenth century's two epidemiological theories: miasma versus contagion, which offer a convenient structure for understanding the degree to which Zavala's views on race and hemispheric possibility differ from Sarmiento's. Given his professional medical background, it is not unreasonable to assume Zavala would have had a passing familiarity with epidemiological debates though he never publicly participated in them. In the early nineteenth century, supporters of the miasmic theory (anti-contagionists) believed that disease was caused by environmental conditions such as poor sanitation and exposure to sewage and garbage vapors. Contagionists, on the other hand, believed in the germ theory of disease: small organisms, which could be isolated and contained, spread disease.[64] As Milton Terris notes, in nineteenth-century Europe these scientific camps were highly politicized with elite, conservative contagionists supporting quarantines that curbed middle-class, mercantile expansion, restrictions concomitant, in the liberal imagination, with the state's defining control of the public body. Anti-contagionists, such as Zavala, were motivated by a passion for rigorous science and were considered quite radical. They resisted the idea, which smacked of the mysticism and ignorance promulgated by the Church, that invisible, little creatures could spread disease (Terris 442).

The miasmic theory of disease invested individuals with more control and sovereignty over their own bodies. Sarmiento's and Zavala's respective descriptions of New Orleans illustrate this difference. "Unfortunately, New Orleans is incurably sick," writes Sarmiento, blaming malaria that "kills those who do not flee from the center of the city." He reads geographic conditions as halting the "contagion" (307).[65] Zavala, though, reads New Orleans' central maladies as heat, humidity, and overpopulation (8, 207). All the "well-to-do people" are able to travel in order to escape the "excessive heat" and thus avoid illness (23).[66] Sarmiento identifies an avoidable contaminant while Zavala reads New Orleans' health problems as the product of interrelated and uncontrollable factors such as weather. Similarly, both Zavala and Sarmiento refer to U.S. slavery as an infectious disease, but they differ on its proper treatment. Their different takes on racial disease reveal their different levels of enthusiasm for and investment in the liberal state and the possibility of the transnation, or a truly "American" political culture.

Sarmiento has an enthusiastic optimism for the hemisphere and reads the racial other in *Viajes por . . . América* as relegated to the natural past. Slavery, however, gives him pause. He blames its presence on the colonial past, calling slavery a "parasitical vegetation which English colonization has left glued to the leafy tree of American liberty," confining it to the colonial past despite its reality in the present (305).[67] Like malaria, slavery can be contained and treated; it is a festering sore threatening the "leafy tree" and must be removed in order to avoid a "black, backward, and vile nation alongside a white one" (306).[68]

Zavala, on the other hand, is much more circumspect and contemplative when it comes to parsing the lived reality of race in both the United States and Mexico. Above all he advocates moderation and heterogeneity as a consistent, philosophical principle. On the question of race he is no less guarded, finding fault with repatriating African Americans and taking care to point out the benefits of racial diversity at every turn. For example, in describing his visit to West Point, Zavala tells his readers that several years hence "a young Indian from the Creek tribe named Moniac held a distinguished place among the students" (184).[69] Moniac excelled at math, which Zavala takes as evidence against Buffon's assertion that human intellectual capacities diminish in the Americas.[70] Slavery, therefore, and broader issues of racial discord cannot be solved by segregation, just as health and disease cannot, in Zavala's view, be reduced to a single organism or activity. Just as water mixed with a little brandy might prevent untimely death, so can racial integration strengthen the body of the nation, as the example of Moniac proves.

In the context of nineteenth-century theories of health and disease, Zavala's reading of racial diversity becomes a radical critique of hemispheric racial epistemes. Race, he argues, relies on the economy of expansion, and expansion, Zavala demonstrates in his reading of waterfalls, leaves fractured colonial subjects in its wake. Slavery, more than a festering sore, evidences systemic problems in the Americas, an argument Zavala underlines by connecting slavery to literacy rates and global capital in his discussion of sugar production. If slavery and ignorance exist in the United States because the United States wants to export more sugar and cotton, as Zavala argues (23, 222), then race as a biological fact is undermined. Zavala's ability to recognize the political and economic expediency of slavery and racial prejudice, and to connect this to the racialization of the Indians at Chalma (35, 234) as well as the Hurons (62, 261), makes visible the future racialization of Latinas/os in the United States. This possibility motivates his arguments for racial diversity as a way of holding out hope for a transamerican future, one Zavala sees in Texas.

Zavala's view of Texas as Mexico's future was relatively unique among his Mexican contemporaries. Texas had long been a thorny political issue for Spain, which struggled to defend the territory against native attacks as well as French and U.S. incursions. The Adams-Onis Treaty of 1819 established a boundary between Spain and the United States, but Mexico gained its independence from Spain in 1821 before that boundary had been officially surveyed. This boundary confusion, coupled with Mexican continuation of Spanish empresario grants in an effort to populate the frontier, brought an influx of Anglo and European settlers that, by the late 1820s, raised questions in the capital about the territory's stability. These threats were compounded by increasing numbers of native groups that had been pushed into Texas by aggressive U.S. policies in the Southeast. At the time, many Mexicans saw Anglo settlement in Texas as a prelude to war.

Zavala, however, true to his philosophy of race as correlative to a systemic, anti-contagionist view of bodily health, sees the diversity of Texan settlers as a potential strength rather than a threat to Mexican integrity. Mexico should no sooner bar future settlement, as it temporarily did in 1830, than U.S. abolitionists should send free blacks to Liberia. Granted, Zavala's own empresario contract did give him a financial stake in this argument. Mercenary aims aside, Zavala sees the racial and national diversity of Texas as the source of the Mexican political sublime that its political institutions must capture. Settlement, Zavala argues, will produce a "new generation" in Mexico that will be "entirely heterogeneous." They will form a free government that is not "a deceit, an illusion, but a reality" (79).[71] Zavala's journey through the metaphorical American body instantiates Texas as the American ür-text, the material space where the Mexican body is remade, the locus of a political healing that might spread "through other states towards the south, and those of Tamaulipas, Nuevo Leon, San Luis, Chihuahua, Durango, Jalisco and Zacatecas" (79).[72]

History, unfortunately, did not bear out Zavala's optimistic vision, causing him to ultimately abandon the Federalist cause and become a supporter of Texan independence. Zavala died in 1836, too soon to witness the eventual annexation of Texas by the United States in 1845, the codification of national boundaries, the increase in racial strife between Mexican and Anglo-Americans, and the quelling of transnational hopes. Many scholars have examined these racial dynamics and their effects on Chicana/o cultural production, but these studies have been carried out largely from a U.S. perspective and have focused primarily on the Southwest.[73] Turning to the Chilean writer Vicente Pérez Rosales's "Algo Sobre California," which documents his experiences in gold rush–era California, encourages a broader analytical scope, pushing further both north and south. Where Zavala suggests a constitutive relationship between the abstract body politic and the physical, racial body, Pérez Rosales shows the codification of that body in legal discourse and vigilante justice, demonstrating—in the evolution of "greaser" and "chileno" as generic terms to indicate racialized foreigners in the San Francisco Bay Area—the truly transnational dimensions of race that shut down the possibility of transamerica in the nineteenth century.

The Chilean Hottentot and the California Gold Rush

In Pérez Rosales's account of his U.S. travels, the idea of a Latina/o racial or ethnic identity emerges as the legal codification of the national and transnational tensions about which Sarmiento and Zavala can only write indirectly. A politician, journalist, and entrepreneur, Pérez Rosales traveled from Chile to California in 1848 in search of gold. He documented his adventures in "Algo Sobre California," which appeared in the June 1850 issue of the Chilean journal *Revista de Santiago* and later as part of his collected writings in 1882 (Brintrup 27). Pérez Rosales paints a picture of the San Francisco Bay Area in the late 1840s as an international crossroads where race emerges as a product of global capital, as part of a colonizing, Anglo-American discourse that elides the complicated histories and social structures of Latin America with racist legislation that codifies national division and firmly shuts a door on Sarmiento's transamerican vision.[74]

Sarmiento, like Zavala, correlates race with space, through which both writers move in racializing ways. Pérez Rosales links the production of space and race similarly, arguing for a reading of both as arbitrary, ideological constructs. His own presentation of himself and his relation to public space mirrors the slippage of race and nation evident in the nineteenth-century San Francisco Bay Area, a slippage most clearly marked in his descriptions of maps that bear no relation to actual land.

In Sarmiento's analysis maps actively and productively transform space, while for Pérez Rosales maps are completely random sketches of unknown terrain, which an irrational market then constitutes as knowledge. This is unfortunate given the utter chaos in which Pérez Rosales finds San Francisco upon his arrival in 1848. Hundreds of people wander haphazardly through the muddy ruts that pass for streets, past tents and shacks that house ephemeral and transitory businesses, all without the protection of any effective law and order. Reliable information about the northern mines is scarce, and what information does circulate is a capricious blend of hearsay and fiction. "Fortunately, a certain Mr. Prendergrast hit upon the idea of gathering gold without budging from San Francisco," Pérez Rosales tells his readers. "Somewhere he managed to find an old map of the viceroyalty of Mexico; and enlarging the part corresponding to Upper California as the spirit moved him, he flooded the city with sketches that, though badly executed and consisting of sheets of cigarette paper, brought a price of 25 pesos each" (232).[75] In these maps knowledge emerges as a relative construct of contingent value.

Moreover, where Sarmiento sees maps as the materialization of conquered nature and historicized race, Pérez Rosales understands both space and race in a state of flux, their meaning determined by social and economic forces. Unable to historicize space, as Sarmiento does, Pérez Rosales, an early gold seeker actively engaged in the construction of space, understands both space and race to be unfolding into the future. His narrative demonstrates the beginning of racial identities that approach our understanding of race relations in the twenty-first century, identities that surface here as the product of economic and geopolitical tensions.

On the Pacific Rim of the western hemisphere, these are rooted in the strained relationship between Chile and Alta California, which have limited interaction during the colonial period but clash repeatedly throughout the 1820s when Chile emerges as the dominant trading power in the Pacific, interfering continually in Mexican-Russian relations.[76] Despite a history of low-grade conflict, Chile supported Mexico against the United States during the Mexican-American War of 1846–48—a conflict Pérez Rosales refers to as "disastrous" (208)[77]—largely in response to widespread antipathy toward the United States after being misled by Joel Poinsett to expect U.S. aid during their struggle for independence from Spain (Faugsted 8). Furthermore, Chile worried that a U.S. victory would allow the United States to establish a Pacific presence that could threaten Chile's regional status. All was forgiven, however, with the discovery of gold in California, news of which reached Valparaiso in August 1848 (Faugsted 15). The discovery sparked mass migration from Chile, prompting major newspapers to declare an emigration crisis (Giacobbi 23). "The streets are full of people from Chile," declared Thomas Larkin, a San Francisco politician (in Faugsted 20). Vicente Pérez Rosales was one of them.

San Francisco was only one of many world cities Pérez Rosales visited in his lifetime (1807–86), which covered a vast and transformative period of Chilean and world history including "Chile's independence, its early nationhood, two foreign wars, two civil wars, the arrival of steamships, railroads, telegraph, the southern and northern expansion of the country's territory, [and] the arrival of European, North African, Latin American, and North American immigrants" (Loveman xvii). His memoir *Recuerdos del Pasado* (1882), a small fraction of his literary output, reflects a remarkably cosmopolitan worldview. "Algo Sobre California," included in *Recuerdos*, is a lighthearted tale of his and his brothers' adventures as fortune hunters in nineteenth-century California. Despite the overwhelmingly humorous tone, however, "Algo Sobre California" covers serious and frightening territory. He describes anarchy in the streets, lynching, and increasing bodily violence against Chilean, Mexican, and other Latin American miners as competition for mining rights increases. The reader witnesses racial formation, seemingly as it happens. Prendergrast's haphazard maps are juxtaposed with racial antagonisms in the Bay Area, and race emerges as something very much like one of those cigarette-paper sketches of an imagined land: endlessly rewritten, never the same, and subject to the whims of its creator.

Social organization through physical metaphors of blood and the like existed before the discovery of gold at Sutter's Mill, of course,[78] but in the wake of gold's discovery, such distinctions take on the modern cast of racial thinking as an Anglo-American majority used first national and then racial distinctions for political and financial gain. Latin Americans in particular were targeted because they tended to operate the most successful diggings (mining operations). "The biggest waves of Latin Americans," writes Leonard Pitt, "came from Chile and Northern Mexico," but for the most part Latin Americans were "lumped together as 'interlopers' and 'greasers'" (53) by Anglo-Americans.[79] This was particularly galling to Chilean miners who prided themselves on their independence, fighting spirit, political stability, and national successes, sentiments Pérez Rosales illustrates throughout his narrative but particularly in his description of a solitary journey he makes from San Francisco to Monterey in search of milk and a little relaxation. After encountering fellow travelers, Pérez Rosales reflects: "As during my earlier encounters with Sonorans and Spanish Californians, I now again had occasion to marvel at how naively these poor people view the invasion and conquest of their homeland by the Yankees. They believe themselves incapable of expelling those whom until now they rightly consider tyrants; but, having seen how vigorously the Chileans have resisted brutal persecution by the Yankees, they are also firmly convinced that the Chileans could expel them if they wanted to" (286).[80] Because the Chileans had forcefully resisted increasing Anglo violence, Mexicans and *californios* viewed Chileans as a sort of talismanic protection against Yankee hostility.[81] Taken in by a *californio* family on his way to Monterey, Pérez Rosales remarks, "For Californians, a Chilean veteran of the diggings was the symbol of personal security, the scarecrow to ward off the outrages of the Yankee, and the brother toward whom one's hand should always be outstretched" (287).[82] Chileans served as moral leaders of Latin American mining communities, which has been corroborated by historians of the period, and Chilean and Mexican mining skill was also widely acknowledged. Both Chileans and Mexicans were very successful wet and dry washers and developed new, useful mining technologies in the field.[83]

"Algo Sobre California" depicts the effects of this mining success as violence against non-Anglos, Latin Americans especially, at the mines increased in inverse proportion to the ease in extracting gold. Chileans, and all foreigners, quickly became scapegoats for mining failures, an animosity that soon developed into calls to exclude "foreign" miners, or to at least heavily tax them. Pérez Rosales narrates the increasing animosity and couples the nativist turn with the explicit racializing of Chileans, whom the "Yankees," according to him, consider as "scion[s] of Africa" (221).[84] He writes of vigilante justice at the mines that migrated eventually to the cities, coming to a head in July 1849 when a group called the Hounds attacked Chilecito, or Little Chile, a tent encampment of Chileans in what is now San Francisco's Little Italy, or North Beach.[85] Tents were destroyed and looted, and people—including patrons of what a contemporary newspaper report described as a "house of Chilean women" (quoted in Faugsted 33)—were beaten senseless in the streets. San Francisco residents were aghast at these events, which prompted them to take matters in hand and swiftly curb the Hounds' authority, but this did little to ameliorate the situation of Chileans in the mines or in California more broadly.[86]

After the attack of the Hounds, public opinion swelled strongly in favor of tighter regulation. The California legislature approved the Foreign Miners Tax Law in 1850. The law stipulated that any non-citizen who wished to mine needed a license to do so, at a cost of $20 per month, an outrageous amount eventually lowered to the much more realistic tax of $3 per month. After repeated revisions and repeals, the law accomplished its clear purpose of controlling the non-Anglo, non-U.S. citizen population in the mines and establishing Anglo superiority in the state. To Pérez Rosales's mind, it "put the finishing touch to the abuses committed against the peaceful and defenseless Chileans," abuses he attributes to the perception of Chileans as black. "Their [the Yankees'] argument was simple and conclusive: the Chilean descended from the Spaniard, the Spaniard had Moorish blood, therefore the Chilean had to be at least a Hottentot or at best something very much like the timid and abased Californio" (271).[87] This transitive deduction is a generous gloss on the fact that as the diggings dried up it became useful for Anglos to think of Latin Americans as racialized others.

Notably, Pérez Rosales does not argue against racial hierarchies; he simply describes Anglo animosity toward Chileans as misguided. Elsewhere in his narrative Pérez Rosales refers to an African customer at his restaurant as "Mr. Fatlips" and a "scion of Africa" (284),[88] and he makes no mention of the Chinese, who suffered similarly. The passage of the Foreign Miners Tax Law equalized the Chileans, the Chinese, and the Mexicans before the law and successfully created a legal other to the Anglo-American with regard to mining rights (Pitt 69). Though Pérez Rosales's views on this process of racialization were not particularly progressive, his narrative demonstrates how categories of race emerge in tandem with flows of global capital.

In addition to creating a legal other in the service of establishing Anglo superiority, as with the foreign miners' tax, laws were also deployed in the service of criminalizing Latin Americans. Certainly there was crime of all kinds in the cities and the mines. Pérez Rosales evokes San Francisco's frontier justice when he describes personal security as dependent only upon "the number of those banded together for mutual defense or the superiority of the weapons carried by the victim of aggression" (266).[89] The difference, as the 1850s progress, came with legislation like the Greaser Laws, which criminalized aspects of Mexican and Latin American culture.[90] Just as Mexicans, Chileans, and other Latin

Americans came to be included under the "greaser" umbrella, so then did increasing hostilities come to render all "greasers" criminal in the popular imagination.

Not only crime but all types of vice were attributed to Chileans especially; many historians still understand Chilean women to be San Francisco's pioneer prostitutes, accusing them of dedicating "the nights to bawdy carousal and to sexual excesses and exhibitions" (Asbury 33). Pérez Rosales says otherwise. He describes the near total absence of women in San Francisco until mid-1849 when some tavern keepers, seeking other avenues of profit, began charging admission fees to view life-size portraits of naked women painted on their walls (289, 488). Nude tableaux of real women replaced these artistic renderings when what Pérez Rosales describes as the first prostitutes, "more substantial gargoyles" (290),[91] were brought to San Francisco on the Panama steamer. The Panama route was the primary east-west U.S. route from 1848 to 1869, making a Panama steamer, for Pérez Rosales, a U.S. ship transporting U.S. citizens from New York to San Francisco (Kemble 3). The women disembarking from the Panama steamer are "gargoyles" in contrast with the extremely modest Chilean and Mexican women who, for example, smoke by "carefully covering their mouths with their shawl while inhaling, and uncovering it when exhaling" (289).[92] In Pérez Rosales's descriptions of Chilean and Mexican sexual mores, we see that immorality lies not necessarily in the sexual act, economic exchange, or gestures thereto but in the public display of such things that render women, to Pérez Rosales's mind at least, "gargoyles."

This sexual diffidence has its corollary in a racial diffidence that makes Pérez Rosales's narrative even more interesting at the level of language. "Algo Sobre California" demonstrates the linguistic mutability of race and space, seen in Prendergrast's maps, at the same time it makes plain the materiality of race, seen in race-based violence such as the Hounds' attack on Little Chile. Throughout his narrative Pérez Rosales maintains a healthy suspicion of racial and national affiliations that can easily change. His experiences purchasing a boat are a perfect example of this.

After, as Pérez Rosales puts it, the mines "had become inaccessible to foreigners" (275),[93] he and his brothers decide to go into trade, for "no one paid any attention to the fact that what was sold inland for a hundred was being practically given away in San Francisco" (276).[94] After purchasing the *Indefatigable* from a Chilean acquaintance, Pérez Rosales prepares to sail inland with his cargo of beef jerky when he is stopped by a customs agent who asserts that his boat is neither "American" nor made of

"American" wood, two requirements for sailing on the inland rivers. Pérez Rosales enlists the help of an insurance agent he knows from Valparaiso, who, in San Francisco, has turned himself into a lawyer but "pretended not to know [Pérez Rosales] or even speak Spanish" (277).[95] The lawyer insists that he knows the boat, though he appears confused enough about its particulars to worry Pérez Rosales. A few days later, however, the lawyer presents him with the necessary paperwork to prove not only that the boat was American but also that it was built in San Francisco. Furthermore, "not only was the vessel a purebred, but so was its name, because instead of *Indefatigable*, which is how the Mexican barbarians who don't know English pronounced it, it was *Impermeable*" (277).[96] Pérez Rosales is not convinced that the lawyer's findings are true, but he does find that enough money and paper can create truth, as well as national identity.

The story of the *Impermeable* also highlights the lengths to which Chileans and other foreigners work to deny their foreignness in San Francisco. The boat's true nationality is unclear, but both Pérez Rosales and the lawyer work to establish it as a "purebred" American. The lawyer, likewise, denies his association with Pérez Rosales. "And this rascal," he writes, claims "he had only been in Chile a short time, when he had grown gray there!" A mere "sign on his door" transforms the insurance agent into a lawyer, his own assertions remove the taint of Chile, and some fairly dodgy paperwork converts the boat into a pedigreed American (277).[97]

Pérez Rosales, however, engages in a fair amount of dissociative self-referentiality as well. He does not dispel the assumptions of neighboring miners that he is French (260, 437), even referring to himself as "the Frenchman" (264, 442). Similarly, he rarely refers to himself in the first person, describing himself as "our worthy Elder" in several places and leaving it to the reader to determine from contextual clues that he is, in fact, that Elder (262).[98] This kind of narrative self-deferral allows for some poignant explorations of self and other in a transamerican context.

In describing inland California, for example, Pérez Rosales writes, "A traveler on the Argentine pampas, if suddenly deposited on a California ranch, would no doubt think he was changing horses at one of the post-stations of that wasteland" (246).[99] Sarmiento, in *Facundo* (1845), had famously described the course of Argentine history as the struggle between the civilized cities and the barbaric pampas. In equating California with Argentina, Pérez Rosales reverses Sarmiento's equation of civility with increased population. He describes the mining territory as a "country made semi-barbaric by the exceptional circumstances it was undergoing" (264).[100] Civilization in the mining territories actually decreases in inverse proportion to immigration; that is, as more people arrive to displace the native presence, the territories descend deeper into barbarity, an observation that mirrors Zavala's rendering of the human cost of U.S. expansion as suicide. In this same vein, Pérez Rosales finds humorous a journalist's comparison of Stockton's specially constructed public gallows with San Francisco's and Sacramento's practice of improvising gallows in trees. The journalist sees Stockton's gallows as "a mark of civilization" (268),[101] which Pérez Rosales find woefully ironic.

Pérez Rosales further undercuts concepts such as "civilization" with elliptical and convoluted references to himself that also highlight the pettiness of national and racial conflict. He first refers to himself as "the Frenchman" to a group of miners planning an attack on a native community. Pérez Rosales tells the miners that though he is ill, the spirit of Lafayette compels him to fight. His colleagues reject his "heroic sacrifice" and allow him to rest (260).[102] Pérez Rosales's tongue-in-cheek description of the miners' national pride coupled with his sympathetic description of the natives' grievances against "the alien intruders who harried them everywhere" (259)[103] constitute an ironic commentary on national conflict and pride, from which he extricates himself by strategically eschewing first-person narration and adopting different nationalities.

Through these textual strategies Pérez Rosales refuses self-identification. His definition of himself in "Algo Sobre California" relies on making himself other in a way that mirrors the textual and linguistic racialization set in motion by the gold rush. Pérez Rosales manipulates the emerging, racial hierarchies in nineteenth-century California with evasions of his "self" that exploit the fact that race and nation can be made and remade as easily as an imagined map or a genuine, "American" boat. In "Algo Sobre California," as in Zavala's *Viaje* and Sarmiento's *Viajes por . . . América*, the transformation of space parallels the creation of race, which in its turn codifies national division in the Americas. Over the course of the three travel narratives an imagined Latina/o other appears in the United States as U.S. hemispheric dominance increases, a dominance manifest in the laws and physical violence that eventually drive Pérez Rosales, his brothers, and thousands of other Latin Americans from the state.

Shifting Literary Terrains

Not all Mexicans and Latin Americans left the United States in the 1850s, however. Many immigrants stayed and continued to seek their fortunes, and many Mexicans were California natives whose families had settled along with the first missionaries in the early 1700s. These *californios* considered themselves Californian first and then only secondarily Mexican, if at all. After 1850 they grappled with "greaser" as the nominalization of the shifting legal and social identity of Mexicans and Latinas/os as subordinate to Anglo-Americans.

Nativism may have created a de facto Latina/o collectivity in the Anglo-American imagination, but many Latin American groups were resistant to such identification. Pérez Rosales maintains Chilean superiority in his narrative, and Mariano Vallejo, to whom I turn in Chapter 2, was certainly no friend to the Chileans.[104] His animosity historically grounds twentieth-century Chicana/o resistance to terms like "Hispanic" and "Latino." That resistance is often understood as opposition to the homogenizing moves of Anglo capital, but it also grows from intracommunal tensions between differently located Latina/o collectivities whose resistance to Anglo hegemony engenders a vision of the past that idealizes the Mexican presence in the Southwest at the expense of other *latinidades*. Pérez Rosales shows California's radical heterogeneity along with the Anglo desire to subsume that diversity into Anglo-dominant historical narratives. As we turn to writers like Vallejo as founding figures in Chicana/o literary history, it is crucial that we keep alive the vision of transnational *latinidad* that emerges in Pérez Rosales's narrative and that we not succumb to the desire to homogenize the Latina/o past of California and the southwestern United States.

Sarmiento analogizes that homogenizing drive to an enterprising, Yankee spirit that he greatly admired and saw as the foundation of transamerican cooperation. Ironically, and unfortunately, it renders impossible his vision of transamerica. In "Algo Sobre California," Mexican and Latin Americans are violently driven from the United States because of that same capitalist entrepreneurship that Sarmiento saw as literally tracing the contours of transamerica. Sarmiento's abstraction of America can neither map the actual terrain nor contain the physical bodies inhabiting it. Zavala lays the philosophical groundwork for this contradiction in *Viaje* when he speaks of the symbiosis of the physical and mental (153) and describes the necessity of incorporating free blacks into the U.S. body politic (143). In "Algo Sobre California" some Americans are transformed into those same black bodies that Zavala describes the United States as having such a difficult time integrating.

In showing the transformation of Chileans into "Hottentots" or "scions of Africa," Pérez Rosales's "Algo Sobre California" is a window into the formation of the United States as a neo-colonial force in the Americas, a process of which Sarmiento, Zavala, and Pérez Rosales trace an almost linear chronology. These three travelers, however, show race made anew in a hemispheric context and the forging of U.S. identities in the crucible of colonial, racial epistemologies. Textually speaking, however, these forces do not result in narratives of oppressed peoples chafing against colonial dominance; rather, we can imagine Sarmiento, Zavala, and Pérez Rosales with heads cocked and eyebrows furrowed, attempting to make sense of an emerging racial language grounded in global capital.

Neither Sarmiento, Zavala, nor Pérez Rosales saw himself as a racial subject, though Pérez Rosales understood that he was being racialized even as he wrote "Algo Sobre California." Rather than subaltern speech, their writing reflects the economic dimensions of Chicana/o and Latina/o "identity" in the United States and the deeply transamerican roots of class and race conflict. Bringing these identities into focus as the product of nineteenth-century economic tensions in the hemisphere allows us to fully grasp Mariano Vallejo's "nation" of global possibility, explored further in the next chapter, as the direct descendant of the debates traced here. Born and raised in California, he poses an eloquent counter to Sarmiento, Zavala, and Pérez Rosales, who were engaged in quite different literary projects. Each wanted to make the United States legible to a Latin American audience, while Vallejo wanted to make the United States legible to itself. As travelers intimately involved in the process of statecraft in their home countries, Sarmiento, Zavala, and Pérez Rosales performed a confluence of textual self and nation; writing the other offered occasion to write Argentina, Mexico, and Chile, to reflect on the traveler's subjectivity and the meaning of being away from home, even the dimensions of home itself, and thus to meditate on the citizen's relation to the state.

Sarmiento, Zavala, and Pérez Rosales are all writing of their travels as *letrados* engaged in statecraft.[105] All were important and influential politicians in their home countries. Each responded in different ways to the processes of modernization set in motion during the nineteenth century that at first offered such promise, as we see in Sarmiento, but resulted in the political and economic subordination of Latin America to the United States, as recounted by Zavala, and the racialization of Mexicans and Latin Americans that Pérez Rosales experienced. Literature takes a different direction in the later nineteenth century, moving from building and venerating the state, as did the three travelers discussed in this chapter, to calling the state into question as an agent of capital fomenting uneven development and the alienation of labor. In Chicana/o literary history, Mariano Vallejo functions similarly as *modernista* writers like José Martí and Rubén Darío, who turned literary aesthetics to state critique.[106] While Sarmiento, Zavala, and Pérez Rosales are active state builders, Vallejo is ultimately resistant to state power in a way that both prefigures *modernismo*'s aesthetic challenge while also asserting the primacy of historiographic romanticism.

2 / *Mexicanidad* at Home: Mariano Vallejo's Chicano Historiography

The work which has been done in three years to cross the Continent is stupendous!
—MARIANO VALLEJO WRITING IN HIS JOURNAL IN 1869

I am tired of the trains, they run with such violence day and night, so full of people, and so many people are killed in collisions that occur every day that it makes one afraid to ride in them. Sometimes they pass over arms of the sea, the bridges sink and those seated within are drowned; other times two trains on the same track come together and it is horrible to see how the people and cars are made into bits.
—VALLEJO WRITING TO HIS WIFE IN 1865[1]

Mariano Guadalupe Vallejo, former Mexican military commander of Alta California and, at one time, the region's wealthiest resident, was, like the travelers in the previous chapter, duly impressed with technologies of U.S. travel, as indicated by the above epigraph from 1869. He also shared those travelers' admiration of the professed liberal, egalitarian, and republican ideals of the United States, as will become clear in the course of this chapter. As the above epigraph from 1865 reveals, however, Vallejo was not blind to the dehumanizing effects of these modern marvels, nor was he unaware of the racialization and proletarianization of California's Mexican American population that followed in the wake of conquest and modernization.

Vicente Pérez Rosales chronicles the beginnings of this process in "Algo Sobre California" (1850), discussed in Chapter 1; twenty-five years later Vallejo covers similar territory in his *Recuerdos Historicos y Personales Tocante á la Alta California* (Historical and Personal Recollections Touching upon Alta California [1875]). Vallejo's *Recuerdos* recount the history of California from its earliest beginnings until the end of the Mexican-American War in 1848. His history encompasses a range of topics and voices, moving from literary history to analyses of political economy and public policy, and scathing critiques of both Spanish colonialism and the early Mexican Republic as well as of California's transition from Mexican to U.S. rule.

In writing his *Recuerdos*, Vallejo offers his own historical vision, but he is also carving out a space for himself and his fellow *californios*. This is not, as Rosaura Sánchez argues in *Telling Identities*, an imaginary space "no longer recoverable except in memory" (1). Sánchez's reading of Vallejo's history and other similar texts as "cognitive map[s] of local and global social spaces" (x) reduces the *californio* engagement with space to a nostalgic conjuring of lost land. Here, by contrast, I read Vallejo as part of a tradition, described in the previous chapter, of viewing the Americas as a work in progress. The California Vallejo imagines is not, as Sánchez would have it, "a liminal ethnic space" (1) but the red-hot center of the late nineteenth-century Americas. Vallejo's cosmopolitanism, his travels, and his interactions with an increasingly international population disprove the notion of nineteenth-century California as a cultural backwater. Quite the contrary, Vallejo was a part of the hemispheric "commonality of Latino expression" (xi) Kirsten Gruesz traces in *Ambassadors of Culture*. Deeply committed to his own community, Vallejo also recognizes the need to develop a global perspective and establish empowering connections for *californios*.

In my reading of Vallejo's *Recuerdos* I am most interested in discerning what U.S. places like California begin to look like when considered in a broad, American, rather than stringently national, context. In this regard, Vallejo's desire to establish global networks of trade and communication is particularly compelling and deserves close attention. In his *Recuerdos* Vallejo writes primarily of California, and scholarship to date has focused on the emergence of California as an imaginary space in his writing. Sánchez's study, for example, posits Vallejo's text as both a representational space in and of itself and a reconstruction of the *californios'* "former spatial and temporal configuration" (4). This textual imagining of California's past grounds, in Sánchez's analysis, "a liminal 'protonational' space neither Mexican nor American" (232) that is eventually rearticulated as an ethnic identity Sánchez understands as incipient *chicanismo*.

Sánchez sees California, and the protonational *chicanismo* it engenders, as a key space of Mexican-U.S. conflict, but I seek a perspectival shift toward understanding California as the global crossroads Pérez Rosales describes and as Vallejo clearly understood it to be. "Geographically," Sánchez writes, "California existed in isolation, with limited contact with the rest of the world" (234), and she treats it as nearly exclusively Mexican. Pérez Rosales's "Algo Sobre California," however, depicts California as a remarkably heterogeneous and multiracial space. Granted, Pérez Rosales is describing post-conquest California, but the diversity and tensions he portrays are part of a long history of intercultural and international conflict in the region, as Vallejo's sweeping *Recuerdos* make plain.

Vallejo's text is not a nostalgic vanity project. The *Recuerdos* paint an American vision of the present and are best read in the context and trajectory of Domingo Sarmiento, Lorenzo de Zavala, and Pérez Rosales, Vallejo's traveling, intellectual contemporaries. Vallejo's text does not craft a protonational "social space and collective identity" (Sánchez 37); it refutes the very logic of patriotism and nationalism. Vallejo's vision echoes in some respects that of his contemporary Francisco Ramírez, a Los Angeles–based journalist whose newspaper, *El Clamor Publico* (1855–59), advocated an international definition of *la raza latina* (Kanellos, "Clamor" 17). Unlike Ramírez, however, Vallejo has a transnational vision that is less a resistant response to U.S. hegemony than a claim staking. Vallejo's global, Californian history is one link in a long chain of American visions; his is a proactive authorial stance that predates, though it is catalyzed by, conquest.

Vallejo wrote his *Recuerdos* at the request of the San Francisco–based, Anglo-American historian Hubert H. Bancroft. In his own memoir, *Literary Industries* (1915), Bancroft describes his relationship with Vallejo and how he convinced Vallejo to contribute to his project of chronicling the history of the western United States, Central America, and South America. Here I consider Vallejo's *Recuerdos* in relation to the seven volumes dedicated to California in Bancroft's *Works*. I envision the two texts in dialogue with each other and read the *Recuerdos* in conjunction with Vallejo's personal archive in Sonoma, the town he founded in Northern California. This includes the papers that Vallejo did not donate to Bancroft's library, which offer an intimate view of Vallejo before, during, and after he completed his manuscript for Bancroft.[2]

In situating the *Recuerdos* in this way I aim to show Vallejo as not simply a voice from out of the shadows illuminating early Chicana/o experience. The differences between his and Bancroft's history of California are much deeper and far more significant. Bancroft's history adopts a depersonalized, authoritative, fact-driven tone. Concerned with an accurate representation of the past, the history documents every claim it makes, the body of the text resting on inches of footnotes at the bottom of each page. Assured of its rightness, the history moves forward like a well-oiled machine, absorbing internal narrative conflicts and reproducing itself several times over in thirty-nine volumes. The text, its mode of production, and its marketing reflect Anglo-American capitalism and nationalism at the turn of the last century. But Bancroft's *Works* are not without their problems, as we will see. He was severely criticized for his "business methods," supposed biases, and lack of objectivity.

Vallejo's *Recuerdos* exploit these fissures in Bancroft's austere, historically objective façade. Where Bancroft's text moves forward in an orderly fashion, Vallejo moves back and forth in time, discussing the U.S. 1848 occupation of California one moment and Junipero Serra's eighteenth-century deeds the next. Far from Bancroft's consistent and predictable prose stylings, Vallejo moves deftly from literary analysis to history to poetry in one page. If Bancroft's text reflects late nineteenth-century Anglo-American capitalist nationalism, then Vallejo's *Recuerdos*, in their exploitation of Bancroft's fissures, must be understood as a self-conscious critique of Bancroft's political ideology.

Vallejo's Journeys

Vallejo's critique of Bancroft is informed by his own idiosyncratic national imaginary, developed in part through his transcontinental trips and one sojourn south to Mexico. In 1869, Vallejo made his second trip east, accompanied by his U.S.-born son-in-law, John Frisbie. As he marveled at the machinery of travel, Vallejo was also quite taken with the grandeur of urban centers such as Chicago, whose streets, buildings, and museums he lavishly praised in his journals. On this trip, Frisbie and Vallejo were lobbying Congress to make the city of Vallejo (named after Mariano) a major port and to increase naval activity at the Mare Island Shipyard, which had been built there in 1854. Vallejo's 1865 trip had been primarily for pleasure.

Yet, the energy and enthusiasm evident in Vallejo's letters and journal entries from 1869 differ significantly from the brooding gloom of his 1865 trip. Then he complained constantly about the hustle and bustle of New York, the noise of the trains, and the unfriendliness of the people. The unbearable cold is another recurring motif in these letters.[3] Further pall was cast over the trip when, from his hotel window, Vallejo watched the crowds mourning Abraham Lincoln, of whom Vallejo was a great admirer, as Lincoln's body passed down Fifth Avenue after his death on April 15 (Empáran 114). On April 30, 1865, Vallejo wrote to his wife, Francisca, that he missed California and was ready to leave "this country which I admire but do not love because its climate as much as the people in general have done many bad things to me and have caused my ruin and that of my family."

Vallejo's claims to admiration are borne out by his personal archive in Sonoma. He kept a copy of the *New York Herald Tribune* from April 15, 1865, boasting a large sketch of Lincoln on its front page. The *Tribune* keeps company with copies of the Declaration of Independence, the U.S. Constitution, the signature page of the California State Constitution, and letters from George Washington and Benjamin Franklin, two of Vallejo's political heroes. Along with his U.S. ephemera Vallejo kept an original, 1822 letter from Simón Bolívar to General José Paes, of Columbia, in which Bolívar warns of continuing unrest in Mexico. Similarly, invitations and newspaper clippings suggest that Vallejo kept up with events in Mexico and Latin America, celebrating various days of independence and meeting with south-of-the-border luminaries, like the Mexican poet Guillermo Prieto, when they visited the Bay Area (Tays 239).[4]

Vallejo's transamerican archive speaks more to geopolitical dislocations than affections, however. Toward the end of his life he had no particular love for either the United States or its southern neighbors, but this disaffection had a circuitous path and developed over a long, eventful life. Born in Alta California in 1808, Vallejo followed his father into a military career. After Mexico gained its independence from Spain, however, the *californios'* sense of isolation from the capital deepened. In an 1879 letter to his son Platon, Vallejo referred to "our people" as "the Spaniards,"[5] and he described Mexico City to his wife as "infested" with Indians.[6] The United States offered little better in exchange. Having initially welcomed Anglo-American settlers with open arms, Vallejo found that incorporation into the union came at great personal and political cost to him and his fellow *californios*, as the moneyed and empowered Mexican Californians referred to themselves.

Vallejo was, initially, an ardent supporter of annexation to the United States. Life experiences—including Hippolyte Bouchard's 1818 invasion of Monterey[7] and the mutiny of Vallejo's own troops in 1829[8]—had led him to believe that neither Spain nor Mexico could defend or develop California; only the United States, in his opinion, could help the region reach its full potential. His later realization that the development of California came at the expense of the *californios* did not, however, soften his heart against Mexico. A drawn-out legal battle against the Mexican government in 1870 confirmed his belief that the country was run by a bunch of thieving, ineffective Indians,[9] and an 1877 business trip to Mexico City left him with crippling diarrhea and something bordering on hatred for all things Mexican.[10]

Vallejo's personal finances in the 1870s somewhat explain his vituperative attacks on Mexico and his general ill will. The global financial crisis of the 1870s, precipitated in the United States by the collapse of Jay Cooke in 1873, affected Vallejo severely.[11] Most of Vallejo's money was invested in the Vallejo Savings and Commercial Bank, managed by Frisbie, which, over-invested in mining and rail stocks, collapsed in 1876. Vallejo was reduced to relying on the goodwill of friends and neighbors and pretending to be crazy so as to forestall his creditors. In a letter to Platon dated October 10, 1876, just one month after the bank failure, Vallejo despairs that "with the last blow to my fortune I shall become older than a centenarian . . . my illusions are gone, they are silent, and my soul withdraws." He tells Platon that, adding insult to injury, the bank is trying to collect from him on a $2,000 loan and that he has given them a "'check against the treasury of the Empire' like in the story which I told you of a fine gentleman who feigned madness in order to pay his debts."[12]

Vallejo's woe, anger, and humor are especially affecting in this letter, but most interesting is the ambiguity of "Empire." To which empire is he referring: Spanish, Mexican, the United States? And what does it mean to write checks, even in jest, against this ephemeral power? The uncertainty of "Empire" mirrors the ambiguous terrain that emerges in Vallejo's travels, which trace an American path toward a nascent Chicana/o national imaginary grounded in a hemispheric consciousness, not the protonationalism Sánchez envisions. While the travelers of the previous chapter chart an increasing sense of exclusion and racialization, Vallejo's American moves produce a murkier narrative. He is betwixt and between empires and at times seemingly indifferent to the competing pulls on his national affections. As he tells Francisca, he does not love the United States, but he hates Mexico, though he pretends ardently to the contrary when speaking to the Mexican press.[13] He is, furthermore, agonizingly uncomfortable in both countries, as well as in transit between and across them. His letters are filled with references to the discomforts, inconveniences, and inefficiencies of travel.

The writers in the previous chapter deployed travel narrative to unite the Americas; but by the time Pérez Rosales arrived in San Francisco Bay, narrations of American space are increasingly narrations of racial hierarchies and the codification of national boundaries. Vallejo's transamerica is historiographic; he does not even bother to narrate his travels, except in private letters. By this I do not mean, as Sánchez argues, that Vallejo occupies and narrates liminal, abstract space. The stakes of his history are real; the space he imagines is grounded. His *Recuerdos* are his check against the Empire's treasury, the remaking of existing terrain, of entrenched and hegemonic spatial imaginaries, into something uniquely American.

The Value of History

With such aspirations, Vallejo's aims in setting out his history are quite different from Bancroft's, though their texts are, as Sánchez has noted, interdependent (32). The *Recuerdos* are part of the collection of oral narratives gathered by Bancroft's staff, regarded as comprising one of the foundational genres of Chicana/o literature. These *testimonios*, which document the lives of Mexican Californians in the wake of the Mexican-American War, have been examined extensively by scholars such as Sánchez, as well as Genaro Padilla in *My History, Not Yours: The Formation of Mexican American Autobiography* (1993).[14] Vallejo's text figures prominently in both studies, and part of my project here is to extend the reach of these scholars' analyses. Although Vallejo and his text share some of the characteristics of the *testimonio* and its presumed narrator, the generic differences in the *Recuerdos* are crucial to understanding the new order of class and race consciousness emerging in late nineteenth-century California.

Such qualities are often overlooked, however, as scholars attempt to reconcile Vallejo's position as a wealthy, pro-U.S., Mexican ranchero with his critique of the United States and his articulations of what they view as proto-Chicana/o politics. Such treatment glosses his enthusiastic endorsement of the free market and disregards his literary and philosophical contributions to nationalist debates in late nineteenth-century California. Reading Vallejo's memoir as an extended meditation on historical narrative and international law, rather than as an elegy for his disappearing community, highlights the complex interpretive processes that enable ethnic identity. In comparing Vallejo with Bancroft, I emphasize how different historiographic modes reflect not just the marginalization of Chicana/os and Latina/os—processes evident in Pérez Rosales's narrative—but also constitutively different views of the nation, laying the groundwork for a liberatory and potentially progressive Chicana/o nationalism. Such an approach also offers a model for Chicana/o critical strategies that situate Chicana/o literature hemispherically.

Close readings of Vallejo's memoirs and personal papers reveal both that his personal and financial troubles, including the depletion of his fortunes after the Mexican-American War and the Land Act of 1851,[15] were not limited to his U.S. interactions and that he did not understand himself as marginalized in the way Sánchez's and Padilla's readings position him. Sánchez's reading of Vallejo relies on her assertion that he narrates a collective identity forged out of loss. However, Vallejo's public assertion that he avoided mentioning personal details in the service of historical truth, which Sánchez cites (9), speaks less to a burgeoning collective identity and more to Vallejo's own history as a public servant frequently accused of self-aggrandizing and self-serving motives.[16] Interpretations such as those of Sánchez and Padilla—who reads Vallejo's and Bancroft's printed disputes over historical documentation as analogous to the U.S. conquest of Mexico—emphasize notions of self, identity, and dispossession, all of which converge in the 1960s in a proletarianized and racialized Chicana/o community. These readings emphasize contemporary realities over past concerns and so limit the range of observations we can make about Vallejo.

Vallejo is less concerned with articulating his self or a subaltern community than he is with writing history and analyzing international policy. Bancroft's and Vallejo's narratives articulate competing modes of nationalism that emerge and gain political force concomitant with sweeping economic changes in the post–Civil War United States. In teasing out the various trajectories of Mexican American racialization in California through an analysis of Bancroft's and Vallejo's histories, we come to see how philosophies of history and economics manifest themselves in narratives of the nation, how these narratives are integral to the construction of ethnic identities, and how they offer more nuanced ways to understand interracial, interethnic, and international relations and texts.

As the United States consolidated its post–Civil War national economy, the *californio* economy continued to fracture, witnessing economic depression, increased industrialization and urbanization, and a move from small- to large-scale capitalist farming. These rapid shifts structured both men's sense of self, yet thinking only in twentieth- or twenty-first-century terms of racial and ethnic conflict and identity does not do justice to Bancroft's or Vallejo's historical narratives.[17] Historical perspective is crucial, but historical narratives are also central to the formation of racial and ethnic communities, and national ideologies are imbricated in modes of historical discourse.[18] Understanding our contemporary reality relies on parsing the past as much as possible on its own terms rather than viewing it through the lens of the present.

My hemispheric reading of Vallejo is not, therefore, anachronistic. My insistence on his global perspective and my argument that this globality is integral to Chicana/o literary history recognize and respond to the reshaping of U.S. national "tradition in a way that recognizes the continuous life of Latinos within and around it" that Kirsten Gruesz argues is imperative in the face of rapidly changing U.S. demographics (211). While Vallejo might not have called himself a Chicano, he is indubitably a vital and significant part of Chicana/o literary history. Reconstructing that history necessitates reading beyond the artificial unity imposed by descent and ethnicity toward a national imaginary that accounts for the historicity of nations, their material effects over time, and how Chicana/o narratives have responded to them.

The force of historical narrative to express a nationalism grounded in economic and political principles becomes clearer in light of Bancroft's and Vallejo's writings about historiography. The following passage, for example, appears in a pamphlet promoting Bancroft's *Works*:

> [T]he true wealth of a nation lies in its accumulated experiences, its storehouses of knowledge, and the hearts and minds of a free and intelligent people. These are the kind of acquisitions that history encourages. . . . What is a nation without history—without its experiences placed on record to be preserved in an enduring form? . . . It is one of the strongest instincts of man thus to remember and preserve, to recite or read, the doings of his forefathers. . . . Some histories have no beginning, no clearly defined starting point, being obscured by the mists of antiquity; others have knowledge of the nation's inception, the causes that engendered it, and the hour of its birth. (*Historical Works* 4)

Although no specific author is attributed to the pamphlet, all texts emerging from Bancroft's workshop underwent a thorough corporate authorship and revision, so it is safe to say that Bancroft would have had a large hand in articulating the above sentiments.[19] Notable here is the clear allusion to Adam Smith's *Wealth of Nations*, the conflation of historical data with "acquisitions" to be kept in "storehouses" and then distributed to foster the "development" of a nation. Compare this understanding of history with Vallejo's historical philosophy expressed in a letter to Enrique Cerruti, Bancroft's assistant who took Vallejo's dictations: "It's very possible that Mr. Bancroft finds 'that the dates which you have sent him are at variance with much that others have written,' but what to do, my friend? Everything I have told you I am prepared to prove with reliable documents and signatures that corroborate my assertions. The history of Alta California is being dealt with and it is necessary to be true and impartial. I am reminded of the words of Cicero who said: 'history is the witness of the times, the light of truth, the messenger of antiquity'" (April 21, 1875).[20] Vallejo avoids economic metaphors and locates the truth of history not in particular facts or dates (which function as engines of progress for Bancroft) but in its rhetorical value as a messenger from the past. Bancroft's insistence on an austere, objective style puts him squarely in line with post–Civil War historiographic developments in the United States. As Peter Novick notes in *That Noble Dream*, after the war historians in the United States, influenced also by academic historical traditions in Germany, moved away from the ornate, highly personalized styles of amateur historians such as Walter Prescott Webb, Francis Parkman, and Vallejo (42). Therefore, it is possible to read Bancroft and Vallejo's stylistic differences in the context of larger historiographic trends, but these stylistic differences speak also to evolving philosophies of the nation and articulations of ethnic identity.

In the late nineteenth century, when both Bancroft and Vallejo were writing, the nation was becoming an increasingly salient idea for Mexican American writers. One explanation for this can be found in the distinction between Bancroft's and Vallejo's philosophies of history: history as a function of the economic consolidation of national identity, and history as a rhetorical link to the past. In the former position, Anglo-American nationalism is tied to the efficiency of capitalist modes of production and the integration of the national economy in post–Civil War America. Bancroft enacts this in his modes of textual production and his publicly stated views on authorship and writing. In the latter position, nationalism emerges as a function of shifting discursive positions Vallejo takes with regard to the past. He becomes the voice of a textual national community that recognizes its porous boundaries, its lack of centripetal force, and its contingent existence in relation to other nations. Thinking in nationalistic terms allows us to understand the two texts' fundamental political differences without applying anachronistic conceptions of race and ethnicity to their authors. Nations, race, and ethnicity change over time, yet they remain definitive arbiters of cultural belonging, adumbrating not only ethnic but also economic identifications and conflicts. When viewed in relation to each other we can see patterns of tension and identification developing in Bancroft's and Vallejo's texts in ways that potentially complicate our received notions of Chicana/o community and continuity. I begin my analysis by examining Bancroft's *Works*, since Vallejo's text emerges in response to Bancroft's project. I focus my discussion in two domains: the mode of Bancroft's textual production, which is accretive in nature and mirrors the expanding national economy, and his literary relationship with Vallejo, which illustrates the uneasy and tenuous position of Mexicans in Anglo society.

Bancroft, a seasoned bookseller by the 1860s, began his historiographic endeavors by amassing a huge collection of books and archival materials. *Historical Works*, the marketing pamphlet cited earlier, describes his library: "The field thus covered [by Bancroft's collection] is equal in area to one twelfth of the earth's surface; and we venture to assert, that never since the world was made, have the early annals of any nation or important section been so thoroughly, so conscientiously, and so intelligently gathered. [Bancroft] alone seized upon the occasion, and stepped in and accomplished the task at the only time and in the only way in which it could be thus so fully and successfully accomplished, and that timely labor of such quantity and quality has never been performed by any other people" (5). In the era of manifest destiny, the scope of Bancroft's library grew along with the imperial reach of the United States. Embedded in the pamphlet's rhetoric of size is also the assumption of Anglo-American supremacy in strength, organization, and intelligence. The belief that an Anglo-American man is best suited to giving coherent, rational shape to a body of disparate materials is further developed in Bancroft's own descriptions of the writing of the histories.

Though Bancroft claims that there is "no particular system or method" to his writing, when he speaks of writing he does so in language that clearly reflects the values of breadth, efficiency, organization, and production described above. His writing system "applies only to the accumulation and arrangement of evidence upon the topics of which [he writes], and consists in the application of business methods and the division of labor to those ends" (*Industries* 331). Bancroft and his team understand writing as an act of winnowing and arranging "precious grains" of historical information, without acknowledging that winnowing itself and the business methods he perceives as value-free are in fact elements of style and method (*Historical Works* 7). When Bancroft speaks of style at all he speaks of it as an afterthought. The work of the author, in his analysis, is to collect, organize, and dispense evidence in whatever "natural or acquired style" he or she chooses (*Industries* 330). Style is not a value for Bancroft, but facts, or historical knowledge—that which is tied to the economic development of a nation—are extremely valuable. "[T]here is palpable and direct money value in [Bancroft's project] for the nation," *Historical Works* assures us (7). Writing history, in other words, makes money.

Bancroft and his History Company use the language of business to describe the project. Fact, raw materials, and finished products hold value for Bancroft far and above the human element of style (labor). We see this valuing of product over labor in Bancroft's mode of constructing the texts, which emphasizes "business methods" and the efficiency of a "division of labor." Bancroft describes this division of labor in *Literary Industries*: the first order of business was to index the library so that relevant material could be found quickly. Then, when beginning a particular volume, another set of employees would compose "rough material," abstract notes about a given topic, culled from the indexed references. Another group of writers arranged and revised the "rough" into a narrative with some chapter divisions. Finally, Bancroft rewrote and revised what his employees had constructed.

Bancroft's system worked well, but it created two major problems for the historian that have some bearing on how we are to understand Vallejo's text in relation to his. Both arise from Bancroft's business methods: the first from how he chose to finance his project; the second from his methodical division of labor. To continue collecting materials and paying employees, Bancroft sold subscriptions to the *Works*, which instigated a barrage of criticisms and disregard of the *Works* that hounded Bancroft until near his death. Eminent figures such as Charles Darwin and Oliver Wendell Homes, who had praised earlier volumes, were upset when their praise was used to sell subscriptions to later volumes they had never seen.[21] Coupled with the perception that he had taken advantage of personal favors was a growing unease within the East Coast literary establishment over Bancroft's success. In his memoir *"Literary Industries" in a New Light*, Bancroft's head librarian, Henry Oak, describes how literary men in the East, "men of more brains than money," were jealous of Bancroft's success. Some felt that such a project as Bancroft proposed, and the manner in which he proposed to carry it out, could "be little better than trash," yet it was proving to be quite good and profitable (12).

The East Coast establishment's criticism gained new force, however, when several of Bancroft's employees began publicly claiming authorship for many of the *Works'* volumes. These writers claimed that Bancroft's much-vaunted "division of labor" was a sham: while it may have been the original intention, in actual practice employees did much of the work on their own.[22] While Bancroft's detractors accused him of stealing their work, for Bancroft the matter was purely a business issue. He maintained that his employees were made to understand at the beginning of their employment that all they produced belonged to Bancroft to use as he saw fit and that they were on his payroll, operating under his direction and using his resources. Beyond a purely legalistic argument, Bancroft felt that the ends justified the means. "I have been able to accomplish thoroughly in fifteen years what [the more limited historian], quite as zealous, industrious, and able as myself, has done superficially in twenty-five years, and what he could not have done as thoroughly as myself in half a dozen lifetimes," he asserts in *Literary Industries* (335). Putting all his faith in the objectivity of business methods, Bancroft saw no truth in his detractors' claims. In conflating his right to publish their work with their claim of authorship, Bancroft invited the assumption that the entire *Works* was the product of hired hands.

Bancroft's histories, despite a long period of disregard, are today seen as excellent sources; with their clear, linear narrative, endless footnotes, and exhaustive explorations of multiple points of view, they are nothing if not scholarly. Nevertheless, the image of Bancroft that remains after considering his texts in light of his business methods troubles the image of the imposing Anglo-American historian whom Genaro Padilla sees textually oppressing Vallejo. Vallejo, a prominent and well-respected man, would have been on equal footing with Bancroft, who, wealthy and well-known as he was becoming, was not without his serious detractors. Though their relationship was not one of dominance and subjugation, Bancroft's writing reveals a marked ambiguity about the Mexican American population he so strongly supported. Bancroft was very vocal in his opinions that the United States had done wrong by its Mexican population; his assertions led the Society of California Pioneers to revoke his honorary membership.[23] Likewise his personal and public writings reveal a profound regard for Vallejo. As late as 1915 Bancroft sent Vallejo's son Platon a draft of a speech in which he wrote of the father, "I never met a man of purer patriotism or kinder heart" (November 12, 1915). Nevertheless, his published writings and unpublished correspondence present a slightly more complicated picture.

In *Literary Industries*, for example, in describing the enthusiasm with which Vallejo took up the project of helping him, Bancroft writes that the history "was a work in which [Vallejo] was probably more nearly concerned than the author of it. If I was the writer of history, he was the embodiment of history. This he seemed to fully realize" (212). The fact that Bancroft and Vallejo barely spoke the same language problematizes Bancroft's assumptions about what Vallejo understood. Even more troubling, however, is Bancroft's positing of himself as the thinking writer above Vallejo, the bodily actor, a move that repeats the liberal rejection of the racialized body that Lorenzo de Zavala understood as slavery's central, ideological problem. Both moves involve the assumption of a position as privileged interpreter, within which is imbricated a sense of superiority, which together make the reader doubt Bancroft's claims to historical objectivity.

Less obviously problematic than Bancroft's subtle racism are the ways in which Bancroft's position permeates contemporary scholarship on the *testimonios*. Vallejo's approach to historical truth and his first-person narrative lead Genaro Padilla to assert that Vallejo was anxious to maintain "personal control" over the *Recuerdos* (89). Padilla assumes that Vallejo's self-identity was inextricable from the act of his writing, a position equally troubling as Bancroft's insistence that he was the writer of history that Vallejo embodied. Both positions assume a transparency between Vallejo's history and his life, ignoring the materiality of the text and denying Vallejo the ability or chance to speak to anything besides his personal experience. In other words, Padilla's reading of Vallejo sees the *californio* as just as much an embodiment of history as Bancroft's. To be fair, Padilla's reading does put Vallejo in the context of amateur literary historians of the late nineteenth century who, Novick notes, wrote out of personal feeling or a sense of moral obligation, making "no effort to achieve the authorial invisibility, which had become normative in the late nineteenth century" (45). At the same time, however, Padilla allows for Vallejo to do no more than write from a sense of moral outrage, when we can also view the *Recuerdos* as gesturing toward larger debates over the nature of the historic text and the possibility of objectivity.

Padilla's argument rests upon the assumption that Vallejo understood his text as the vehicle through which he could speak truth to power, offer a counternarrative. Padilla makes much (and even takes the title of his own book) from Vallejo's supposedly telling Cerruti that though he is willing to dictate his memoir, he "will not be hurried or dictated to. It is my history, and not yours, I propose to tell. . . . If I give my story it must be worthy of the cause and worthy of me" (*Industries* 211). This scene appears in Bancroft's memoir, but the archive suggests Vallejo's actual words were slightly less declamatory.

While archival evidence does not reveal Vallejo denying he ever spoke such words, it does reveal similar statements with, however, decidedly different implications, suggesting that Bancroft altered Vallejo's speech to serve his own ends. Bancroft gets this scene from an 1874 letter written by Cerruti to Bancroft in which Cerruti informs him that Vallejo does indeed have many documents, but they are difficult to read for they have been half eaten by moths. More infuriating to Cerruti, though, is Vallejo's reluctance to let the documents travel to San Francisco. Vallejo wants Cerruti to examine the documents at Vallejo's home, carefully, "since he says that history must be written slowly and not like a Yankee on horseback" (March 3, 1874).[24] The moment shows up again in Cerruti's memoir, *Ramblings in California* (54), combined with parts of another letter, suggesting some authorial invention on Cerruti's part. In neither his letter to Bancroft nor his memoir, however, does Cerruti make any reference to Vallejo calling his *Recuerdos* "my history, not yours." Vallejo insists that he must tell the history in "[his] own way" (*Ramblings* 54), but he does not say that he must tell his own history. This discrepancy is significant for in viewing Vallejo as the embodiment of history Bancroft denies him the ability to think rationally, analytically, or creatively about the narrative he was writing in "[his] own way." Bancroft assumes a writerly objectivity, but putting words in Vallejo's mouth merely makes his point about the difference between writing and embodying in a different way. If Vallejo is writing "[his] history, not [Bancroft's]," then he is simply acting, not thinking.

Bancroft thinks Vallejo is writing his own history, while Vallejo thinks that he is writing history in his own way, a semantic difference that bears heavily upon how each conceived his historical project. Bancroft viewed Vallejo's narrative as a highly personalized, subjective account based, at times, in opinion more than fact; again we can recall here the emerging "professional" historian, described by Novick, which Bancroft clearly sees himself as (Novick 42). Vallejo, on the other hand, both in the *Recuerdos* and in his private correspondence, is nearly obsessed with objectivity. In a letter to Cerruti he asserts, "I have not had, nor do I have the intention or desire to deviate from the truth" (April 21, 1875).[25] And in the "Prologo" to his *Recuerdos* he writes, "I propose nothing less than to bequeath to posterity a true history of the facts, just as they have taken place, in which each actor, each town, and each city will appear according to his or its just merits" (I:iii/iii).[26] Vallejo is very concerned to represent what he understands as truth. To read his work as subjective, or to think Vallejo understands himself as bearing a synechdochal relation to the history of Alta California, obscures the value of this truth and lessens the force of the arguments we can glean from his text, namely, that historical texts necessarily reflect authorial bias and that the self is composite, not in the communal sense that Sánchez imagines but contingent and textually constructed.

Vallejo's *Recuerdos* comprise law, letters, historical facts, and his own musings on a range of topics. Vallejo calls it a "compendium of the true history of California" (IV:422/320).[27] Calling his history a compendium gives us some idea of its underlying tensions. While the *Recuerdos* are exhaustive in scope, a compendium is still a summary, and yet Vallejo asserts that the history is "true." Any abridging, however—any narrative, in fact—involves authorial choices and biases, Vallejo's protestations to the contrary notwithstanding. Though Vallejo makes many anxious gestures toward truth, his use of *compendio* (compendium) suggests that he was not so naïve as to think his text was bias free, or that any text could be, and he freely shares his opinion on many topics, which Bancroft does only to adjudicate between documentary evidence.

That Vallejo and Bancroft take different approaches to voicing their own opinions within their narratives suggests both a difference in their view of historical truth and a difference in their understanding of the relationship between themselves and their national economies. Bancroft's labor dispute with his employees over the question of authorship and his attempts at complete self-negation in the *Works* suggest the obfuscation of individuality and the alienation from labor characteristic of an expanding capitalist economy. On the other hand, Vallejo's very present textual self and his reliance on letters, documents, and personal relationships in the construction of his narrative suggest the paternalism of the Spanish *hacendado*, who operated within a market economy structured around the patriarchal family. In this system, peonage was class based and hereditary (similar to the southern U.S. plantation economy), the landowner was physically responsible for his employees, and wage labor was a foreign concept.

Their disparate approaches to historical truth also denote a difference in the textual construction of self. Bancroft sees his self as extradiscursive, as a perceiver and processor of information. Vallejo, however, argues that the self as subject is constructed through a variety of national, legal, and moral discourses. History, in other words, does not exist outside our selves; we construct it when we write it, thus confusing the notion of historical truth. When Vallejo quotes Cicero saying "history is the light of truth," he is asserting not that knowledge of the past is fact based and irrefutable but that our construction of past narratives constitutes a truth we tell about ourselves. Vallejo's constant references to and obsessive concern with truth can be read not just as an anxious attempt to offer counternarratives to the many racist, Anglo histories of California in circulation at the time of his writing but also as recognition of the impossibility of knowing the truth and the past.

Text and Countertext

What to make, then, of this tension in Vallejo's narrative between objective truth and the textually constructed self negotiating simultaneous truths? Vallejo may tell us that he believes "that history should be just as Cicero painted it, 'the light of truth, as well as time's witness'" (I:45/33), but then he also tells us that history lies.[28] At several points in the narrative Vallejo makes overt, emphatic, and performative references to truth and assures his readers that all he says can be verified in records. But his claims to truth become slightly shaky when he veers into the realm of memory. In volume 1 of the *Recuerdos* Vallejo tells of the 1815 arrival in Monterey of Governor Solá from Mexico, a time of growing animosity between the colony and its Spanish rulers. He describes the political tensions between Spanish loyalists, such as Solá, and those who desired Mexican independence. Vallejo then describes the ball held in Solá's honor in detail from a letter written sixty years after the fact in 1875. He claims that though the letter relies on memory, it "is a true reflection of the facts, manner of thinking, and customs which ruled amongst us in 1815" (I:130/95).[29] Though the letter may be inaccurate in some ways, it has historical value for Vallejo because it adumbrates a subjective truth.

Vallejo views historical memory, that which purports to objectivity, as much less benign in its approximation of truth. Vallejo's tone in telling how California's San Quentin earned its name is dismissively jocular, yet the anecdote gives Vallejo occasion to meditate on the transmission of stories through time and how linguistic details convey depths of meaning in their misinformation. Quintín was a lieutenant of chief Marín, who ruled the Licatiut that blocked *californio* settlement north of San Francisco through violent warfare and occasional, murderous invasions of the *californio* villages there. After a particularly bloody battle between Solá's and Quintín's forces, the *californios* took to calling the place where it occurred the Punta de Quintín. Vallejo writes:

> [I]t was reserved to the Americans to change the name of this place and to call the "Punta de Quintín" "Point San Quentin." Whatever may have been the North Americans' motive in effecting such a change I do not know, but I think it can be attributed to the fact that a great number of them came to California in the belief that the inhabitants of this country were mostly Catholics; with the aim of ingratiating themselves to them they added "San" to the names of the towns and villages they visited. I recall upon different

occasions having heard mention of Santa Sonoma, San Monterey, and San Branciforte and guided by this custom they added San to Quintín's name; about this behavior I have no comment except to admit the Latin saying "there's no arguing with taste." If "San Quentin" pleases them more than the simple "Quintín" then let them have their vision and their saint, I'm sure I don't envy them. (I:148/190)[30]

While Vallejo quips that there is no quarreling with taste, his true point is how language misinforms and can be deployed to erase memory and enforce a hegemonic view of the past. In calling the Punta de Quintín "San Quentin" the Americans are excising the Licatiuts from the region's cultural memory and creating a false and condescending "Catholic" past for the place.

Contained within this seemingly lighthearted story is an argument about the work of history: claims to veracity aside, all historical narrative is in some way an act of violence, erasing one memory to replace it with another. Vallejo's claims are to a truth that moves beyond historical fact and transcends the content of his story. The disjuncture between word and deed we see in the story of the Punta de Quintín becomes increasingly pronounced as Vallejo moves through his narrative. The more he recognizes the linguistic manipulation of others, the more his text bears the formal brunt of his realizations. Although Vallejo continues to use his recollections as evidence after this discussion of Quintín, his invocations of memory begin to be coupled with abrupt generic shifts that correlate to his growing dissatisfaction with and alienation from both the United States and Mexico.

Once the text moves into the time of which he has personal memories, Vallejo begins to intersperse his narrative with personal recollections, seemingly at random. He remembers his interactions with Solá and regales his readers with anecdotes about Father Magín and other Mexican priests in the region (I:257/194). These incorporations of the personal would seem like irreverent touches if they were not always coupled with discussions of political conflict. Immediately after the story about Father Magín, Vallejo begins writing of Mexico's independence from Spain and the tricolor flag of the fledgling republic. The pattern of political conflict spurring a personal memory and then motivating a generic shift continues throughout the *Recuerdos*, but around the time of Vallejo's marriage there appear the added elements of literature, literary criticism, and analysis.

At Vallejo's wedding Governor Echeandía informs the newlywed that he, Vallejo, will have to leave immediately after the wedding dance on a military campaign. As with the emergence of Mexican independence in the text, the announcement of a new political conflict inspires the invocation of memory. "I still recall the toast by señor Echeandía and I think it opportune to reproduce it, for, although forty-three years have passed since then I still recall it with pleasure" (II:190/155).[31] Vallejo quotes the toast, and of course we must take his claims to faithful reproduction with a grain of salt. What is interesting here, though, is not whether Echeandía actually said what Vallejo remembers but that this invocation of personal memory is coupled with a love poem to Vallejo's new wife. Vallejo depicts himself composing the romantic poem, replete with passionate embraces and eternal kisses, extemporaneously. Padilla discusses this moment also, commenting that the "lavish prose in this section discloses Vallejo's ease with—and in—the past" (95). But this is not all prose; it is poetry, sprung out of personal recollection, a double generic shift instantiated by the emergence of political conflict in the narrative.

The wedding scene is not the first moment in the *Recuerdos* where Vallejo places importance on literature, specifically poetry, but it is the first instance where literature is coupled with the invocation of memory and political conflict. These moments in the text suggest that literature is tied, for Vallejo, to the inevitability of political conflict, and they show how conflict is imbricated in the instability of truth, language, and memory. Poetry also gains importance when Vallejo tells the story of how Don Joaquin Buelna, a Santa Cruz judge, fought off a rumored attack on his person with poems. According to Vallejo, Buelna sent copies of his poems to his supposed attackers, who were so frightened of the poetry's power that they gave them to a priest for safekeeping. After relating Buelna's story, Vallejo critiques the poetry, claiming, "The *décimas* are terrible. They have no literary merit whatever, but they secured political and domestic peace for Buelna. This proves how well-grounded was the ancient Latin proverb—'A tiny spark overlooked has often started a great conflagration'" (I:220/164).[32] From this tiny spark Vallejo takes a great lesson about the power of literature. While Vallejo scoffs at the superstitions of Buelna's attackers, he does not deny that poetry can have significant power.

The moments in Vallejo's narrative in which he appears to be merely analyzing literature or commenting upon someone's literary tastes always link up to moments of political commentary or policy analysis.

Vallejo takes pains to emphasize the distance between literary quality and quality of character, institution, or event. Buelna, for instance, is a good man but a terrible poet. Nicolás Alviso's poems commemorating Hippolyte Bouchard's pirate raid on Monterey are excellent but the event was devastating (I:204/152). Don Joaquín Maitorena is not a bad poet but he is a drunkard and represents Alta California poorly in the Mexican Congress of 1824 (II:19/15). When, in volume 1, Iturbide's government sends Canon Fernandez to Alta California to exact oaths of allegiance to the new constitution from the province's authorities, Vallejo describes him as a handsome man with excellent literary taste but with a taste also for diplomacy and intrigue, the kind of man who "has been the cause of three-fourths of the revolutions that have destroyed Mexico, and more-over the republics of Central and South America, in the past fifty years" (I:284/216).[33]

On the one hand, then, literature and literary analysis serve in the *Recuerdos* as signs of misrepresentation, deceit, and disappointment. Still, however, there exists a tension between this idea of literature and the positive political power to be had via access to books and education, such as in Vallejo's account of how he faced excommunication by the Catholic Church in order to acquire a library including Voltaire, Rousseau, and other books the Church had banned (III:111/92). Although Vallejo consistently links literary discussions to either invocations of memory, which are necessarily fallible, or to political conflict, deceit, and intrigue, he nevertheless continues to use literary discussions to make complex political and personal points. His discussion of early Alta Californian political life is loaded with poetic analysis. He can only convey his love for his wife through poetic language, and desire for abstract knowledge can be described only through a discussion of the literature he and his friends read.

Vallejo's discussion of the books banned by the Church follows the same pattern as that of all his literary appeals. Talk of Rousseau and Voltaire is followed immediately by a relation of the scandals of Governor Mariano Chico's administration and Santa Ana's surrender to Sam Houston. Of Santa Ana Vallejo tells us: "While he was captive, he relegated his glorious antecedents to oblivion, recognized the independence of Texas, and, to the great disgrace of the Mexican Republic, it was humbled to the government of the United States which, despite existing treaties with a sister republic, had incited the rebellion of a group of its citizens against the president of the Republic" (III:127/104).[34] We see two important things happening in this critique of Santa Ana's behavior. On the one hand, we see Santa Ana deviating from his public image as a staunch defender of the Mexican Republic, showing his craven self in his capitulation to the Texans' demands. On the other hand, Vallejo references a duplicity that goes beyond just the individual. He points to treaties between the United States and Mexico to show how the United States ignored them. He argues that what is written has little bearing upon what actually happens.

Vallejo treats the 1824 Acta Constitutiva (the Mexican constitution) in like fashion. Political conflict in the *Recuerdos* motivates a generic shift, a move from straightforward narrative to poetry, or a letter, or an anecdote. Similarly, this discussion of the constitution, in which Vallejo highlights the discrepancy between the written word and actual practice, sparks a generic shift in which Vallejo moves from his own narrative to including the entire text of a law or official political document. In introducing the 1824 Acta Constitutiva Vallejo comments that very few copies of it survive, and since he considers it important he will include the entire thing. He predicts that after reading it, his readers "will be able to judge as to the manner in which this document has influenced the well-being of the Mexican Republic which during the passage of the last forty-seven years has so many times been the plaything of the ambitious aims of certain of her renegade sons who, deaf to the wail of anguish . . . ceaselessly and pitilessly slashed at the vitals of that motherland which owes to them all her grief and lassitude" (II:32/26).[35] The constitution of 1824 is inspiring, if ineffectual. The new government facilitates the rich getting richer and the poor getting poorer while the seven million natives in Mexico "are studiously kept in barbarism and ignorance" (II:41/34).[36] This disjunct between word and meaning recalls the slipperiness of language notable in Vallejo's account of how the Punta de Quintín became San Quentin. While that story serves as an example of the ways in which Vallejo appreciates the mutability of literary and historical language, here, less benignly, the mutability of language intersects with attempts to write the nation.

As a document that delineates the nation the 1824 Acta fails. According to Vallejo, none of the things it promises came to pass, and while it sets up Alta California as a protected department of the Mexican Republic, after the Acta, Mexico continued to mistreat and mismanage the province even more severely. The nation, as both a thing and an idea, holds little significance for Vallejo outside of concrete, economic realities. The documents with which it defines itself prove to be just as inconstant and shifting as the changing place-names of the northern frontier. Just as those changing place-names spoke to larger political and cultural forces at work through language, so does the failure of national documents to create a nation speak to government corruption and the untenability of patriotism or Mexican nationalism as guiding principles in his action.

The *Recuerdos* display an acute suspicion of national pride throughout. The only time Vallejo experiences "all the fervor of [his] Republican soul" is when he is denouncing Governor Chico for his "boasting publicly of his wantonness and disregard for the good opinion of virtuous people" (III:120/99).[37] When, in the midst of the Mexican-American War, Governor Micheltorena (the last Mexican governor of Alta California) distributes broadsides intended to arouse the *californios* to resist occupation, Vallejo calls them documents that "bore the stamp of absurdity rather than patriotism" (IV:303/229).[38] Vallejo grants that such a thing as patriotism can exist, but calls to take up arms in defense of Mexico will not arouse it in him.

Mexico's inability to govern Alta California effectively is the *Recuerdos'* leitmotif, arising throughout the narrative and sparking abrupt generic shifts or pointed literary analyses. Mexico's failings are due in part to its distance from the outlying territory but also to simple neglect or disregard. At one point, Vallejo tells us, Mexico's president Bustamante, forgetting that he had already appointed a governor to Alta California, accidentally appoints another one. "This should cause no wonder, however," Vallejo assures his readers, "for it is well known that the presidents of the Mexican Republic only remembered about California when someone visited them personally or we through our deputy caused some letter or present to reach their hands" (IV:35/26).[39]

Though Mexico may have neglected California in many ways, the central government still managed to send governors and extract resources from the region. The governors were, in Vallejo's opinion, much like the loose-living Governor Chico, "for the most part people devoid of any attributes that might ennoble a mandatary" (III:172/142).[40] Vallejo supports the move for *californio* independence from Mexico in 1836, resting his political argument—ironically, given his suspicion of laws and treaties—on the immutability of the laws that, he argues, the Mexican governors neglected to follow. A similar tension is evident in Vallejo's rendering of his nephew Juan Alvarado's declaration of independence: "California is free and will sever all her relations with Mexico until the latter ceases to be under the heel of the present dominant faction called the 'Central Government'" (III:196/164).[41] While the *californios* resented Mexican rule from afar they nevertheless wanted to maintain ties to Mexico as an equal partner in the federation.

In between expressing his own lofty political sentiments and relating Alvarado's declaration, Vallejo digresses momentarily into a discussion of the poetry of Castillo Negrete, a lieutenant of then governor Nicolas Guttiérrez, who was opposed to independence. Vallejo says he does this consciously because "as an impartial writer it is incumbent upon me to draw aside the veil concealing the motives which caused the erudite but ill-intentioned poet to vilify the successful opponents of Guttiérrez" (III:194/163).[42] By this he means that though Negrete and others justified their behavior to the Central Government by arguing that foreign forces were inciting rebellion in Alta California, in "truth" they harbored personal grudges against those fighting for federal status. Again we see here a discrepancy between literary and personal quality: the poetry is not bad, but the politics, in Vallejo's estimation, are. Even more telling, however, is Vallejo's self-consciousness regarding his digression. He claims it is borne out of an obligation to objectivity, but this sliding between genres in a discussion of Alta California's federal status hints at deeper unease concerning claims to liberty in the form of the nation-state.[43]

In the *Recuerdos*, Vallejo refers to himself as a "*californio* born in this beautiful land that used to belong to the Mexican Republic" (III:170/140).[44] This is, of course, an instance of strategic essentialism, given his self-identification elsewhere as Mexican or Spanish, as the spirit and situation moved him.[45] Nevertheless, he clearly sees California as a space apart from Mexico, and from this reference to himself we see this carries over into his own self-identification. Though he may have understood Alta California as independent, that does not indicate he thought of it as a separate country. Indeed, Vallejo's suspicion of narrative (shown in his generic indecision), language (shown in his continual emphasis on the distance between word and reality, as well as in his literary references), and nations (shown in his overt diatribes against both the United States and Mexico) indicate a deep distrust of nationalism and its constituent narratives.

That distrust crystallizes in Vallejo's discussion of the Hijar-Padrés colony. The colony was a subsidiary of the Compañia Cosmopolitana, which sought to export Californian products. Its directors desired military authority in California while the *californios* wanted them to be merely civil directors. The company argued that only with military control could they fully bring about their plan of liberation through trade for Alta California. Vallejo and others felt that the colonization plan was really a ruse to plunder the missions under the protection of the highest government authorities. According to Bancroft, however, while it appeared that "certain members of the colony under the leadership of Padrés were engaged in plots to secure the territorial government by force," there is "no real evidence to support the claim that the colony was out to despoil the territory." Bancroft notes that colonization had long been thought to be the best way to settle Alta California, and many "intelligent men" had long ago realized the impracticality "of attempting to continue the old monastico-missionary régime" (*Hist. Cal.* III:264–80). Vallejo disagreed with Bancroft and saw the colony's deployment of liberation rhetoric as a manipulation, for its own personal gain, of Alta California's yearnings for independence (II:386/315).[46] Patriotism is problematic for Vallejo, as are calls to liberty in the voice of the nation-state. Given his reliance on rhetoric to adumbrate historical truth, Vallejo's suspicions of nationalist rhetoric suggest that the nation must have a strong economic and juridical base. His writings on trade and monetary policy demonstrate how this base is, for Vallejo, international in scope and so destabilizes any notion of monolithic, isolationist nationalism.

From the beginning of its Spanish settlement Alta California had global prominence, and since the Mexican declaration of independence from Spain in 1810 the major governments of the world had been seeking ways to take advantage of Mexico's weakness. Vallejo saw the world's intrusion in Mexican affairs as one of the key factors retarding its progress, yet he also recognized that a healthy world trade was necessary for Mexico's and Alta California's success. For Vallejo, the key to political strength did not lie in passionate defenses of patriotism or empty calls to liberty but in finding a way to be open to the world and prosper from what it had to offer. Unfortunately he found, as he did with the Hijar-Padrés colony, that being open to the world also meant making oneself vulnerable to it.

Vallejo warmly welcomed immigrants from the United States, admiring their ingenuity and work ethic. In the *Recuerdos* he writes, "The arrival of so many guests filled us northerners with happiness, for we saw with great pleasure that many groups of industrious people had come from the other side of the Sierra Nevadas to set up camp amongst us" (III:384/307).[47] But he also held that U.S. rule did not benefit the *californios*. In addition to his own fiscal losses, Vallejo lamented in the *Recuerdos*, "How beautiful it would have been had the exaggerated enlightenment which the Americans have brought to California not perverted our patriarchal customs and relaxed the morality of our young people" (I:65/47).[48] He sees the moral decay as the outgrowth of the gold rush and so many aggressive adventurers coming to seek their fortunes in California.

Vallejo's distrust of foreign influence was not limited to Anglo immigration to California, however. There is no love lost between Vallejo and the French, whom he sees as "a showy people with a tendency for windy sentiments and [for whom] it is very difficult when in a foreign country to forget the customs of their own country which are so different from the majority of other peoples'" (III:279/234);[49] and he sees the Masonic factions in Mexico as "instrumentalities of foreign politics," responsible for the civil wars retarding Mexico's progress (II:55/45).[50]

Vallejo's feelings about a perceived global threat to Mexican sovereignty highlight his policy analyses for Alta California now that "European civilization was coming upon [them] with giant strides" (III:238/202).[51] Like literary analysis, policy analysis plays a large role in the *Recuerdos*, coming often in the form of inserting the entire text of actual laws as well as his own proposed laws, coupled with a brief discussion of the pros and cons of the legislation. A closer look at Vallejo's ways of writing about international relations and trade offers some insight into his articulations of nations and nationalism.

The *californios* had long had a global view of the world. Early in the nineteenth century Russia had established a stronghold, near what is now known as the Russian River, from which they traded fur with the native tribes and the *californios*. Vallejo had negotiated with the Russians to purchase arms in the 1830s, continued negotiations with them as the *californios* sought to curb Russian smuggling throughout the decade, and maintained business and political relations with them after he had been appointed to the northern frontier. Vallejo dealt similarly with representatives from various countries and business enterprises. One of the main *californio* complaints when they declared independence was Mexico's restrictive trade legislation that hindered California's full development in global markets. After the declaration of independence, Alta California passed a law for itself encouraging free trade with the rest of the world. Vallejo includes the entire law, commenting, "during the brief passage of time that Alta California remained separated from the government of the mother country which had so oppressed us . . . the citizens of the universe were cheerfully invited to prosper in a broad field under the shelter of wise and prudent laws" (III:211/179).[52] That prosperous period, unfortunately, was short-lived.

Although free trade had a short life in Alta California, Vallejo, always looking ahead, continued to write and promote policies encouraging development. He wrote, printed, and distributed his own plan for increasing the population of the northern frontier and revitalizing the treasury.

He argues that since the republic is unable to provide resources to Alta California, "those of us who feel these ills most immediately should undertake to create their remedy, if we be moved by a lively desire for national prosperity, while simultaneously bearing our own private interests in mind" (III:344/279).[53]

In these fiscal propositions Vallejo refers to a nation but only in the context of economic prosperity and not any abstract or ill-defined sense of kinship. The "nation" in his proposal is separate from the republic, so when he speaks of the nation he is not speaking of Mexico. Alta California was never an entirely separate state; although Vallejo refers to it as the Free and Sovereign State of Alta California, complete independence was never desired, only equal federal status. So what is the nation for Vallejo? What does he mean when speaks of national prosperity, and what is the political form he imagines for himself and his fellow *californios*?

In telling the story of Governor Micheltorena's negotiations with Commodore Jones of the U.S. Navy (who, under the impression that the United States and Mexico were already at war, had mistakenly taken command at Monterey Bay), Vallejo reconstructs the private meeting, putting these words in Micheltorena's mouth: "The happiness of nations is not made by many leagues of land, rather it is made by the people and by order . . . wise laws are more useful to the states than subjection and . . . development is the soul of stability and not coercive management" (IV:323/245).[54] Vallejo goes on to heartily approve of Micheltorena's realizations, which must be read as Vallejo's own since he was not at the meeting and can only reconstruct it via hearsay but also because he praises it so highly. In this understanding, the nation is defined not in terms of land but of law, and economic enterprise allowed free development in the good faith of its people.

Vallejo's understanding of the nation gives even greater insight into his enthusiastic support of the 1827 report of the Junta de Fomento de Californias (Committee on Californian Development) of the Mexican Congress. Their plan called for the formation of the Compañía Asiático-Mexicano, which would foster trade between California and the Pacific Rim. Had it "been carried into effect [it] would have given the port of Monterey great maritime importance," Vallejo recounts (I:300/230).[55] Vallejo includes all sixty-four articles of the proposed legislation including detailed information about tax concessions, the privileging of Californian products, attendant colonization plans, and routes of import and export in which Monterey serves as the gateway to the rest of Mexico. Vallejo thinks it an excellent plan and is sure that had it not been for

Mexico's civil unrest the law would have been put into effect and California would have become one of the most prosperous points on the Pacific Rim. In his endorsement of the Compañía Asiático-Mexicano, Vallejo offers an example of what an open and prosperous global engagement could be. In rhetorically separating California from Mexico with regard to economic prosperity, here and in his dispatch concerning the treasury, Vallejo shows how a worldly engagement can be predicated less on war and more on discursive community.

By including actual laws and proposed legislation in the *Recuerdos*, Vallejo delimits his imagined community, which, bounded by law, is necessarily discursive. Legislation concerning the Compañía Asiático-Mexicano never comes to fruition, as is the case with several of the laws he includes. By counterpoising these with laws that actually do come to pass, and by pointing to the ways in which the United States, Mexico, and their agents disregarded other laws, Vallejo points to the distance between what is written and what happens. The distance between law and action is analogous to the distance, or slippages, between language, history, and narrative evident throughout his text, as well as in his generic shifts and the importance he places on literature as a constitutive component of his history. In those cases, however, Vallejo's focus is the language, while in his discussion of law his focus is on action. The difference between language and action, for Vallejo, signals a shift in his conception of community: the literary analyses are tied to intracommunal reflection while the legalistic moves later in the *Recuerdos* reflect an extracommunal focus. That is, emphases on law, both real and imagined, delineate the global shape of a changing *californio* consciousness; that these laws tend to be related to trade suggests an economic understanding of the global.

Because the trade legislation Vallejo discusses either never comes to pass or is short-lived, we might be tempted to view it as just one more way in which the *Recuerdos* narrate loss. Yet, in relating what did not happen Vallejo offers us the textual possibility of what *could* happen. "Que lindo hubiese sido," he says, how beautiful it would have been, if the *californios* could have had "American" progress without the attendant moral degradation (I:65/47). The grammatical structure of this counterfactual (the imperfect subjunctive) is reflected in the narrative structure of the text, especially in the discussion of law.

The generic instability of the *Recuerdos* signals unease about politics, language, and history. The text moves back and forth across genres, never settling comfortably in one place for long. The lure of the borderlands is seductive here; we could say that in its generic indecision the text lives in the margins troubling the narrative center, marked by a text like Bancroft's. We could say that in its narratives of loss and oppression the *Recuerdos* speak truth to the oppressive lie of Anglo-American historians like Bancroft. To do that, however, would ignore both Bancroft's attempts to give voice to the *californios* as well as the very troubling aspects of his narrative; it would also do a disservice to Vallejo's work.

"Que lindo hubiese sido" to have had progress without moral decrepitude, to have had free trade in Alta California, to have had a Compañía Asiático-Mexicano. "Que lindo" if Hijar and Padrés had really meant to liberate Alta California, if smuggling could have been curtailed, if the United States had honored the Treaty of Guadalupe-Hidalgo, and Castillo Negrete could have lived up to the promise of his poetry. Yes, Vallejo is angry, and yes, his stories of loss, oppression, and racialization are important to study, but it is also important to look at how he tells these stories. The different strands of his argument necessitate different genres, and the text's constant shape-shifting reveals not a voice on the margins but a voice with global aspirations.

Chicano Historiography for a Hemispheric Future

Vallejo's global aspirations are manifested in attempts to link the hemisphere economically, culturally, and politically, as we see in his *Recuerdos* and as is borne out in his 1877 trip to Mexico two years after completing his manuscript for Bancroft. Vallejo and Frisbie traveled south in the hopes of obtaining railroad concessions from the government of President Porfirio Díaz, newly elected in 1876 on a platform of economic recovery and modernization for Mexico. "The day that Mexico has a railroad which devouring distances unites it with California, commerce and industry will flourish," Vallejo told an approving reporter from the *Monitor Republican* in Mexico City.

Vallejo and Frisbie's trip garnered less positive press in the United States where, according to an article in San Francisco's *Daily Evening Post*, rumors abounded that the two were carrying out secret orders from the U.S. government to "acquire territory or provoke war."[56] Frisbie dispelled these speculations, clearly articulating to the *Post* reporter his belief in Mexico's profit potential and outlining his plans to lobby for the Díaz administration in Washington. After his total financial collapse, Frisbie was energized by Mexico, moving his family there in 1878 and building a multimillion-dollar fortune with the help of a grateful Díaz (Empáran 274).

Frisbie enjoyed a personal relationship with Díaz as well. The Mexican president and his wife were *padrino* (best man) and *madrina* (maid of honor) at the wedding of Frisbie's daughter, Sarah, who was also Vallejo's granddaughter. On their 1877 trip, Vallejo and Frisbie had free access to Díaz. A note, accompanying a photo of Díaz, in Vallejo's Sonoma papers bears the president's signature and the message: "General Vallejo can enter the President's mansion at any hour that he pleases without more than notifying the guard." This level of access suggests the high esteem in which Vallejo was held, both in California and Mexico, further dispelling any notion that he would have considered himself marginalized. At the same time, his access to power and his desire to link the Americas by rail are troubling.

During the Porfiriato, the time of Porfirio Díaz's presidency (1876–1911), Díaz generated vast wealth for his allies in Mexico and abroad by maintaining brutal control of his opponents and further widening the divide between Mexico's rich and poor. His policies, as discussed in the next chapter, set the stage for the Mexican Revolution. To connect Mariano Vallejo so directly to Díaz is to render him culpable, at least in part, of the class and race warfare that characterized early twentieth-century Mexico and pushed thousands of Mexicans, fleeing both Díaz and the poverty he left in his wake, into the United States.

Such a perspective on Vallejo is deeply problematic for Chicana/o studies, and yet it is also the point of situating him hemispherically and globally. To be fair, Frisbie, not Vallejo, grew rich with Díaz's help. Though Frisbie was largely responsible for the decimation of Vallejo's personal fortune, due both to the bank collapse and various unfortunate land deals, and despite his dependence on Vallejo to open business doors for him in Mexico, household records indicate that Frisbie sent only $50 every other month to Vallejo after moving to Mexico (Empáran 147). Nevertheless, Vallejo's willing participation in Frisbie's schemes, coupled with his disregard for Mexico and antipathy toward indigenous populations, adumbrate the profoundly racist context out of which a Chicana/o national imaginary emerges.

The creation of racialized others through various discursive means grounds the emergence of nations and nationalisms in the Americas, as all of the authors discussed here so far have demonstrated. Chicana/o articulations of racial oppression must thus always be considered in this long history of intracommunal Chicana/o racism, which we see in Vallejo's letters and memoir. The story of Chicana/o literature, however, and the cultural history of a Chicana/o national imaginary is the story of grappling with this conflict between the desire to transcend the nation's fundamental, racial logic while still retaining its organizing force, a conflict enacted in Vallejo's competing stances on travel, illuminated in this chapter's epigraphs. Such vast and contradictory philosophical terrain is also mirrored in the formal complexity of Vallejo's *Recuerdos*. In that dual history of himself and California, Vallejo attempts to encompass everything: what happened, what did not happen, and what it means when the two do not match up. The text thus offers not just a narrative of loss but also a narrative of future possibility. Ignoring this future possibility means ignoring half of Vallejo's narrative; it also means remaining entrenched in ways of reading that refuse to see invocations of the nation as anything other than an ethnic entanglement or capitalist imperialism. Vallejo's attempts may not be fully successful, but he is clearly trying to articulate a nationalism predicated not on ethnic isolation and oppression but on global engagement, bounded by trade legislation dedicated to the common good, aims reflected in his approach to historical narrative.

PART TWO

INHABITING AMERICA

3 /   Racialized Bodies and the Limits of the Abstract: María Mena and Daniel Venegas

The hemispheric utopia of globally integrated trade imagined by Mariano Vallejo moves, at the turn of the last century, slowly from imagination to reality, with questionable motives and decidedly mixed results. What Mexico gained economically it lost in social cohesion as the Mexican Revolution rocked the country during 1910–20. Tens of thousands of Mexicans fled to the United States as warring factions battled for control over Mexico's future and its past. The works of María Mena and Daniel Venegas reflect two disparate factions of the Mexican revolutionary diaspora that eventually do become part of a Chicana/o collectivity in the United States. A comparative reading of Mena's short stories and Venegas's novel, *Las Aventuras de Don Chipote*, highlights each writer's conflicting and contradictory alliances. As the dimensions of Mexico shift, as the landscape is restructured and the people drift, Mena's and Venegas's observations of Mexican schisms migrate as well into astute analyses of cultural, political, and racial conflicts in the United States.

The political discord Mena and Venegas respond to resulted in large part from Mexico's increasing economic dependence on the United States in the early twentieth century, of which the exponential increase in Federal Direct Investment (FDI) from the United States to Mexico after the Mexican-American War was the largest sign. U.S. companies invested heavily in Mexican railroads, mining, agriculture, and civic infrastructure. Spurred by the liberal economic policies of Porfirio Díaz—whose 1876–1911 presidency is known as the "Porfiriato" and who welcomed Vallejo and his son-in-law John Frisbie with an open door policy in 1877, as discussed in Chapter 2—by 1910, U.S. interests owned nearly half of Mexico's national wealth (Fernandez and Gonzalez 38). Díaz's plans displaced hundreds of thousands of Mexicans as U.S. companies turned communal landholdings and indigenous farms to the purposes of industrial agriculture, railways, and mining interests. Mexicans moved en masse toward the cities, Mexican mining centers in the northern states, and the United States in search of work (Fernandez and Gonzalez 44).

Díaz's strategies to strengthen the Mexican economy resulted in the literal remaking of Mexican space as the landscape changed drastically, populations shifted, and poor, Mexican workers established enduring migration routes. The continual flow of people and resources across the U.S.-Mexico border, combined with increasing U.S. involvement in Mexican and Latin American affairs, render it difficult to clearly distinguish the United States from its hemispheric neighbors. John Frisbie compellingly illustrates this entanglement: born on the East Coast, he married into the prominent, *californio* Vallejo family. Then, after financial ruin in the United States, Frisbie made another fortune in Mexico with business interests that provided substantial earnings to U.S. investors. Where, in the example of Frisbie's life, as discussed in the previous chapter, does Mexico end and the United States begin?

The question of national boundaries and hemispheric unity is the lingering American question posed in the travel narratives of Domingo Sarmiento, Lorenzo de Zavala, and Vicente Pérez Rosales, the subjects of Chapter 1, as they struggled to articulate a transamerican vision from the United States, the incipient center of hemispheric, imperial power. The Monroe Doctrine, part of President James Monroe's 1823 address to the U.S. Congress, was, as Rachel Adams notes, "as much an early manifestation of U.S. imperial designs as it was a blueprint for hemispheric solidarity" (*Continental Divides* 10). When Monroe stated that the United States would understand any act of aggression against its southern neighbors as an act of hostility toward itself, he supported South and Central American independence while simultaneously asserting U.S. interests in the region. In 1845 President James Polk made explicit what was only implicit in Monroe's address: not only was the western hemisphere closed to European colonial interests, but Europe ought not interfere with U.S. efforts to expand to the Pacific. President Theodore Roosevelt further clarified Monroe's ambiguities in 1904 when he told Congress that the United States had the right not only to oppose European intervention in the western hemisphere but also to intervene in the domestic affairs of its neighbors if they proved unable to maintain order and national sovereignty on their own.[1]

The United States' avuncular, helping hand, which Porfirio Díaz enthusiastically grasped, has often cloaked imperial designs. Díaz's fiscal complicity with the apparent U.S. desire to enforce unity through its own, expanding national borders fanned Mexico's revolutionary flames. As Mexico's rich grew richer, its poor were cast aside in the name of progress. Reformists like Francisco Madero, who assumed the presidency after Díaz fled the country in 1911, chafed against Díaz's flouting of the Mexican constitution and his flagrant abuses of human rights, while revolutionaries like Ricardo Flores Magón combated the workings of multinational capital with an anarchist political program dedicated to global human rights and proletarian uplift.

Flores Magón, a young lawyer turned opposition journalist and editor, founded Regeneracíon, one of the earliest and most vocal anti-Díaz groups. The political party he organized, the Partido Liberal Mexicano (PLM), explicitly opposed any new debt and saw Mexico as exhausted and exploited by foreign powers (Flores Magón 134). Persecuted relentlessly in Mexico, Flores Magón and his allies carried out their work in the United States and Canada as Flores Magón fled from Díaz's agents, first to St. Louis then to Toronto, Los Angeles, and ultimately Fort Leavenworth where he died in 1922. His death marks the end of an era in Mexico's revolutionary history, and his work offers a hermeneutic framework for the transnational forces to which María Mena and Daniel Venegas, the two writers under consideration in this chapter, were both responding. Flores Magón's activity was covered extensively in the U.S. press, especially during the early days of his exile, when Mena was a recent immigrant, but also well into the 1920s when Venegas arrived.

One of the journalists covering Flores Magón was John Kenneth Turner, who wrote for the *Los Angeles Express*. Inspired by his conversations with the Mexican anarchist in exile, Turner traveled to Mexico in 1908 to investigate Flores Magón's allegations against Díaz. Turner published several pieces about his trip in *American Magazine*, the first of which, "The Slaves of Yucatan," documented rampant slavery on the henequen plantations of Merida. There can be no doubt that Mena read Turner's pieces in *American*. The magazine published her "Gold Vanity Set" in November 1913, the same month and year that *The Century* published "John of God," another of her stories. Clearly, she was familiar with, and anticipated a positive response from, the journal. Furthermore, her stories directly echo Turner, both linguistically and ideologically.

Turner opens "The Slaves of Yucatan" with the question, "What is Mexico?" (3), a query that captures the early twentieth-century zeitgeist of that country. Mexican revolutionary politics coalesce around the question of what, and where, Mexico is. After 1911, the three main revolutionary forces in Mexico were reformers like Francisco Madero, native Mexican rebels like Pancho Villa in the north and Emiliano Zapata in the south, and Flores Magón's anarchist PLM working toward the overthrow of capitalism and the liberation of humanity. Each of these groups had their own Mexican visions. Despite the tendency of official histories to co-opt Flores Magón into the liberal revolution, Flores Magón and Madero had split by 1911. Flores Magón called Madero "an advocate of the capitalist exploitation that oppressed the Mexican people" (Verter 80). For him, by 1910 the revolution had transcended the nation to become a revolution of humanity against capitalism.

By contrast, Madero and the reformers who followed him were heavily invested in Mexican particularity, an investment that led from an initial interest in indigenous rights to a fetishization of indigeneity that avoided real reform. Such tokenism raised the ire of Madero's early allies Zapata and Villa, who were working for substantial agrarian and Indian reform, on which it was becoming increasingly clear Madero would not deliver.

In the struggle to define revolutionary Mexico and to reclaim and restructure Mexican space in the wake of Díaz's deprivations, the racial body thus emerges as a contested space. Mexico seeks to contain its indigeneity, the state's racial other, in an idealized past, while the United States seeks to contain Mexico. The construction of national space thus also becomes the construction of a national race. Space and race converge repeatedly in both Mena's and Venegas's writings, as when, in "Doña Rita's Rivals," Rita loses her way in Mexico City's red-light district, filled with women of ambiguous race and of a decidedly lower class than herself (79), only to find what she is later looking for on Calle del Niño Perdido (Street of the Lost Child; 80). Don Chipote's raced body marks space similarly in Venegas's novel, most apparently when he is made to shower before crossing into the United States at El Paso (35). In this scene, his clothes shrink when passed through a fumigator, and he finds himself turned away at the border, his rejected body squeezed into clothing that barely contains him (36).

Don Chipote in shrunken tatters is a stark visual of how the struggle to contain and demarcate national space produces an excess: real, racialized bodies whose physical needs remain unmet by a Mexican state that fetishizes them while pushing their laboring bodies to the periphery.

These bodies are then rejected, in principle, by the United States, which nevertheless depends upon their labor. Finally, these bodies become boundaries in their own right, a no-man's-land of racialized space, which Mena and Venegas attempt to narrate, that drifts back and forth across the U.S.-Mexico border.

The two writers respond to these racialized bodies and their relation to the meaning of Mexico in vastly different ways. Both champion Mexico's indigenous population, but they also seek to limit its mobility and signifying power. Mena does this by turning indigeneity into an historical relic. In "The Birth of the God of War" (1914), for example, a grandmother silences her granddaughter's appreciation of Coatlique, who gives birth to the Aztec god of war, with "a vision of a feathered Apache coming to carry" (69) her away. The story introduces Aztec myth less in celebration and more to assure readers that it is rooted firmly in Mexico's past. The Aztecs are pacified and domesticated through the granddaughter's depiction of "gentle Coatlique" (69), which stands in sharp contrast to Aztec renditions of her, such as the massive Coatlique Stone, which pictures Coatlique, whose name means "snake skirt" in Nahuatl, wearing a skirt made out of snakes, a necklace of human hands, hearts, and skulls, and with two serpents, rather than a head, sprouting from her neck.[2] In "The Birth of the God of War," by contrast, Aztec cosmography appears quaint, non-threatening, and historical.

Venegas's approach, on the other hand, is to contain indigeneity by advocating against immigration. Mexicans should remain in Mexico, his novel argues, in a performance of conservative nostalgia that is highly suspicious of revolutionary politics. Mena and Venegas are both wary of protestations of reform and revolution that cannot deliver on their promises; yet, their writings are also engaged in answering Turner's question: "What is Mexico?" Their work embraces and refutes otherness; they try to both define and embody an idealized Mexico while simultaneously critiquing the essentializing logic of an idealized nationality.

Their surface differences—Mena's work betrays a self-consciously feminist, anti-racist agenda, while Venegas's decidedly does not; Mena is sympathetic with calls to reform, while Venegas's novel explicitly contends that the revolutionaries have made matters worse for ordinary Mexicans—do not obviate this core similarity, a contradictory stance on the value of indigeneity that parallels the United States' conflicted embrace of Mexico and lies at the heart of later twentieth-century theorizations of Chicana/o subjectivity. Both writers express a conservative reaction to the radical transformations of Mexican spaces wrought by forces of U.S. capital that also redefine the Mexican body as it passes north of the border. Though neither aligns with Flores Magón's anarchism, I situate my readings of their work within the debate over the meaning of Mexico and of revolution, seeing their musings on these questions as refractions of what it means, for them, to be Mexican in the United States in the 1910s and 1920s.

María Mena's Divided Loyalties

For María Mena, being Mexican in the United States meant fleeing the revolution. By her own accounts her family grew wealthy during the Porfiriato. She lived a privileged life, was educated at private, international boarding schools, and was multilingual. To escape the turmoil wrought by the revolution, Mena's family sent her to live with family friends in Manhattan in 1907, when she was fourteen years old. In New York Mena's writing career flourished. She married Henry Chambers, an Australian playwright, and included D. H. Lawrence among her friends. Despite her rarefied upbringing and an adult life led safely ensconced in the upper-middle-class, cultured echelons, Mena writes mostly of Mexico's indigenous poor. Her stories satirize the pretensions of Mexico's wealthy elite, castigate mercenary reformers with no true concern for native Mexicans, and have an undeniable feminist agenda.

Her patrician background and the delicateness of her prose have led to her mixed academic reception, however. Raymund Paredes, perhaps her harshest critic, writing in 1978 calls her "a talented storyteller whose sensibility unfortunately tended towards sentimentalism and preciousness" (85). Her "portrayals are ultimately obsequious," Paredes continues, asserting that "if one can appreciate the weight of popular attitudes on Mena's consciousness, one can also say that a braver, more perceptive writer would have confronted the life of her culture more forcefully" (85). More recent critics have taken Paredes to task for this harsh view. Leticia Garza-Falcón, for example, reads the gentility that Paredes calls "incapable of warming the reader's blood" (85) as "a distinctly feminine quality and a question of subtlety of language" (136) overshadowed by the confrontational stance, exemplified by Paredes, of *movimiento* writers and critics. Likewise, Tiffany Ana López appreciates how Mena's "work stands in dialogue with the historical events that influence her as a Mexican woman." López sees Mena as a "cultural insider" (24) whose work responds directly to outsider representations of Mexicans, especially those appearing alongside Mena's writing in *The Century*, the journal that published the bulk of Mena's stories.

López and Garza-Falcón appreciate Mena's stories as feminist critiques of U.S. nationalism, a reading that is only bolstered by considering her in the context of nationalism on the other side of the border. Written in the midst of the Mexican Revolution, her stories confront the materiality of the nation and the vexing question of the lived experience of actual natives in a national context. Mena's stories seek to understand the native presence as part of a Mexican past, highlighting at every turn national inconsistency and the ways in which the nation constrains and idealizes women and natives. Her stories provide radically different notions of community and nation than those reflected in the myth of Aztlán, against whose idealized communality Paredes measures her. A central contradiction in her work arises, nevertheless, from the tension she maintains between making natives central to a definition of the Mexican nation while simultaneously distancing Mexico from its native present.

Yet Mena's stories also work against this same containing logic. The Aztecs in "Birth" may be historical relics, but the grandmother specifies an Apache rather than a generic "Indian" abductor. Invoking the Apaches raises the specter of present, native resistance and argues against the historicizing logic of the grandmother and granddaughter. Apache territory was truly transnational, extending across the southwestern United States and into Mexico. They tried to ally with Spain, Mexico, and the United States in turn, aiding the Pueblos in their 1680 rebellion against the Spanish, resisting reservation life, and conducting raids well into the 1880s. The Apaches were not entirely historical at the time "The Birth of the God of War" was written, and they were certainly not easily caricatured, assimilable icons of nativity.

Mena makes the case against cultural consumption—the idea that the other can be objectified and put to ideological use—throughout her work. In "The Education of Popo" (1914), for example, the wealthy Arriola family imports a wide range of "American" processed foods, brought in "on the backs of men and beasts," in order to publicize their status (47). The Arriolas are the Mexican elite, grown wealthy during the Porfiriato, while the poor "men and beasts," or Indians, are left to bear the burden of Mexican modernity. Similarly, in "John of God, the Water Carrier" (1913), native Mexicans are subsumed into the machinery of progress. The "spirit named 'modern improvement'" (19) has been inspiring Mexico City's middle classes to install "American force-pumps" (20) in their homes, thus rendering John and his ilk obsolete.

Native resistance to such consumption and obsolescence is most apparent in "The Gold Vanity Set" when the American traveler Miss Young arrives in Petra's village, camera in hand. She wants to capture images of the native, but Petra turns her face away, resisting the colonizing gaze (3). In each instance Mena argues against the fetishization of the native other, which, while a commentary on Mexican race relations and revolutionary politics, also stands as an indictment of the United States' paternalistic and exoticizing view of Mexico.[3]

In the Mexican context, white reformers and native Mexican rebels figure prominently in Mena's stories along with characters representing the excesses of Díaz's regime. Neither is favored with unconditional sympathy by any of Mena's narrators. Middle- and upper-class pretensions come under attack, but the stories maintain contradictory positions on the native Mexicans. Though Don Ramón calls them "the children of the youth of the world" in "The Gold Vanity Set" (8), their behaviors are described as far from ideal. Similarly, all aspects of revolutionary fervor are offered up for criticism.

Mena's stories critique every Mexican demographic, paying closest attention to white Mexicans who live comfortably under Díaz; white Mexican reformers; clueless U.S. citizens; and saintly, if stupid, Indians. In bringing these disparate populations together the stories respond repeatedly to the first sentence of "The Slaves of Yucatan": "What is Mexico?" (Turner 3). Mena's stories simultaneously attempt to answer Turner's question while denying its querying logic. The stories embrace and reject the nation in the same manner in which they flirt with indigeneity. What emerges consistently in Mena's stories is the idea of "nation" as the root source of Mexico's problems. What is Mexico? It is that which creates limiting ideologies of race, class, and gender that ultimately impede progress. Mena may very well be producing a vision of Mexico for U.S. consumption, but she also resists the idea of consumption, rejecting the idea that the two nations are separate enough for one to consume the other but also resisting the objectifying logic of consumption, as Petra does when Miss Young tries to take her picture.

Indigeneity is, for Mena, the irreducible difference that precludes consumption, or the transgression of national boundaries. Petra's resistance signals race as a barrier to transnational connection, despite the narrator's desire for the women to reach an understanding predicated on their gender. If Mexico and the United States are so interconnected elsewhere in Mena's work, however, what difference do race and gender make for the stories and for international diplomacy? What is Mexico?

According to Don Ramón in "The Gold Vanity Set," the Indians physically constitute Mexico. "They are our blood," he tells Miss Young (10). But then is he, a non-native, really Mexican? Or is the story arguing that all Mexicans are native, to a certain extent? Indigeneity may offer the proto-feminist granddaughter in "The Birth of the God of War" a means of transcending the colonial logic of gender, but the state that constrains her is still predicated on indigenous fantasy.

"The Gold Vanity Set" and "Doña Rita's Rivals" illustrate this contradiction at the heart of Mena's work: race and gender are both the means of oppression and the tools of its transcendence. This is evident in "Doña Rita's Rivals" where Jesús, Doña Rita's son, speaks at length about Indian reform. At the same time that Jesús understands the Indians' condition as a function of policy, the story connects him to Indians by blood in describing him as "not drunk in the competent Northern fashion, but borracho, in the poignant, morbific mode of Indian blood" (76), and in detailing his ability to play "Indian airs" (85) on the violin without making the same mistakes as when playing an "ornamental piece" (74). Furthermore, while the story mocks the practice of determining social class through women's clothing (70), it marks political divisions through the aging, female body (84). What is the nation? Perhaps a set of impositions upon the bodies of women and Indians; or perhaps the nation is rooted in the body. Mena's stories are indecisive, wanting both to define the nation and reject the nation's materiality.

"The Gold Vanity Set" also tries to establish an anti-racist, woman-centered environment but like "Doña Rita's Rivals" winds up beholden to misogynistic and colonialist conceptions of subjectivity. As the women in "Doña Rita's Rivals" fail to establish a connection across class and race, so too do Petra and Miss Young bypass a meaningful connection. But if "Doña Rita's Rivals" is invested in figuring out what race means, "The Gold Vanity Set" is more interested in what its characters *think* race means. The latter pays particular attention to what race looks like to the various characters, which means that the narrator does far less focalizing than in "Doña Rita's Rivals." The narrator stakes no clear position but does appear to critique Petra's mystical understanding of the vanity set just as energetically as Miss Young's vaguely condescending magnanimity is mocked. As in "Doña Rita's Rivals," neither woman in "The Gold Vanity Set" is very compelling.

Key to both stories is women's inability to form meaningful relationships with other women. Doña Rita's class prejudice and sexual conservatism prevent her from seeing Alegría and her sister, the prostitute

Piedad, as anything except rivals. In contrast, Miss Young and Petra do form a bond in "The Gold Vanity Set" over their subservience to men, but this is an idealized connection. In each story the narrator's position is clear: Doña Rita's pretensions are mocked and Miss Young is praised for allowing Petra to offer the Virgin her vanity set. Petra seems to give Miss Young access to her inner self, suggesting that, above and beyond incorporation into the state, cross-racial connections between women allow for a transcendence of the state's petty concerns, indicated by Doña Rita's patrician values. However, these womanly bonds, represented by the embrace or rejection of the Indian, prove problematic and contradictory as Miss Young's feelings for Petra occlude the structural inequities that condition their relationship, and Jesús' embrace of the native leads to a near-death illness.

Both stories present fully developed characters struggling against the constraints of culturally defined womanhood, but the stories stop short of making that same argument about race. The state makes women; on this point the stories are clear, but they seem unaware of women's subsequent roles as race-making agents. Women, no one more so than the Virgin Mary, police the boundaries of the state. Mary imparts a mystical surplus value to Miss Young's vanity set for Petra, who trades the ivory powder and rouge for her husband's love and affection. Miss Young, meanwhile, relinquishes the set in exchange for confirmation of her superiority to Petra, an exchange mediated by the Virgin. In "Doña Rita's Rivals" the Virgin represents state militarism when Jesús depicts Rita as both Virgin Mary and Joan of Arc in two poems, where she polices the boundaries of both heaven and Mexico.

The significant role played by the Virgin Mary in both stories alludes to the excessive value placed on women's bodies in each story. "Doña Rita's Rivals" opens, in fact, with a disquisition on class hierarchies as mediated through women's clothing. At the top of the social pyramid are women *de sombrero*, followed by women *de tápalo*, who wear shawls. Women in shawls condescend to those *de rebozo*, a long, woven Indian cloth, the wearing of which horrifies the same *señoritas* who will "delight to dignify the national investment by wearing it coquettishly at country feasts" (70). These prefatory descriptions illustrate two important points: first, if women *de sombrero* wear the *rebozo* performatively, then the "national investment" in Indians is performative as well, existing only on the surface of things just as the *rebozo* sits upon the shoulders; second, we learn that even families *de rebozo* "have consolation" (70). The prostitute, whose body is consumed, not decorated, is pariah to all.

Doña Rita subscribes to these class prejudices, which preclude her approval of her son Jesús' love for Alegría, a woman of shawl. Further, she can neither appreciate nor understand Jesús' desire to help Indians, who are picturesque if "ignorant of all save the saints, who do not help them." The narrator, interrupting Rita's meditation on indigeneity, observes that the Indians are "slaves in all but name" (73), echoing Turner's description of slavery as a state defined "not in the name, but in the conditions thereof" (9). The narrator notes further that the "social superstructure . . . rests on their backs—for they are the people, prolific of labor and taxes—but otherwise they do not count, unless it be with God" (73). At the outset, then, the story sets up a distinction between the politics it will argue and Doña Rita's patrician archaisms.

Doña Rita's prejudices lead to actions with a human consequence when Alegría commits suicide after meeting with Rita.[4] Doña Rita, the narrator suggests, is over-invested in material objects of dubious value like her carriage (70) and the statue of her husband (72). Jesús' political ideals also come under attack, however. His dedication to Indian reform is signified by his love for Alegría, whose skin the color of "burned milk" and "delicately aquiline" nose (71)—another allusion to Turner, who describes the Mayan henequen slaves as having "slightly aquiline" noses (9)—suggest a mixed-race heritage. The narrator specifically designates Alegría as lower class, but her race is as ambiguous as Jesús' commitment to it. Doña Rita is able to deflect Jesús from both Alegría and Indians on the afternoon of Alegría's death by employing a series of feminine wiles and distractions in the form of imported commodities like champagne and "that barbarous *fonógrafo* from the United States" (74).

That record player is as multivalent as the story's other core symbols. U.S. commodities and capital waylay true reform, but they also, paradoxically, facilitate it, as the story's treatment of music, recording, and politics makes clear, and as the word's being written in Spanish, rather than English, suggests. One the one hand, the *fonógrafo* aligns Doña Rita with the influx of foreign capital into Mexico during the Porfiriato; on the other hand, the record player actually rekindles Jesús' revolutionary zeal at the end of the story. Though Jesús is an accomplished violinist, the record player suggests the reproducibility and dissemination of music unavailable to live performance. At the close of the story, Jesús and Piedad, Alegría's prostitute sister, imagine music's revolutionary potential as a function of its ability to travel and be reproduced, intimating that the very conditions generating American and Mexican wealth are the same conditions that will occasion its dissolution. This dissolution, ostensibly the first step in genuine Indian reform, is suspect, however. Piedad's enthusiasm for his music sets Jesús "all on fire with a new scheme of patriotic service," but he has heretofore been a weak and decidedly unrevolutionary character. In the story Jesús does not interact with, let alone play revolutionary music to, any Indians. His newfound reformist zeal seems, therefore, like a *rebozo* that he can put on and take off at will.

But reform, the story suggests through Doña Rita's anxiety about aging, is inevitable. As Doña Rita's faith in her "quality" passes with the freshness of her looks, so does Jesús' patriotism rekindle with the blossoming of Piedad's. Doña Rita discovers that "generals' widows pass the age at which smiles are cogent" when she is unable to collect on her dead husband's pension (79). As her body depreciates, Piedad's value grows. Doña Rita cannot "bear to look upon the face of Piedad, which now shone with the cloudless enchantment of childhood" (84). Though the narrator takes a negative view of politicizing women's bodies in the story's opening paragraphs, correlating class with women's clothing, here corporeality is instrumentalized in the service of political argument. The narrator allegorizes reform as a womanly competition that Doña Rita is physically unable to win. She fails to come between Jesús and his true loves, and Alegría and Piedad bring him closer to Indians and revolution.

That Piedad is equally capable of inspiring Jesús as was her virginal sister bolsters the narrator's assertion that sin is a function of the state. "Now, Piedad was a unit in a system under official regulation," the reader learns, "and she had a number, like a cab, in the archives of the Departamento de Sanidad Pública" (81–82). So while Jesús can declaim the "purity" (83) of her soul, the narrator can argue that the idea of sin is a means of controlling women. Piedad, however, motivates an uninspiring political program. Jesús and his fellow reformers are imposing their own vision of uplift without native input. Piedad convinces him that he can achieve more by inspiring the Indians to their own revolution. Jesús agrees, but it is not certain that he is the one to fan the revolutionary flames of indigenous Mexico. Piedad is an astute critic, but such is the political program that she, as an overtly sexual, fallen woman, inspires. She connects Jesús to Indians in a material way. Themes of contagion, infection, and pollution are used to describe Jesús' politics, suggesting an inescapable bodily logic of race.

Whether Piedad can be seen as a voice of real reform or not, race is still presented as a material reality, however much the story wants to attach political valence to the Indian. And in both versions women, however socially determined, maintain the boundaries of the state. Piedad is

Jesús' gateway to the Indians, and Doña Rita, as the Virgin Mary, stands at the gateway to heaven. Though "Doña Rita's Rivals" depicts a woman-centered world wherein the politics of race and class are redefined, that world is still beholden to colonial conceptions of gender, represented by the fact that Jesús narrates the constructions of femininity within which the women operate. He writes the poems featuring his mother as Joan of Arc and the Virgin; he absolves Piedad of sin; and Jesús, ultimately, determines his own reformist program, despite Piedad's interventions.

The characters in "The Gold Vanity Set" are similarly constrained, and like Jesús and Piedad, they fail to redraw the boundaries between native and non-native. The story hinges on *how* its female protagonists, Miss Young and Petra, view each other. It dwells on technologies of viewing like Miss Young's camera, her mirror, and her guidebook, all of which condition the characters' visual perceptions of self and space. The first words Miss Young, part of a group of American travelers in Mexico led by Don Ramón, speaks are about Petra: "Oh, what a beautiful girl! I must get her picture" (3). The book and the lens shape Miss Young's view of Mexico. The guidebook has already narrated for her what she will see, and Petra is a marvelous object. Miss Young sees her clearly, and yet she does not see her at all since her book and camera obscure that vision.

Petra, by contrast, looks away from Miss Young. When she sees the camera she "start[s] like a frightened rabbit and [runs] inside" (3). Later, serving the Americans in the bar, Petra is all "oblique looks" and silence, "followed by the admiring looks of women and men" (3). In all these descriptions of seeing, the verb "to see" is never used. Miss Young "catch[es] sight" (3) of Petra at first, and the scene in the bar uses "look" rather than "see." To see is to visually discern something, while to look is to direct one's gaze. This verbal difference indicates that just as "Doña Rita's Rivals" could not bring women together meaningfully, so too will the women in "The Gold Vanity Set" achieve only a surface knowledge of each other. Abstract boundaries of race and class have material consequences, represented in the story by objects, like Miss Young's vanity set, that enable looking rather than seeing.

The vanity set's mirror does not allow Petra to see, only to be "startled" by her reflection. "She had always imagined that she had red cheeks, like the girls in Manuelo's songs" (4). Saddened by her difference from these women, Petra is quickly distracted by the "powder of ivory tint" and the "red paste" contained in the set's other compartments. Petra does not see herself until she "perceiv[es] esthetic improvement" (5) from the white powder and rouge. The changes wrought by the vanity set convince Petra that "the gold treasure was blessed," and its practical value is taken over by a "fantasy dimly symbolic and religious" (5), a belief confirmed when Manuelo, overwhelmed by her transformation, swears to the Virgin Mary that he will never beat Petra again. His oath is answered by thunder and lightning, convincing Petra once and for all that "the golden treasure was a blessed thing, most pleasing to the Mother of Guadalupe" (7). The vanity set becomes useful to Petra in abstract rather than practical terms as religion emerges as another occluding object, or discourse, in this story about clouded vision.

Religion blurs the class differences between Petra and Miss Young. In Petra's view, Miss Young is too simple-minded to appreciate either her vanity set's significance or her wealth. Miss Young, on the other hand, decides that the Virgin can keep her vanity set if it saves Petra from a beating (11). Miss Young's reaction demonstrates not that she is too simple-minded to understand Petra, just that she has the luxury of not caring. She rejects any vision of herself that the Virgin offers, just as she rejects Don Ramón's attempts to explain indigenous Mexico. When he describes Indians' visceral connection to the past, Miss Young replies, "They certainly are picturesque" (10), denying any depth to her visual field. She does not want to understand why the Indians appear to her as they do. The Virgin pushes her to dig deeper and Miss Young has a physical reaction to her: she chokes and must leave the church, where Manuelo waits to serenade her at the story's end. Miss Young will not allow herself to see that Petra's faith in the Virgin allows Miss Young to possess the wealth she does.

The class disparity between Miss Young and Petra is mediated by race, which is both a significant and insignificant difference in "The Gold Vanity Set." Miss Young is uninterested in Don Ramón's racial philosophizing, and she disavows the significance of color in determining one's relationship to the vanity set. "Well, if those cheeks of hers weren't their own natural color this morning, I must say her complexion makes a stunning blend with my rouge," she tells Don Ramón (8), arguing that the set is of equal value no matter what one's color. On the other hand, Don Ramón is right that Petra has taken the set. His explanation relies on a racial logic that cannot put its finger on the materiality of race, only its lingering traces (7). Race can only be unimportant for Miss Young because of its extreme importance for Petra and Don Ramón.

Don Ramón understands the Indians' race as a series of affective qualities. He speaks of "their passion, their melancholy, their music and their superstition" (10) as the things that keep them "children of the youth of the world" (8). The Indians symbolize the past for Don Ramón, and while he cannot articulate the materiality of their race, he can say that they serve as a material link to the past for Mexicans, a link upon which the Mexican understanding of nation is predicated. The Indians "are our blood," he tells Miss Young (10). The Indians, therefore, physically constitute the Mexican body, the nation, but Indianness is defined by abstraction rather than materiality. Furthermore, though they constitute the nation, "the world of today . . . ignores them; but we never forget that it was their valor and love of country which won our independence" (10). Because the racial logic of this short story is unclear, Don Ramón's paternalism cannot be taken at face value. Indeed, this position appears to be offered for critique.

In criticizing Don Ramón's paeans to Indian history, "The Gold Vanity Set" takes Mexico to task for basing its national identity upon an invented idea of Indianness that relies on the linearity of history to keep Indians firmly rooted in the past, which is, paradoxically, exactly what the grandmother in "The Birth of the God of War" does. Don Ramón cannot define Indianness, and Petra, fascinated with Miss Young's white powder, disavows the materiality of race as much as the other, non-Indian characters in the story. To define Indians by their relationship to the past rather than their material significance for the present (in terms of, among other things, their enforced labor, as Turner describes it) renders racial conflict an historical relic and divests it of any real significance. This is an active effort for Don Ramón, while Miss Young, who benefits from Don Ramón's historicizing racial logic, exemplifies the U.S. belief in a "picturesque" Mexico.

Race has primary importance in this story where each character disavows, or ignores, its significance. Again, it is the Virgin, "the benignant figure of the national saint" (10), that makes this erasure possible. The Virgin brings all three characters together and carves out a space wherein they are equal: Don Ramón and Petra both kneel before her and Miss Young leaves the church. The Virgin makes the logic of difference unnecessary. She flattens distinctions and contains the nation within her. At least, this is what the characters' behavior suggests. But the Virgin is described as a "figure of the national saint," as a representation, not as the thing itself. She is both the representation and, if "figure" is understood as a verb instead of noun, the process of representation.

The double valence of "figure" asserts that allegorizing nation as woman contains and neutralizes not just difference but also the normalizing logic required to make difference invisible. The "figure" of the Virgin is "almost hidden by the gifts of the faithful" (10), suggesting that faith renders citizens blind to the politics of representation and civic incorporation. The Virgin makes invisible the racial politics of a state that cannot adequately incorporate the Indians, and she is exotic enough to obfuscate the production of Mexico for a U.S. audience.

Both "Doña Rita's Rivals" and "The Gold Vanity Set" display the instability of race. The incomplete or failed connections between women gesture toward a desire for gender to transcend the limits of the nation, but women are ultimately pressed into the service of the nation in policing the racial boundaries of the state. Both Doña Rita and Piedad serve as racial conduits narrated by Jesús, while Miss Young and Petra's actions are both circumscribed by Manuelo's serenades. We see also in these stories the uneasy conflation of race and nation, a desire to vitiate race of its significance coupled with a statist logic that relies on the exclusion of racial difference.

Both stories argue that gender is social, discursive, and abstract but stop short of making this same argument about race. Racial thinking reifies the national boundaries that Miss Young and Petra's gestures toward a transnational feminism seek to move beyond. But the questions of race and its relation to the nation-state are central to working through what it means to be Mexican in the United States, intrinsic to any critique of transnational capital. In Daniel Venegas's work, as in Mena's, race is primarily a function of class. Las Aventuras de Don Chipote does not directly address the question of race, which lingers at the margins of the narrative, surfacing only in elliptical references to class or the wounded, male body. As in Mena's work, Venegas's novel does self-consciously note the link between gender fetishism and nationalism, but unlike Mena's stories, in which that realization serves as an impetus to transcend the nation, Venegas's novel retreats into the same isolationist nationalism it criticizes.

Daniel Venegas's States of Gender

The shift from Mena's transnationalism to Venegas's nationalism can be explained, in part, by U.S.-Mexico diplomatic relations in the years between 1916, when Mena stopped publishing her stories, and 1928, when Venegas published his novel. Tensions thawed, cross-border cultural exchange flourished, and Mexican president Plutarco Calles worked to encourage tourism and foreign trade.[5] The friendliness of the upper echelons belied, however, the tensions, isolationism, and hostile nationalism that flared on the ground—and that Venegas's novel reflects so sharply.

As Nicolás Kanellos notes in his introduction to *Las Aventuras de Don Chipote,* little is known about Daniel Venegas, its author. Reviews in Los Angeles's Spanish-language press reveal that in the 1920s he ran a vaudeville group, Compañía de Revistas Daniel Venegas, which performed his plays about labor, gender relations, and popular culture in theaters that catered primarily to the working class (Kanellos, "Introduction" 12). Venegas also "hand-set the type and fully illustrated all the stories and comic reportage for his *El Malcriado,*" a weekly, satiric newspaper, which he wrote on his own (Kanellos, "Recovering" 448). Apart from the public record, Venegas remains a mystery. What little else is known is gleaned from his autobiographical gestures in *Don Chipote,* which fictionalizes Venegas's essay "El Vil Traque," appearing in the April 7, 1927, issue of *El Malcriado,* which discusses Venegas's own experiences working on the Santa Fe railroad.

Venegas's autobiographical statements distinguish him from the tradition of early twentieth-century, U.S., Spanish-language presses, and this distance offers one place to begin thinking about his novelistic project. Though a native, Spanish-language, U.S. press had existed since the nineteenth century, the U.S. Hispanic press blossomed during the Mexican Revolution as many intellectuals and cultural workers, such as Flores Magón, migrated north. As exiles, these writers, editors, and activists worked to maintain their Mexican identity, efforts that developed into a privileging of their ideal *mexicanidad* over and against the degraded state of poor, revolutionary Mexico. Such a tendency is also evident in Mena's stories, which produce idealized visions of Mexico that reflect the presses' class biases. For example, large publishing concerns such as Casa Editorial Lozano in San Antonio and Los Angeles had different editorial missions from the "weekly and occasional publications" of immigrant workers (Kanellos, "Recovering" 440). The large houses addressed the concerns of the immigrant laborers but in a paternalistic way that spoke to the deep class and racial divisions within Hispanic communities (Kanellos, "Recovering" 442–43).

According to Nicolás Kanellos, the Hispanic press was less interested in aiding assimilation than in defending their communities against racism ("Recovering" 439). They saw themselves protecting not just against racism but also against the moral turpitude of the United States. They did so by "promoting the idea of a *méxico de afuera,* a Mexican colony existing outside of Mexico, in which it was the duty of immigrants to maintain the Spanish language, keep the Catholic faith and insulate their children from [the] low moral standards practiced by Anglo-Americans" (Kanellos, "Cronistas" 4). The ideology of *méxico de afuera* was nationalist and extremely conservative in its efforts to preserve Mexican identity in exile. It tended toward a bourgeois, elite classism and was decidedly anti-woman.

The idea of *méxico de afuera* was communicated largely through the *crónica*, a series of short, satiric pieces chronicling a community "through a burlesque of fictional characters who represented general ignorance or who were adopting Anglo ways as superior to those of Hispanics" (Kanellos, "Cronistas" 10). *Cronistas*, those who wrote *crónicas*, poked fun at uneducated immigrants who mixed Spanish and English, were overly impressed with Yankee technology, assimilated Anglo patterns of consumption, or facilitated their compatriots' exploitation by working, for example, as labor contractors. *Cronistas*, who saw themselves as the "conscience of the community," were largely male (Kanellos, "Cronistas" 21). Mexican women—the center of language, family, and culture—came under the most fire in the *crónicas*, as in Julio Arce's *Cronicas Diabolicas*, which were widely syndicated throughout the Southwest and exemplify *cronista* conservatism and misogyny.[6] Though the *cronistas* tended, as did Arce, toward an elitist perspective, Kanellos's research reveals a body of working-class, immigrant *crónicas* and he places Venegas in this tradition.

In contrast to the immigrant labor press that sprang up around certain industries and communities, such as nineteenth-century Cuban tobacco workers in southern Florida and their socialist papers, a tradition of working-class print journalism emerged at the same time that evaded rigid ideologies and based itself largely in workers' experiences (Kanellos, "Recovering" 445). With an emphasis on oral expression drawn from lived experience, jokes, and popular culture, especially vaudeville, "these authors documented the experiences of Hispanic immigrants, often autobiographically, and often employing the vernacular dialects of their working-class readers" ("Recovering" 446). While writers like Arce may have used the *crónica* to promote the cultural conservatism of a particular class, the Puerto Rican *cronista* Jesús Colón wrote of tenement life in New York and the Latino con men who preyed upon residents there, and the Afro-Cuban journalist Alberto O'Farril wrote a tragicomic series about a mixed-race laborer unable to find work during the Great Depression (Kanellos, "Cronistas" 18). Though Colón and O'Farril may express considerably more progressive class politics than Arce, they are no less culturally conservative, spilling much ink on the threat posed to the sanctity of Latino culture by the American flapper (Kanellos, "Recovering" 447).

The American flapper is also a major figure in *Don Chipote* for, sympathetic as the novel is with the titular character's plight as an immigrant railroad worker, Chipote is criticized for his slavish attentions to a flapper who nearly causes him to forget his family in Mexico. Venegas's other writings display a similar disregard for women. For example, an issue of *El Malcriado*, included in the Spanish-language edition of *Don Chipote*, mocks bobbed hair and unattractive waitresses, thus displaying a range of contradictions similar to those of other Mexican writers in the United States in the early twentieth century. These authors railed against perceived injustice but had difficulty perceiving their own injustices against others.

On one level, *Don Chipote* reflects just this sort of blind spot. That is, the novel is pro-worker and pro-immigrant, and the author takes pains to identify himself as such and distance himself from the narrator. This pro-worker position leads to similar misogyny as seen in the culturally conservative writing of Arce, Colón, and O'Farril. However, the novel works against these positions in several important ways. The novel simultaneously promotes and critiques a classist and misogynistic nationalism. This double move reflects, if not Mena's self-conscious transnationalism, then at least the internal contradictions of race and citizenship at play in her stories.

Mena's work emphasizes the instability of Mexico and *mexicanidad*. The shifting place of the native Mexican is analogous to the evolving and rapidly shifting meaning of Mexico in the turn-of-the-century United States. Mexico occupies a similarly murky place in Venegas's writing. In an editorial for *El Malcriado* Venegas argued that Mexican journalists in the United States "had to consider themselves before the rest of Mexican society, as guides towards a future of active solidarity and true patriotism for all exiles."[7] They should act as guides toward dignity and respect for the workers and the country of Mexico but from an exiled position. Journalists should foster "true patriotism," Venegas writes, a claim that puts him in line with proponents of *méxico de afuera* who saw their charge as the preservation of an ideal *mexicanidad* in exile. But Venegas goes on to claim that "journalists are also workers,"[8] which seems at odds with a more conservative, journalistic class identity. Journalists as workers throws into question what "true patriotism" is, if not an elitist ideal of Mexican identity, something with which Mena's Doña Rita might identify. Kanellos writes that *méxico de afuera* was perpetuated primarily by "cultural elites," expatriates who thought "Mexico had been so transformed by the 'bolchevique' hordes who had conducted and won the Revolution that the only true Mexican culture survived in exile" ("Recovering" 441). Who but a *bolchevique* would describe a journalist as a proletarian worker? And why would an elitist preserver of Mexican culture in exile write a novel advocating a return to Mexico?

The novel's deployment of the author as foil to the narrator renders Venegas's authorial identity a crucial element of the novel's meaning making. *Don Chipote*'s plot is mediated through three focalizers: the characters, the narrator, and the author, who exists as a textual element within the narrative. The characters in the novel are the primary focalizers, and the majority of the action is viewed from their competing perspectives. An active narrator glosses their actions, however, creating much of the text's meaning. For example, when Don Chipote eagerly disrobes for the required shower and disinfecting at the Ciudad Juárez crossing, he believes it is a relatively insignificant barrier to U.S. entry. The narrator, on the other hand, comments, "There thou hast it: Don Chipote actually taking pleasure in the first humiliation that the gringo forces on Mexican immigrants" (35).[9] This both provides political color commentary to the scene and demonstrates the narrator's intellectual superiority to Don Chipote.

In the course of Chipote's adventures the narrator declaims against immigrants' unjust working conditions, Mexican revolutionary politics, and an immigrant culture of Mexican denial and female immorality. This political self-righteousness grounds the narrator's empathy with Don Chipote's plight, but it is predicated upon the ironic distance the narrator can maintain from the characters: Chipote's pathos derives from his naïveté, and the narrator is unable to describe this naïveté apart from a base physicality. As much as the narrator's commentary highlights the structural inequalities of the Mexican immigrant laborer's relationship to the United States, these comments also serve to keep those workers in their place in terms of a Mexican class hierarchy. The narratorial asides build upon this sense of superiority, especially in regard to bodily functions and general civility. After Don Chipote's delousing, for instance, he is turned away at the border. Cast adrift in Ciudad Juárez, Don Chipote wanders into a mariachi concert, after which the plaza becomes deserted and Chipote falls asleep. The clock strikes eleven, then midnight, "and Don Chipote gave no more signs of life than some flat chords he let escape from his mouth and one or another through private channels."[10]

Don Chipote's flatulent disempowerment speaks to his proletarian position in relation to the narrator's intellectualism. Chipote is body while the narrator is mind, and though the narrator is empathetic to the body's privations, the narrative privileges mental dexterity.

The narrator thus exemplifies the elite *cronista* mocking Chipote's peasant ways. These ways include being mistakenly impressed with his friend Pitacio's ridiculous outfit, which Don Chipote takes as a sign of Pitacio's prosperity in the United States and which our narrator notes "was not of very good quality" (24).[11] They also include Chipote's being overly impressed with Yankee technology in a letter to his wife, Doña Chipota. "If you could just see how sharp these gringos are! Because there are some things out here that even make Skinenbones gawk with his mouth wide open" (75), he tells her.[12] Chipote can neither read nor write and must engage a scribe to write a letter to his wife. His illiterateness and the tone of awe in the letter, which mirrors Chipote's and his friend Policarpo's slack-jawed walk through El Paso upon their initial arrival (36, 44), evoke the *crónica*.[13]

In the midst of all this praise, however, Chipote calls the gringos "demons," a point lost in the English translation above. The original Spanish reads: "¡Si vieras que demonios son los gringos!" (69), and the demonic is worth dwelling on here. Chipote's letter is less about the technology that so impressed him and Policarpo initially and more about the working conditions on the *traque*. Chipote describes his duties as well as the fact that his foreman cannot pronounce his name, often calling him by "a nickname that I don't understand too well. I think it's something like 'Godam Sonovagun'" (76).[14] "Demonios" clearly has a double valence in Chipote's letter, signifying both ingenuity and inhumanity, a reading corroborated by the letter's placement immediately after a description of the author's own experiences working on the *traque*.

"The author of this novel, not too long ago, had to join up with the infamous traque, like the majority of those who come from Mexico, and he took perfect account of the abuses which foremen commit against the workers," the narrator reports, distinguishing the authorial persona from the narrator's (70).[15] The abuses of which the author took note range from spitefully placing workers in dangerous positions to actual physical abuse, including murder. Invoking the author complicates the narrator's status as *cronista* and inaugurates the novel's more complex political and literary arguments. The author is introduced by the narrator in the third person, which slips into the first person as the story progresses: "He took perfect account," but, the end of the same paragraph reads: "that foreman worked us like dogs, only making us desperate" (70).[16] This slippage between author and narrator, the move from "he" to "us," is a significant one. The author physically inserts himself into the story and collapses the distance between author and narrator. The narrator has, up until this point, maintained an ironic distance from the characters, but materializing the author as a character that shares experiences with Chipote and Policarpo complicates this distance and undermines the narrator's ironizing work.

Don Chipote features characters whose naïveté, coupled with the unscrupulousness of the various characters with whom they interact, creates the need for the narrator, an elite *cronista*, to step in and maintain the purity and integrity of Mexican culture. However, a very strong authorial persona competes with the narrator. *Don Chipote*'s critique is twofold. On the one hand, we have political commentary documenting the injustices faced by Mexican immigrants to the United States and discussing the merits and failings of the revolution. On the other hand, we have a literary critique in which the novel unwittingly deconstructs its own literary tradition. Since that tradition is predicated upon a set of conservative beliefs, parsing the novel's social commentary requires fully grasping its literary intervention. Venegas, as Kanellos argues ("Introduction" 5), wants to tell the story of immigrant labor, but that is not the only work his novel accomplishes.

Telling the story of immigrant labor gives voice to the country bumpkins mocked in the *crónicas*. This would appear to put Venegas at odds with the *crónica* tradition. *Crónicas*, however, retain the bulk of their critique for peasants who aspire to be "American." The moral of *Don Chipote* is similar: Chipote is redeemed when he returns home with Doña Chipota. Both Don Chipote and the *crónica* tradition privilege a pure, unadulterated Mexico, but they disagree on where that Mexico is located. For the *cronistas* true Mexico is in exile, preserved and maintained by those promoting an ideology of *méxico de afuera*. *Don Chipote*, on the other hand, locates Mexico not in the exiled intellectuals but in the Mexican peasantry. The novel takes issue with the *crónica*'s class bias when the author uses his own class identification as a platform for his political observations.

Two types of class conflict, intra and inter, are apparent in *Don Chipote*, while U.S. injustices fall to the background. Intraclass conflict occurs when members of the same class delude each other about U.S. opportunity. Chipote, for example, is persuaded to try his luck in the north when Pitacio, apparently successful, returns from his sojourn there.

Pitacio's success is a ruse, however, evidenced by the narrator's opinion of his shoddy clothing, of which Chipote is mistakenly enamored. The narrator asserts, "The United States is full of these Pitacios" (28)[17] who are too proud to admit their failure in the United States and thus continue to spread their lies in Mexico. Unfortunately "Chicanos" believe these lies, and it is "for this reason, more than the poor conditions in which the Revolution has left the country, that more and more people emigrate each day" (28).[18] The narrator sympathizes yet again with immigrant labor but sees their exodus as motivated less by the revolution and more by their compatriots' betrayal and their own gullibility.

While the narrator criticizes the self-deceptions of the working class, the most vitriol is saved for elite Mexicans whose disregard for the working class fuels the interclass conflicts in the novel. "Can there be any greater wickedness than these bastards," the narrator asks about immigrants who, "passing themselves off as gringos[,] refuse to speak their own language, denying even the country in which they were born?" (51). This critique can be read as an elitist take on the need to preserve culture. But, from these "bastards" is "where the harshest epithets about us have come" (51).[19] Words like "cholo" and "stupid" are "their things to wound recent arrivals from Mexico."[20] The "bastards" here have a double resonance, therefore. The narrator calls them "the worst thorn in the side of the Mexican *bracero*" (51),[21] a thorn in the side of the *worker*, not the *cronista*. Furthermore, if words wound, then these epithets harm recent arrivals just as much as the cultured elites. The "bastards" may be ignorant peasants overvaluing Anglo culture, but they may also be the elitist proponents of *méxico de afuera* betraying their compatriots by savaging them in the press. The *malditos*' shifting identity destabilizes the novel's political critique by simultaneously supporting and undercutting a *méxico de afuera* ideology. *Don Chipote*'s intervention, therefore, is both a literary and political one: a critique of a genre and a revaluation of the politics underpinning that genre.

The class disparities the novel highlights are also disparities of race—seen in the use of "cholo" as a word that wounds and in the offense Policarpo takes in the rude behavior of the "gringo prieto" (44)[22]—but they do not lead to a critique of nationalism, as they do in Mena's stories. The novel believes in an ideal Mexico and in national responsibility. The narrator in *Don Chipote* sees immigration to the United States as the result of Mexico's failure to provide for its citizens (24, 33) rather than as the result of U.S. economic intervention in Mexican affairs, as does Mena. While Mena's stories suggest the impossibility of conceiving Mexico and the United States as separate entities, *Don Chipote* merely takes the latter to task for its cruelty and disregard for Mexican labor, eschewing systemic critique. Where Mena's stories offer no clear vision of what it means to be Mexican in the United States, Venegas's novel argues that there can be no greater evil than Mexicans who choose to transgress the national boundaries of culture (43). On this point of believing in a national ideal *Don Chipote* is in accord with *méxico de afuera*, and while the novel takes progressive stands on the politics of class and race, it is much more conservative when it comes to questions of gender.

For both Venegas and *méxico de afuera* the national ideal is intricately bound up with intractable notions of gender. That is, women, in both the *crónicas* and *Don Chipote*, bear the burden of representing the nation. The national problem, for both, is a gender problem. In *Don Chipote* this takes the form of the two nations being represented by two women: Doña Chipota stands for Mexico, and Don Chipote's love interest, "a flapper who waits tables" (125),[23] stands for the United States and the dangers of its influence.

After waiting several months, to no avail, for Don Chipote to send for the family, Doña Chipota takes the family to Los Angeles to find him. Desperate to win his flapper's love, Don Chipote has entered a talent contest at a local music hall "frequented by pretty much all the Chicano riffraff,"[24] including Doña Chipota and her traveling party. "Shameless one! Bad Husband!" she calls him, rushing the stage on which he is about to perform. Doña Chipota physically assaults Don Chipote; the police are brought in, and the entire family winds up in jail, from which they are deported home to Mexico. They return to their old lives as tenant farmers, secure in their knowledge that "Mexicans will make it big in the United States . . . WHEN PARROTS BREAST-FEED" (160).[25]

The authorial persona is not noticeable in passages concerning Doña Chipota and the flapper, suggesting that the author and narrator are united in their reading of the flapper as a dangerous temptress compared to the safety of hearth and home represented by Doña Chipota. Don Chipote has an ethical responsibility to Mexico, while his dalliance with the United States was an amoral aberration. But this reading, like so many things in the novel, cuts two ways. During the night he spends in jail Don Chipote dreams of his flapper. At the point of consummating their love an evil witch appears to turn Don Chipote into a braying mule (153, 154). The witch may be Doña Chipota, in which case Don Chipote is still morally compromised if Doña Chipota occupies the ethical high ground. The witch may also be the United States, however. While in Los

Angeles Don Chipote briefly begins to explore his personhood: he cares for his appearance, he engages in leisure activities, he imagines himself in romantic narratives, and perhaps most significantly he places himself on the stage, as a performer. When he sends a picture of himself home to Doña Chipota she does not recognize him at first because of his new clothes (122, 124). But in the United States, Don Chipote can never be fully human; he will always be a laboring animal. Doña Chipota can show him that truth, but she does not define its parameters.

The witch may also represent the *cronistas* who assert the inhumanity of the working class, who betray their culture by turning against their own in the press. Forces beyond his control turn Don Chipote into an animal in his dream. His rough edges are grounded in his physical being, while the narrative works to show Don Chipote's self as an active performance, at least when he is in the United States. The witch, however, intervenes in Don Chipote's construction of self, asserts his inhumanity, and relegates him to an ideal Mexico. In Mexico, Don Chipote realizes he will only be successful when parrots breastfeed, when creatures step out of their natural place. The novel thus argues that Mexicans have a moral obligation to remain in Mexico, while also arguing that to do so is to accept one's inhumanity. The national ideal, in other words, dehumanizes the citizenry. In this sense, then, *Don Chipote* undermines the idea of a *méxico de afuera*, the need to preserve an ideal *mexicanidad*, and advocates more fluid notions of nation and subjectivity.

Women are presented equally ambiguously in *Don Chipote*. Doña Chipota and the flapper are deployed as national signifiers, but the novel works against this equation as well in describing the first vaudeville show Don Chipote attends. The scene opens with a performance of the song "Sangre mexicana" ("Mexican Blood"), after which the curtain lifts to reveal "a practically naked singer."[26] Though the narrator finds her unattractive, to the Mexican audience for whom she performs "she was out of this world" (116).[27] While the opening song works to create a sense of Mexico as rooted in the body, the narrator's mocking tone deconstructs that notion and pokes fun at the audience and the performer. The singer may be an ugly warbler, but "the Chicano community goes crazy when something reminds them of their blessed cactus land" (117).[28] The audience is criticized not just for enjoying a poor performance but also for their reaction to national representation. They go crazy, and the narrator thinks them ridiculous.

The narrator's mocking language and tone suggest not only that any national representation is flawed but also that the desire to represent the nation is misguided. The nation does not reside in its songs or dances but in its people. If an audience goes crazy for "their blessed cactus land" then they are paying too much attention to its representation and not enough to its materiality; to idealized visions of Mexican bodies as light skinned—the singer's legs are described as "streams of *atole*" (116)— rather than Mexico's actual, dark, indigenous population.[29] The novel's earlier authorial interjections can be understood in this context as a criticism of the elite *cronista*'s view of the nation. Venegas does not take issue with the national ideal, simply its composition. For him, the people, not abstractions of propriety, comprise the nation. To be overcome by representations of the nation, as the Mexican audience is in the vaudeville scene, is to be guided by sentiment rather than reason, and sentiment, in *Don Chipote*, is a potential liability.

Sentiment is also traditionally the domain of women in its literary articulations. Not so in *Don Chipote*, where men are incapacitated by sentiment and the women are eminently practical. At several points in the novel Don Chipote is described as longing for his family, sometimes to the point of tears. He is extremely attached to his dog and develops an affectionate bond with Policarpo. The two men care for each other lovingly, cooking, cleaning, hugging, and ministering to each other from El Paso to Los Angeles and through Don Chipote's deportation. And Don Chipote is so desperately in love with his flapper he even consults a faith healer (125, 122). His attempts to make his flapper feel meet with little success, and Don Chipote is left spinning his wheels in sentiment that precludes action.

Like the flapper, Doña Chipota avoids sentimentality. She does have feelings, but she is able to mobilize herself and her family in the face of those feelings. She can act as well as feel. Moreover, she must help Don Chipote to feel correctly when she encounters him in Los Angeles. Sentiment, per se, is not bad; the tendency of sentiment to override action is, however, problematic. *Don Chipote* positively links sentiment to action in the figure of Doña Chipota, as well as in grounding sentiment in the male characters' physicality. Don Chipote has a physical reaction to his emotions, but the clearest link between sentiment and materiality comes with Don Chipote's injury on the *traque*.

Early in the narrative Don Chipote, overworked and exhausted, plunges a pickaxe into his own foot (78, 85). This injury brings him and Policarpo even closer together as Policarpo nurses him on the way to the company hospital in Los Angeles. Illness, injury, and death mark U.S. literary sentimentality. In the context of *Don Chipote* and the early twentieth-century Hispanic *cronistas*, shifting the grounds of sentiment from abstract notions of a national ideal to the physical bodies of its male characters subverts the gendered logic of *méxico de afuera*. The body is made to signify differently in this shift, moving from a reflection of ideal sentiment to the materiality of race and class. The tragedy in *Don Chipote* is not necessarily that the Chipotes return to Mexico and remain poor but that they run up against the abstractions of the nation. Neither an idealized *méxico de afuera* nor the economic hegemony of the United States can incorporate their classed and elliptically raced bodies.

Transnational Bodies and the Sexuality of Citizenship

Mexico slips and shifts, expands and contracts throughout the writings of María Mena and Daniel Venegas. This national shape shifting has its corollary in the multivalent Mexican bodies that populate their work. In the early twentieth century, demographic shifts and political upheaval combined to produce a heterogeneous, Mexican diaspora who very gradually came to understand their conflation in the Anglo U.S. imagination over the course of the Mexican Revolution. As their particular bodies become one general body, so too does Mexico morph from a particular set of geopolitical realities into a conglomeration of national fantasies and ideals.

Later in the century, as Mexican diasporic communities adjust to their relative permanence in the United States, diversities of class and race continue to trouble attempts to define Mexican America. The body and its desires continue to stand as conflicted indices of race and nation in Jovita González and Eve Raleigh's novel *Caballero*, written initially in 1937. That novel, which I explore in the next chapter, attempts to move beyond the national proscriptions apparent in both Mena's and Venegas's writings but is ultimately limited, in ways structurally similar to the restrictions evident in Mena and Venegas, by its own adherence to the heteronormativity of the liberal state.

4 / More Life in the Skeleton: *Caballero* and the Teleology of Race

This is not Modernismo, but it is true, it is the reality of a new life, the certificate of the intense force vital of a continent.
—RUBÉN DARÍO, "MODERNISMO" (372)

In 1996 Texas A&M University Press published Jovita González and Eve Raleigh's *Caballero: A Historical Novel*, which the two had written sometime around 1937.[1] The novel tells the story of the fictional Mexican Mendoza y Soría family and how they deal with the transition to U.S. rule in the wake of the Mexican-American War. Although scholars had long known of the existence of the novel (in several articles González had published in the *Southwest Review* and *Publications of the Texas Folklore Society* the novel was reported "in progress" [Limón, introduction to *Caballero*, xviii]), the manuscript itself was not discovered until 1992 when Isabel Cruz, González's literary executor, donated her papers and those of her husband, E. E. Mireles, to Texas A&M University at Corpus Christi. As Thomas Kreneck, the head of Special Collections at Texas A&M's Bell Library, describes in his "Recovering the 'Lost' Manuscripts of Jovita González," once the papers had been archived, scholar Cynthia Orozco determined that one bundle of papers bound in twine was indeed the rumored novel's manuscript. José Limón worked with Kreneck and coeditor María Cotera to prepare *Caballero* for publication. *Dew on the Thorn*, another González novel found in the Mireles archive, followed from Arte Público Press in 1997 (Kreneck 77–79).

The publication of both novels revolutionized scholars' understanding of Jovita González's importance for the development of South Texas and Mexican American literature.[2] González was already recognized as a significant scholar of Mexican American folklore and South Texas history. Her master's thesis in history from the University of Texas at

Austin, "Social Life in Cameron, Starr, and Zapata Counties" (1929),[3] has long been recognized as a foundational source text for the study of Mexican American culture and history along the U.S.-Mexico border, and her many articles in the *Publications of the Texas Folklore Society* and *Southwest Review* are essential reading for scholars writing cultural histories of the region. Conjoined with her scholarship, González's visibility as president of the Texas Folklore Society (1930–32), her activism in both the Corpus Christi and San Felipe school districts, and her work with the League of United Latin American Citizens (LULAC) in South Texas render González an important figure in Chicana/o studies.[4] And this was all before the discovery and publication of her novels.

González's novels presented a new set of questions with which scholars now had to grapple: What was the relationship between early Chicana/o intellectuals and the predominantly Anglo institutions of which they were a part? How did early Chicana intellectuals carve a place for themselves? What constitutes a resistant narrative, and how is it different from a narrative of resistance? What is the history of Chicana/o literature? Chicana/o studies has always grappled with these questions, but Jovita González's novels—with their sarcasm, irony, outspoken women protagonists, and scathing political commentary skewering both Mexico and the United States—cast them in a new light.

In the body of work following the publication of *Caballero* and *Dew on the Thorn* scholars have pursued these questions with renewed interest, and no one scholar has been more influential in addressing them than María Cotera. Cotera's epilogue to the 1996 edition of *Caballero*, "Hombres Necios: A Critical Epilogue," set the parameters for subsequent discussions of the novel. In it, Cotera places *Caballero* in the tradition of works by contemporary Chicana writers such as Ana Castillo and Cherríe Moraga, arguing that the novel voices a "trenchant critique of the patriarchal world view" and "deconstructs the myth of the warrior-hero while politicizing the domestic sphere" (339). Both Cotera's book *Native Speakers: Ella Deloria, Zora Neale Hurston, Jovita González, and the Poetics of Culture* (2008) and her published articles carry on this line of argumentation. Cotera has shaped Chicana/o literary studies' current view of González's work as resistant to both racist configurations of Mexican Americans and the patriarchal misogyny of her imagined community.

In this chapter I reorient extant readings of the novel from a specifically U.S. to a broader hemispheric context. Aesthetics offer an initial point of entry into this approach. A third of the way into *Caballero*, Luis

Gonzaga, a young Mexican artist, wanders into Bony's saloon in Matamoros, where his family, the respected Mendoza y Sorías, spends their winters. He would not normally deign to enter such a déclassé establishment, but he is compelled by a black-on-white painting of a skeleton he glimpses within. Though the bar is a known gathering place for the U.S. soldiers stationed in town, and "it was far beneath any gentleman to go there" (102), the quality of the painting pulls Luis Gonzaga in for a closer look.

The bulk of *Caballero* is devoted to the courtships and eventual marriages of Luis Gonzaga's sisters, Susanita and Angela, to U.S. soldiers. Underlying the novel's romantic plot conventions, however, are aesthetic and philosophical concerns captured in this brief scene about Bony's skeleton. The aesthetic questions raised by the skeleton and the political issues they adumbrate ground this chapter's comparison of *Caballero* to Mexican philosopher José Vasconcelos's essay "La raza cósmica" (1925) in order to develop a hemispheric picture of the novel's aesthetic and ethnographic intervention. Bringing the two into conversation foregrounds the hemispheric dimensions of the instability of race and highlights the writers' shared articulation of what Ramón Saldívar refers to as "New World Modernism" (394). Saldívar also uses the term "subaltern modernity" (17) to indicate a hemispheric project that observes processes of modernization from below and situates the modern outside Europe. Bringing these terms to bear on *Caballero* locates the novel's literary project both within and beyond U.S. racial and aesthetic boundaries.

Bony's saloon is a space wherein these aesthetic boundaries are first self-consciously blurred in *Caballero*. As such it stands as an allegory of a profoundly reimagined American space suggested by the ambiguous sexuality of Luis Gonzaga and Captain Devlin, the painter of the skeleton that initially attracts Luis Gonzaga. Their non-reproductive, queer, quasi-romance stands outside the generational family time, defined by Judith Halberstam as the span of time within which values are transferred that build a sense of familial, cultural, and patriotic sentiment, and unite the family's story to a national story (5). Generational and national time are represented in the novel by Luis Gonzaga's sisters. Though *Caballero* makes much of Luis Gonzaga's and Captain Devlin's artistic life together, in one of the novel's many conflicts and contradictions, it tightly contains the radical potential of their union.

Their first encounter is wholly artistic. Luis Gonzaga enters and draws his own version of the skeleton that has been painted by Captain Devlin of the U.S. Army. "With a change of angle here, a tilt of the skull, an added line or two, he made of the skeleton a crying drunkard, a dancing girl, a soldier, a mocking devil . . . then he drew it exactly as it was; yet not exactly, for it had a life which the other lacked" (102). Devlin congratulates Luis for his talent and asks to have one of the pictures. "The world rocked and shook for Luis Gonzaga. This man an *Americano*? But he had always been told that they were coarse, sometimes clever enough to simulate gentility but without the inner grace which was its true test" (103). Despite the congruence of substance and sign in Devlin, however, his art tells another story. Describing it, the Captain says, "I should make a good map. . . . So many feet, so many miles, here a hill, there a valley" (156). A comparison of the two skeletons proves the truth of his self-critique. Captain Devlin's is exacting, but Luis Gonzaga's has "a life which the other lacked." One represents; the other has soul, suggestion.

It is tempting to link the representational questions raised by their artistic differences to the ethnographic philosophy espoused by J. Frank Dobie, one of González's mentors and professors. In *Dancing with the Devil* José Limón describes Dobie's assumption that it was the job of the folklorist to editorialize the information gleaned from subjects. The folklorist took factual data and made them into something new, something with a life and style of its own (50–55). Perhaps Luis Gonzaga stands as an argument in support of Dobie's ethnographic approach. If so, however, one wonders why the authors would choose to ground that support in such ambiguous, imperfect characters. Captain Devlin walks with a cane, and Luis Gonzaga is prone to tearful, emotional outbursts. Furthermore, their relationship remains undefined throughout the novel, sexually suggestive but not explicit.

The difference between Captain Devlin's and Luis Gonzaga's art coupled with the novel's consistent linking of linguistic access to social power suggest deep reservations about language's ability to represent the real as well as an exploration of how narrative functions. If visual art has more purchase on the real, the authors implicitly question whether traditional ethnographic or historical narratives are fully adequate to capture history; and so we might come to read Luis Gonzaga as an argument in support of native ethnographic speakers, rather than of Dobie.

One is still left wondering, however, why this argument is made with Devlin and Luis Gonzaga. Thinking of the artistic distance between the two as an argument in favor of the native ethnographer who turns to fiction, as Jovita González did, in order to explore the gaps in ethnography's colonizing discourse allows us to consider *Caballero* along with the work of Zora Neale Hurston and other New Negro culture workers who engaged similarly with ethnography.[5] *Caballero* challenges ethnography's colonizing gaze, as do the New Negros, but its challenge cannot be understood in entirely the same way. At bottom, the New Negro artists challenged the idea that culture could be scientifically presented.[6] This argument does seem to be in play in *Caballero*, but it is conflicted and couched in aesthetic questions imbricated in racial politics that follow a north-south, hemispheric trajectory rather than modernism's east-west transatlanticism.

Caballero is most productively read not in the context of European modernism but in terms of Latin American *modernismo*, a distinctively different aesthetic project, commonly understood as grounded in the work of the Nicaraguan writer Rubén Darío, from whom this chapter takes its epigraph. While *Caballero* is not as metaphysically oriented as some *modernista* works—Darío was heavily influenced by Pythagorean ideas of divinity and saw the poet as uniquely positioned to disseminate the messages of the higher spheres—it does trade in notions of fate and eternity: the characters into which Luis transforms the skeleton recall the traditional figures on Mexican *lotería* cards,[7] "Devlin" is a near anagram of "devil" (though Devlin, a doctor, is less a trickster and more of a healer), and the plot of the novel hinges on the opposition of destiny and free will. Luis's skeletal sketches are also clear allusions to the work of José Guadalupe Posada, the Mexican printmaker, illustrator, and political cartoonist whose *calaveras* (skeletons) circulated throughout Mexico in the early twentieth century as commemorations of current events and satirical indictments of the Porfiriato. *Caballero* thus situates itself within a hemispheric debate over the aesthetics of art and politics, straddling the divide between *modernismo* and *vanguardismo*, a movement more similar to European modernism.

Though, as Julio Ramos argues, *modernismo* sought to redefine the relationship between literature and the public sphere established by nineteenth-century *letrados* like Domingo Sarmiento, *modernistas* like Darío still engaged political questions. As an aestheticized response to modernity, *modernismo* grounds a host of political projects. In Mexico it can be read as the precursor to post-revolutionary *indigenismo* examined in Chapter 3. *Modernismo's* search for Latin America's aesthetic truth underpins the search for an essential *mexicanidad* (a search arguably begun in the 1820s by the Romantics in post-independence Mexico), manifest in what María Mena understood as the fetishization of indigeneity, or at least the overly earnest attempt to define modern Mexico through recourse to the native.

Out of these attempts to forge a definitive link between the native and modern Mexico emerges the transcendent racial philosophy of José Vasconcelos, a leading intellectual and political figure of post-revolutionary Mexico. Though *Caballero* does not refer to Vasconcelos by name, the novel appears to engage him directly, and it is not unreasonable to assume that Jovita González would have been familiar with him and his writings. Vasconcelos's career as a politician and public intellectual took him across Mexico and the United States. He spent his childhood in southern Texas, and in 1910, as a supporter of Francisco Madero, he fled Mexico for the United States where he worked to generate northern support for the anti-Díaz candidate. Vasconcelos moved back and forth between Mexico and the United States throughout the 1910s until 1921 when newly elected president Álvaro Obregón appointed him minister to the recently formed Ministry of Public Education, a post Vasconcelos left in 1924 to pursue a lecturing career that took him around the world and eventually to a professorship in Hispanic American sociology at the University of Chicago (Juárez 58). Before officially announcing his candidacy for president of Mexico in 1928, Vasconcelos worked tirelessly to ensure broad support in the United States. "Mexican Americans in Texas, New Mexico, and California," asserts John Skirius, "were the first to hear Vasconcelos campaign for president" (490). As an educated, politically active Tejana, Jovita González would have had some knowledge of Vasconcelos; but, here I am less interested in establishing indisputable influence and more concerned to show the similarities and contrasts between the two writers' racial philosophies.

Vasconcelos, as is González for Chicana/os, is an extremely complicated and conflicted figure in Mexican history, however. A member of the progressive, anti-Díaz Ateneo de la Juventud, early in his intellectual career Vasconcelos participated in the crafting of an indigenist national narrative that saw the Spanish conquest as an originary trauma and independence in 1821 as a breaking of oppression's chains. Chicana/o activists in the United States have borrowed heavily from this narrative and have celebrated this aspect of Vasconcelos.[8] The later Vasconcelos, on the other hand, saw the celebration of Mexico's Indian past as an oppressive strategy supported by the United States in order to balkanize Mexico and retard progress (Marentes 14). He repudiated his early work, including "La raza cosmíca," claiming Mexican history began with the conquest, with the advent of the national idea. In and of itself this theory is inoffensive but becomes increasingly so when considering Vasconcelos's transformation into a relatively paranoid and racist "Indophobe" toward the end of his life (Marentes 17). This aspect of Vasconcelos's career conditions his reputation in Latin America but tends to go unnoted among his Chicana/o venerators.

Vasconcelos's contradictions make the comparison to *Caballero* incredibly rich and productive. Critics have also read *Caballero* as making conservative and problematic arguments in favor of Mexican assimilation into U.S. culture. Vasconcelos and *Caballero* are both deeply conflicted on the question of race and its significance for Mexicans and Mexican Americans. This conflict is a constitutive feature of Chicana/o literature and culture, which, in comparing *Caballero* to Vasconcelos, appears to grow as much from a Mexican and Latin American cultural milieu as from racial politics in the United States. The colonizing embrace of indigeneity against which María Mena and Vasconcelos react is rearticulated by mid-twentieth-century Chicana/o activists' celebration of Chicana/os' indigenous roots; evident in each move is the profound instability of race and fear of the ever-shifting other who traverses racial and national borders.

Scholarship on *Caballero*, however, remains concentrated on the United States. Readings often center on LULAC, a fairly conservative political organization with which González was actively involved. LULAC was formed in 1929 to combat discrimination against Mexicans in South Texas; one of its primary goals was to help settle Mexican immigrants and assimilate them into U.S. culture. LULAC, a staunchly middle-class organization, was motivated in part by the desire to uplift poor Mexicans who, according to LULAC, threatened political gains the organization had already made. LULAC worked against the racial discrimination of Mexicans but not against racism per se, arguing vociferously in several instances that Mexicans "were white and therefore had such privileges coming to them as admission to white schools and public places" (Marquez 31).

Scholarship on *Caballero* has tended to focus closely on the relationship between Jovita González's politics, as evidenced by her work with LULAC, and her ethnographic work, which critics see as culminating with *Caballero*. As a counternarrative to Anglo hegemony *Caballero* fails, in some estimations, because of its assimilationist, racist, and classist politics, which echo those of LULAC.[9] Two things undermine such an easy elision of LULAC's philosophy with *Caballero*'s politics. First, as María Cotera has continued to remind readers, the novel is a joint effort with Eve Raleigh, and though it is not generally discussed as such scholars should always keep its collaborative qualities in mind. Second,

Caballero is a novel, not an ethnographic work. In parsing the meaning of *Caballero*, we must ask what fiction allows the authors to do that ethnography does not.

Caballero clearly imagines itself as undercutting the patriarchy of Mexican nationalism, but to do so does not necessarily imply wholesale support of U.S. nationalism. The novel promotes LULAC's conciliatory positions on issues of race and class but not without hesitation and contradictions. This ambivalence is seen in the authors' use of allegory and their deployment of historical conventions in ways that neither romanticize history nor root it firmly in the past. *Caballero* is about the gender, race, and class of nationalism. Bound up with these plot-level concerns, however, is an interest in literacy, representation, and narrative control that simultaneously support and undercut LULAC's positions.

At the level of form, in other words, despite its purposeful, progressive interventions, *Caballero* appears to be working against many of its plot-level assertions. For example, when Padre Pierre explains to Captain Devlin his theory that procreation between the Mendoza y Soría women and Anglo-American men will strengthen the racial stock of each national group, he evokes Vasconcelos on race while undermining LULAC's assertions of Mexican whiteness. But Vasconcelos's theory is itself contradictory, and it is unclear whether *Caballero* is celebrating him or taking him to task; in fact, the novel winds up doing both. In "La raza cósmica" the tension between nationalism and internationalism, which Padre Pierre traces, mirrors the tension between evolutionary and circular notions of historical time: Vasconcelos's theory is progressive but he denies an evolutionary logic to race. Thus the central tension in the essay is between material and abstract notions of race, which *Caballero* deploys, consciously or not, as a tension between form and content that can be read as a commentary on the viability of historical narrative. In so doing *Caballero* performs and even, in some instances, takes issue with Vasconcelos's contradictions, revealing a deeper, hemispheric, racial instability manifest in Chicana/o narrative.

Vasconcelos and the Mystical Eugenics of Taste

While *Caballero* calls to mind the racial theories found in Vasconcelos's "La raza cósmica," which directly counter LULAC's, the essay's internal contradictions result in an even broader critique of race, history, and narrative than *Caballero* appears to intend. "La raza cósmica" bears the undeniable influence of the "Ateneo," and yet its embrace of the Ateneo's mysticism is ambiguous. In the early twentieth century the Ateneo countered the positivism of the Porfirista, *científico* elite with a "spiritual alternative to ... materialism," a philosophical approach that characterizes the bulk of Vasconcelos's work (Marentes 2). Revealing his interest in and study of ancient religions, his early writings, including "La raza cósmica" and his book *Estudios industíanicos* (1920), demonstrate his lifelong spiritual quest for a deeper, mystical explanation of life's meaning.

"La raza cósmica" also bears the influence of post-revolutionary Mexico's Indianist movement, which encompassed the struggle for indigenous land rights and political representation as well as attempts to venerate indigenous over Spanish culture. Vasconcelos, however, according to Nicandro Júarez and others, "never held these views," believing in the need to assimilate rather than isolate native Mexicans from modern Mexican culture (67). "La raza cósmica" is Vasconcelos's attempt to do just that while also celebrating Latin America's *mestizaje* (racial mixing). True, as many critics have noted, his sociology of race lacks scientific rigor. As the Peruvian intellectual José Mariátegui, Vasconcelos's contemporary, noted, however, the essay's great strength lies not in its strict adherence to method but in its privileging of imagination and the role of the artist (Marentes 81).

The artist, according to Vasconcelos, will propel humanity into a third stage of existence. "La raza cósmica" offers a theory of race that is at once mystical, historical, and geographical, rooted in time and space yet transcending both through aesthetic, artistic vision. In the first stage, social groups struggled for power and dominance. The second stage, in which, according to Vasconcelos's formulation, we currently reside, is intellectual and political; reason prevails and manages the forceful gains of the first stage with borders, nations, treaties, and laws to regulate ethical and political norms. The third, coming stage is the spiritual, or aesthetic, era, grounded in inspiration, love, and joy (69/29).[10]

Movement into the third stage relies on the integration of four racial "trunks" Vasconcelos identifies: "the Black, the Indian, the Mongol, and the White" (9), whose movements around the globe mark the development of humanity.[11] Vasconcelos sees racial unification as having begun with the colonizing efforts of the Spanish and the English, whose differing views of their American roles became the central conflict of contemporary humanity, "a conflict of Latinism against Anglo-Saxonism; a conflict of institutions, aims and ideals" (10), writes Vasconcelos, indexing indigenous reality to European history.[12]

More troubling to scholars than his reading of indigeneity through a European lens is Vasconcelos's assertion that the Spanish conquest marked the beginning of Hispanic America's "transcendental mission" (9) to integrate the races.[13] Despite the colonial move of privileging the European power, however, the bulk of Vasconcelos's argument is paradoxically anti-colonial. He sees Hispanic America's mission thwarted by nationalist divisions that preclude the unity necessary to achieve full racial integration in the Americas and lift humanity into the spiritual era. This national division is perpetuated and inspired by Anglo forces, who are currently the dominant race but do not understand their dominance as transitory (51/11).

"La raza cósmica" is dedicated to dispelling popular ideologies of racial dominance, inspired in part by the work of Artur de Gobineau. Vasconcelos took issue, in particular, with Gobineau's assertion that social progress depended upon racial purity (Juárez 60). In stark contrast, Vasconcelos's theory depends upon miscegenation, leading to a fantasy of racial and national unity that glossed over the realities of class and race inequality in Mexico. In this sense, Vasconcelos's theories of indigeneity have much in common with the work of the Mexican Eugenics Society, which saw integration of the Indian as a means of racial uplift (Stepan 151). In the United States, eugenic, or hereditarian, ideas took a somewhat different form, more hostile to integrative ideas. Thus, Vasconcelos, who lived a resolutely bi-national life between the two countries, must also be read in response to the work of such racial thinkers as Madison Grant and Lothrop Stoddard. Grant's "attempt to elucidate the meaning of history in terms of race" in *The Passing of the Great Race* (1916) asserted the "immutability" of physical characteristics to factors such as nation, language, and environment (xx). Stoddard, likewise, in *The Rising Tide of Color Against White World-Supremacy* (1920) argues that "the basic factor in human affairs is not politics but race" (5), hence whites must work to ensure their continued world domination by curbing procreation by people of color.

Vasconcelos writes against Grant and Stoddard but also against the scientific study of race prevalent in the United States and Mexico, where eugenic thinking was the purview of institutionalized medicine and geared toward bettering the national stock (Stepan 56–58). Vasconcelos, by contrast, describes a "Universopolis" of love and beauty resulting from the completion of Hispanic America's racial mission (25). He eschews a quantifying logic of race that falls "into the puerility of the description of utensils and cranial indices" (8).[14] For Vasconcelos, race is a dynamic, not an object; history is not a linear narrative but a pattern of "transcendental hypotheses" (8).[15] Race, for Vasconcelos, is the means by which the nation can be transcended, not necessarily improved. Though he believes true internationalism would benefit only the current ruling powers, Vasconcelos advocates a universal and transcendental dimension to patriotism (52/12). He supports a Latin Federation, as did Simón Bólivar, and sees independence movements as "the puerile satisfaction of creating little nations and sovereign principalities" that replicate an evolutionary logic of race and perpetuate the colonizing forces of Anglo capital (15).[16]

Vasconcelos eventually repudiated these ideas when his thought took a conservative, reactionary turn after his loss of the Mexican presidential election in 1929. In *Breve Historia de México* (1937), for example, where he argues that Mexican history begins with the conquest, Vasconcelos describes Mesoamerican cultures as barbaric and ignorant, a sharp departure from seeing their reintegration as humanity's best hope. Though many critics see these positions as irreconcilable, Luis Marentes argues that even "La raza cósmica" is fraught and conflicted. "It is too easy to hang on to one of the apparently pure Vasconceloses, be it the radical revolutionary or the reactionary conservative," he writes, concluding that "the thought and practice of the later Vasconcelos are intimately related to their earlier incarnation" (31). Marentes points out that for a theory of Latin American liberation, "La raza cósmica" relies too heavily on a European context and is too skewed in favor of *latinidad* to be truly "cosmic" (79). Vasconcelos questions racial selection, not the idea of race, and his theory is less about "blending racial traits" than a hope that those traits "Vasconcelos thought inferior would be absorbed into the superior" (Marentes 91).

Another, related contradiction that Marentes does not note can be found in Vasconcelos's treatment of historical and racial time. He argues, in response to the prevailing eugenic theories of the day, against evolutionary readings of race but develops a racial teleology that places the Indian firmly in the past. He claims that the Spanish and English have been charged with "reintegration of the red world" (9)[17] but then also says, arguing against neo-indigenist romanticism, that "no race returns" (16).[18] Vasconcelos's theory of reintegration is, in fact, quite linear and denies the right of native return. As Marentes argues, however, it is less productive to point out Vasconcelos's flaws and more useful to contemplate how the tensions and conflicts in his theories resonate with "the broader theoretical debates and practical implementation of national identities in which [he] intervenes" (185). In bringing Vasconcelos to bear on *Caballero* I am most interested in this temporal contradiction and how the novel unwittingly puts aesthetic pressure on it. Vasconcelos's inability to reconcile racial time is expressed in the inability of Padre Pierre, *Caballero*'s French priest, to reconcile the intersections of race and class.

Race is the conflicted linchpin in *Caballero*'s political project, serving as a marker of both class and nationality. The novel argues that race is both surmountable and insurmountable, and it is this conflict that ultimately complicates equating the novel's argument with LULAC's philosophy. The conflict of race as both real and imagined also aligns the novel with Vasconcelos's essay. Vasconcelos argues against any notion of the essential Indian but then bases his ideas on "the reintegration of the red world" (9) into contemporary culture.[19] For both texts race is simultaneously material and abstract.

While for Vasconcelos the problems of race were largely theoretical, Jovita González would have had to deal with the real-world effects of racial thinking like Grant's and Stoddard's. As Alexandra Stern has shown, the militarization of the U.S.-Mexico border and the racialization of Mexican Americans in the United States was very much a public health project informed by eugenic thinking. The typhus quarantine along the border, which imposed humiliating rituals of delousing and fumigation upon Mexican laborers seeking entry into the United States, began in South Texas in 1917 and ended around the time of *Caballero*'s writing.[20] Happening, as they did, in her own backyard, González would have been familiar with these procedures as well as the unrest they caused (Stern 61). She would also have been aware of the class disparities in this medicalization of race. Stern notes that "most middle and upper-middle class Mexicans were able to bypass disinfection because they . . . arrived on the train via first class, were well coiffed or dressed, or could furnish a doctor's waiver" (65). Race here becomes a function of class, a slippage visible also in *Caballero*, where race is simultaneously rooted in the body and a discursive construct created or dismantled with a note from one's doctor. This vacillation between abstraction and materiality destabilizes the political claims of both the novel and "La raza cósmica." In Vasconcelos, the instability of race precludes the emergence of his Universopolis, and in *Caballero* racial tensions reveal the confused relationship between the novel's form and its ostensible political allegiances.

Padre Pierre, the French priest of the Matamoros parish, sounds strikingly like Vasconcelos when he explains the Mexican rancheros' racial philosophy to Captain Devlin, the American doctor. Though he antedates Vasconcelos by a good sixty years, Padre Pierre's affinity with Vasconcelos is a temporal parallel to Devlin and Luis's ahistorical rendering of Posada's revolutionary graphic arts, making plain the novel's desire to be understood in the political, cultural, and intellectual ferment of early twentieth-century Mexico and Latin America. Padre Pierre describes ranchero racial ideology thusly: "The high-class Mexican firmly believes that in him is perfection of race and most of them, like the Mendozas and their wives' families, have married so the blood strain remained pure and in its class. It became a fanaticism with many of them. And it does bring the best—for a time. Up to a certain point. Don Santiago's family has interested me beyond others because I believe that Nature, knowing her own inexorable laws, gives her best before she must give deterioration. Should Susanita or Angela marry one of the boys in their circle their children will be ordinary in looks and intelligence, their tastes and tendencies be downward" (157–58). Padre Pierre explains that like many aristocratic cultures, the Mexicans in the novel believe in inbreeding to maintain the purity of their blood, but he contends that such a strategy will meet with only limited success. His judgment here recalls Vasconcelos, who believes "that [racial] vigor is renewed with graftings, and that the soul itself looks for diversity in order to enrich the monotony of its own contents" (33).[21] The current Mendoza y Soría children are the best that nature can offer, claims Padre Pierre, explaining the wealthy Mexican family's attachment to racial purity, or *limpieza de sangre*. Padre Pierre is of the mind that nature will thwart this man-made fascination with "clean" blood by seeking out other avenues to maintain the perfection of the Mendoza y Soría genes, such as causing the children to look outside their "circle" for mates (158).

Padre Pierre offers a middle way out of the racial détente between clean and dirty blood by suggesting that nature will find a way to preserve the best in the Mexicans. His words call Vasconcelos to mind, who argues that in humanity's third stage marriage will become "a work of art" in which "beauty and happiness will determine the selection of a mate with infinitely superior results than that of a eugenics grounded on scientific reason, which never sees beyond the less important portion of the love act" (30).[22] Procreation and racial perpetuation are those "less important" aspects with which the Mexican rancheros in the novel are concerned. Padre Pierre sees the rancheros' conflation of racial purity with national superiority as their great hubris, arguing that it will eventually lead to Mexican deterioration. Here, again, his words put the reader in mind of Vasconcelos, who believes that all races and nations assume the inevitability of their superiority. Of national flags Vasconcelos writes, "each of us takes pride in our humble rags" (11) without appreciating the irony that such racial and national isolation retards human evolution.[23]

Padre Pierre's racial and national critiques conjure Vasconcelos, but González and Raleigh do not allow his progressivism to carry over into analyses of class. Padre Pierre maintains a strict class division in his racial analyses. The upper classes have access to Vasconcelos's "creative feeling and convincing beauty" (29), which allow them to mate and marry across national and racial divisions.[24] The laboring classes, however, are relegated to the less cerebral domain of lust. When Captain Devlin suggests "Nature has been doing a lot of stirring" among the American soldiers and Mexican prostitutes, Padre Pierre replies that he is referring not to "sex attraction" but to "love, as God gives it." Padre Pierre describes the enlightened, transracial inhabitants of Vasconcelos's Universopolis, not Devlin's "half-breed, that creature of inner strife and vagary" produced by the unions of the lower classes (158). Love, he says, must be forward-looking, not "retroactive" (158); similarly, Vasconcelos argues against a romanticization of the past (56/16). Padre Pierre's distinction between love and sex, or mind and body, is also a class distinction. "Sex attraction" is reserved for the servants and prostitutes, those living a life of the body and physical labor, while true love is reserved for those living a life of the mind: the rancheros and the noble American soldiers.

If race is, in part, a function of class, as Padre Pierre's musings suggest, then the insurmountable class divisions he describes mitigate strongly against his own theory of racial transcendence. He cannot account for the "half-breed" Captain Devlin mentions, the creature of "inner strife" upon whose back the hacienda economy, so like the U.S. plantation economy, flourishes. On the hacienda, as on the plantation, the peon belongs to the master. In both places the masters propagated more peons, thus producing "half-breeds," a point the authors address directly in the story of Gregorio, Rancho La Palma's orchard tender (297). While Padre Pierre can criticize American slavery (45), he stops short of criticizing the hacienda system, allowing the peons to experience only "sex attraction" and not true love. The half-breed, it would seem, has no place in Padre Pierre's national imaginary of true love.

This might be a function of Padre Pierre's similarity to Vasconcelos, who imagines a future with neither race nor nation, thus rendering the half-breed obsolete. However, González and Raleigh remain much more grounded in the materialities of race and nation than does Vasconcelos, materialities that González, at least, saw LULAC as addressing, though the novel retains some suspicions about the organization's underlying principles. It is possible to read Padre Pierre as endorsing LULAC's economic liberalism and assimilationist program, but such a link is almost too easy. First of all, Padre Pierre is French, which vastly complicates the national question. Though France has a rich, imperial history in Mexico, Napoleon's 1808 invasion of Spain does enable Mexican independence.[25] Thus, while Padre Pierre may be the voice of assimilation in *Caballero*, his French identity highlights Mexican sovereignty and allows the novel to be somewhat reserved in its support of LULACian assimilation.

María Cotera makes an even more compelling case against reading Padre Pierre as a wholesale endorsement of LULAC. The authors, she notes, engage in a gendered critique that aims at the heart of LULAC's organizational structure, which mirrored that of the patriarchal family ("Native Speakers" 416–17). *Caballero*'s emphasis on women's and queer agency and desire evolves into an elaborate reworking of Padre Pierre, Vasconcelos, and national heteronormativity. Padre Pierre is a lens through which both Vasconcelos and LULAC pass in *Caballero*, but there are things for which Padre Pierre cannot account, such as the contradictions of class and a racial teleology imported directly from Vasconcelos. Padre Pierre traces a linear path for nature to follow, but nature is not nearly so obedient. Desire, that which Padre Pierre suppresses, follows its own logic and disrupts the utopian projects of racial transcendence offered by Vasconcelos and Padre Pierre.

Caballero's Histories of Desire

Though *Caballero* offers women's desire as a plot point to counter the male rancheros' patriarchal dominion, its introduction signals a deeper interruption of the narrative and racial logics within which the novel is working. While for both Vasconcelos and Padre Pierre desire is geared toward reproduction and progress, *Caballero* undermines such chronology. Its formal strategies, which play with temporality and historicity, push toward something other than the relegation of race to the mists of time. Vasconcelos sought to define the place of the Indian in modern Mexico and in so doing establish a theory of *mestizaje* that celebrated Latin America's racial heritage and charted a future course. *Caballero* is similarly trying to define the place of the Mexican in U.S. culture, but the novel assiduously avoids Vasconcelos's racial teleology.

Caballero's temporal concerns are rendered aesthetically; that is, they manifest as questions of form, representation, and allegory. *Caballero* rejects Vasconcelos's historicizing logic, presenting desire as an irrational phenomenon that is less an engine of progress than a problem of narrative. *Caballero* draws force from the interplay of form and content and uses desire as the conceptual bridge between the two. Desire for the other (body, nation, place, story) drives the engine of the plot, but most significantly it drives the engine of the novel's narrative critique. Desire forces the split in the novel between the material and the abstract, a tension highlighted and repeated throughout the novel. For Vasconcelos, desire, which he calls the "mysterious eugenics of taste" and "enlightened passion" (30),[26] is the guiding spirit of the third stage of human development. The second, intellectual stage represses desire, but in the spiritual third stage desire will be allowed free reign to liberate the will. *Caballero*'s most enlightened characters, for whom the novel has a relatively happy ending, follow their desire, thus signifying humanity's new stage.

The novel introduces desire in the foreword, which gives the reader the history of Rancho La Palma de Cristo, the homestead of the Mendoza y Soría family, around whom the novel's plot gathers. Here the reader learns how Don José Ramón claimed Rancho La Palma in 1748 as payment for his many years of service to the viceroy of New Spain and proposed, late in life, to the young Susana, whose father forced the marriage upon her (xxxvii–xxxviii). Susana, "[b]itter against the fate that had given her the rare blond beauty only to move her where it would shine unseen," survives the death of all but one of her children and lives long enough to voice the novel's central formal concern of the tension between the material and the abstract to her grandson. Upon dying Susana admonishes Santiago about his duties as the future master of the hacienda. "It was your grandfather's dream, which he built into a reality. It was my entire life. Santiago, be worthy of Rancho La Palma and the things for which it stands" (xxxviii–xxxix). Her dying words foreshadow the novel's concerns with nationalism, gender, race, class, and their aesthetic implications. Being worthy of the "things for which [Rancho La Palma] stands" is an ambiguous task. Rancho La Palma stands for Spanish religious and cultural traditions, as well as the subjugation of women to male authority. Susana's admonition to Santiago presents the future don with the opposition between the "dream of a great hacienda" and Susana's exploited life, but the reader is unsure of which Santiago is to be worthy: the abstract dream or the material life, or if perhaps she means for him to be worthy of the fact that the two run at cross purposes.

The tension between the abstract and the material that we see here in the opposition between "dream" and "life" is deployed throughout the foreword, and it also underscores the novel's thematic preoccupations. The charge of being worthy of ambiguity foreshadows Don Santiago's misguided obsession with land and ownership at the expense of his family. The foreword also presents issues such as women's roles within national fantasies of territorial expansion, the invisible yet necessary labor of the darker, peon class (the descriptions of the building of the hacienda are wholly in the passive voice and their living quarters are described as potential guest rooms), and the material passing of time (the foreword begins and ends with specific dates, 1748 and 1846) and juxtaposes them with the abstract instability of the things for which traditions stand.

In juxtaposing time with abstraction, *Caballero* makes an argument about historical narrative. The novel's project is, in part, to convey historical knowledge about Mexicans and Anglos in the aftermath of the Mexican-American War, but the novel, at every turn, refuses a causal relationship between past, present, and future. González and Raleigh's turn to fiction as a narrative mode to convey historicity challenges ethnographic and historical knowledge constructs that would place Mexicans squarely in a past that grounds a triumphal, assimilated future. Johannes Fabian makes this theoretical point in *Time and the Other* (1983) when he argues that anthropology constructs its other in terms of a spatio-temporal distance, an act he calls the "denial of coevalness" (31) or the "allochronism" of anthropology (32). Narratives of race are never innocuous representations of experience, Fabian demonstrates, but are shot through their very formal structures with ideologies of dominance, submission, modernity, and the nation-state. While *Caballero*, on the surface, seems to perpetuate such narrative dominance, its attention to language and temporal play undermine that oppressive allochronism. In other words, racial thinking underlines our understanding of time, narrative, and history, and so *Caballero*'s challenges to these paradigms read as a critique of racial hierarchies that deviates from Fabian's into the literary world of metaphor and allegory.

In writing "La raza cósmica" Vasconcelos, too, was motivated by a desire to challenge an evolutionary logic of time that relies on a racialized understanding of global history. Vasconcelos, however, sought to tell a new story, while *Caballero* gets at the logic of storytelling itself. *Caballero*, although it purports in its subtitle to be "a historical novel," does not offer its readers a counternarrative of new causes and effects. It destabilizes the necessary relation between causes and effects, calling historical narrative into question with allegories of writing as interracial romance. The difference between Luis Gonzaga's and Captain Devlin's art is the difference that desire makes; it is that which makes them different from each other, and it is also that which creates distance between their art and what it represents. The two men's desire for each other here functions allegorically, creating distance between sign and signifier and pointing to contingencies of human knowledge that transcend their sublimated love. Reconfiguring the relationship between historical cause and historical effect forces a reconsideration of assumptions about language's ability to capture the passing of time; it asks the reader to reevaluate what he or she considers to be historical knowledge, in addition to how race conditions the link between knowledge and historical narrative.

Most scholarship on *Caballero* has taken for granted that the authors seek to present a more balanced and fair version of Mexican and U.S. history, even while lauding "American" ideals of individuality and the free market. In addition to these self-conscious aims, a tension over representation and the construction of historical narratives runs throughout the story, which undercuts the novel's celebration of "American" values. Therefore, while the novel is perhaps engaged in a kind of counternarrative to racist Anglo and sexist LULACian hegemony, it also recognizes the limits of counternarrative.

Luis Gonzaga's skeleton tells more of a story than Captain Devlin's, but this does not mean that Luis Gonzaga's skeleton tells the whole story. Rather than offering a compelling, historical, counternarrative, *Caballero* offers a narrative critique through its turn to fiction and allegory. The novel's descriptions of transgressive desire highlight the racism, classism, and sexism of nationalism and demonstrate the failings of historical narrative. We see this in the novel's alternation between historical and ahistorical narrative, between descriptions of events rooted in time and events that are timeless and universal. The tension in *Caballero* between the historical and the ahistorical is played out textually in the tension between the tropic (symbolic or representational) and the allegorical.

González and Raleigh show the rancheros' nationalism to be predicated upon assumptions about the race, gender, and class of the Mexican national subject. Various characters in the novel subvert those definitions of the national subject, but we can also think of the Mexican nationalists' self-conception as a kind of historical narrative. Doing so, we can then read the other characters' resistant actions also as narrative critique. The rancheros' nationalism is a story that understands the past, as culture and tradition, to inflexibly shape the present. For example, Alvaro and Don Santiago expect the past to condition Luis Gonzaga's,

Susanita's, Angela's, and Doña María Petronilla's behavior just as clearly as it has conditioned their own. Luis Gonzaga and the women, however, have other ideas about how to tell their own stories.

In turning to fiction to narrate history, González and Raleigh make space for their characters' actions to signify beyond the level of plot. Luis Gonzaga and the Mendoza y Soría women's transgression of the heretofore obvious link between the past and present allegorizes narrative critique as transgressive desire. Luis Gonzaga's romantic adventures demonstrate the tenuous claims language has on representation, suggesting the contingent relationship all narrative has to knowledge. Angela's and Susanita's marriages focus these critiques even more on the question of historical narrative's relation to racialized knowledge. The questions of representation raised by Luis Gonzaga's story are here, in the stories of his sisters' marriages, mapped onto notions of time and narrative. Angela's marriage to Red McLane is tropic, representational, and resolutely historical, rooted in time and pragmatism. Susanita's romance with Lieutenant Warrener, on the other hand, exists in a world of metaphor and simile; it is timeless and ahistorical. If Luis Gonzaga's story forces the reader to consider the relationship between language and knowledge, the tension between the temporal and the ahistorical in Susanita's and Angela's stories raises questions about the relationship of narrative to knowledge and the racial logic of historical narrative, questions central to the evolutionary logic of race Vasconcelos sought to deconstruct in "La raza cósmica." Historical narrative assumes a causal relationship between past and present, but *Caballero*'s characters' actions and their relationships to the past suggest that there are some motivations and effects that historical narrative cannot capture. Their rejection of past influence signals a rejection of the racialization of time and knowing.

Angela and McLane develop a relationship based on mutual respect, not romantic love. When a friend accuses McLane of wanting to "marry a Mexican girl from the higher class because it'll be to [his] advantage to get the Mexicans on [his] side," McLane does not deny it, though he does genuinely like and admire Angela. Angela returns the sentiment, accepting McLane's marriage proposal, which sounds more like a business proposition—he tells her of his fortune and how she can use it to benefit her people—than a profession of love. Angela and McLane represent one model of Mexican and American union: a pragmatic, mutually beneficial approach to living and working together, based in a common appreciation and understanding of U.S. law and the English language, as Padre Pierre advises the rancheros to embrace early in the novel (56). Angela and McLane also represent one way of telling Mexican and American history: incorporating both sides of a story into an objective, fact-based account. Angela and McLane join forces to meet their individual needs, and together they write both the story of their marriage and the future of Texas. Susanita and Lieutenant Warrener are another matter entirely. Their romance is described not as a thing that needs crafting or writing but as something that has always existed.

The authors describe their first meeting as a moment outside time and out of this world:

> Eyes as blue as the still heaven above met eyes green as a summer sea. And the sun halted a moment. The world waited. The crowd melted away and disappeared and left only a vast silence wherein lived only these two.
>
> Once to every man. Once to every woman.
>
> If God is kind—. (60)

Their love is naturalized into sky and sea and exists outside of time and history. It inhabits the world as a ubiquitous force, looking only for people to hold its place. The contrast between their story and Angela and McLane's story is easy to see; also worth noting, however, is the way language breaks down in this description of their meeting. Sentences turn to phrases, and the final phrase is incomplete. The love between Susanita and Lieutenant Warrener tells a different story than Angela and McLane's, and it requires different forms of expression.

This sense of Susanita and Warrener being outside time and history is further emphasized as the novel continues. At the governor's ball they dance a "schottische, the new dance but lately introduced" (93). They are both new, and not new, for when Lieutenant Warrener tells Susanita he loves her, the authors describe the moment as "A minute of time. A fragment of eternity" (118). While the thematic tension between Susanita's and Angela's romances is one between love and pragmatism, the two romances also express the difference between the historical and the ahistoric.

Angela's marriage is the linear narrative of Mexican and American union and political advancement; Susanita's is the timeless tale of desire that subverts such neat narration. Much in the same way that Luis Gonzaga's skeleton has more life than Captain Devlin's, Susanita's romance resists the constraints of historicity and its attendant racial logic. Susanita and Warrener's love is not evolutionary; it does not represent the white apex of romance but exists outside time and race. They inhabit Vasconcelos's third stage. As the "ahistoric" story, however, Susanita and Lieutenant Warrener's romance is characterized by internal tensions between new and old, or temporal and atemporal: they dance new dances but exist in fragments of eternity. The contradiction between eternity and novelty suggests a tension in the authors' own narrative critique. On the one hand, being eternal and outside time allows for love and individual free will to form the basis of citizenship and national belonging; the cultural baggage of the past does not affect their love. On the other hand, this vacillation suggests that their individuality is temporally contingent. Susanita and Lieutenant Warrener cannot be their eternal selves without the confines of time. Though González and Raleigh may wish to portray them as having escaped the past, the past has irrevocably conditioned Susanita and Lieutenant Warrener's present.

But it may also be that Susanita and Lieutenant Warrener, having escaped the past's restrictive hold on the present, are embarking on a new adventure. Their eternal love will produce new citizens with new understandings of patriotism and the nation-state. This is also true, and it aligns Susanita and Lieutenant Warrener with *Caballero*'s self-conscious critique of Mexican nationalism and support of "American" ideals. But while the novel does appear to be actively promoting LULAC's political philosophy yet subjecting it to a gendered critique, *Caballero*'s formal qualities appear to be subverting those aims. While González and Raleigh might want for Susanita and Lieutenant Warrener to exist in a politically neutral space in which their individuality and eternal love are allowed free reign, the two lovers cannot be freed from the constraints of their past. While González and Raleigh might want to create a historical narrative that serves as the grounding for a political union between Mexico and the United States, their characters' transgressive desires appear to thwart those aims.

Caballero's interracial romances suggest the potential of transgressive desire to reshape our understanding of ethnic and national belonging, not through bicultural reproduction but through a flexibility absent in the rancheros' patriarchal nationalism. The authors state explicitly that multiple trajectories of desire, allowed to cross ethnic boundaries, will reinforce and strengthen Mexicans, in Padre Pierre's racial philosophy, while stoic maintenance of the old ways will cause Mexicans to deteriorate, as with Doña María Petronilla, so inbred that the authors first introduce her as "gliding like a black ghost down the portico steps from her room" (3), or die, as with Don Santiago and Alvaro. However, these desires function also as narrative critique, driving a wedge between sign and signifier, narrative and knowledge.

Luis Gonzaga's relationship with Captain Devlin provides the theoretical background for the critique of historical narrative occasioned by Angela's and Susanita's marriages. The difference between the two marriages—pragmatism versus true love, time versus eternity—speaks to the novel's tension between content and form. Angela's marriage treats the plot-level concerns of the story and traces a utopian fantasy of intercultural communication. Susanita's marriage functions as a narrative critique of Angela's marriage. Susanita and Warrener are meant to exist outside time, yet the slippage between eternity and historicity suggests the present's historical condition, the contingency of historical knowledge, and the necessity of national narratives. In this, Susanita and Warrener trace the limits of Vasconcelos's possibility. Universopolis may be the ideal, but internationalism only favors extant superpowers (Vasconcelos 52/12).

Caballero's ethnographic and historiographic critique dismantles patriarchal, national fantasies; but like Vasconcelos, the novel remains entangled in the national and racial language it seeks to escape. This leads critics to read *Caballero* as a failed resistance narrative, or novel of assimilation, and yet it raises a great many provocative questions. González and Raleigh portray fantasies of the past as rhetorical deployments of women and patriarchal gender norms, whose self-expression forces ideological revision. They also show the causal relationship of past and present to be a function of historical narrative. When *Caballero*'s desiring characters drive a wedge between sign and signifier, past and present, they ask us to reconsider what the past has to do with the present, what it means to construct historical narrative, and finally, how race conditions knowledge and temporality.

Tracing the Skeletal Remains of Race

In its attempts to parse the meaning of Mexican America, *Caballero* avoids the historicizing logic of race that lies at the heart of both historiography and Vasconcelos's racial theories. Vasconcelos stakes a claim against evolutionary readings of race, yet his theory points toward a racially conditioned future. *Caballero* pushes against Vasconcelos's teleology with its deployments of form and allegory that appear to sidestep Vasconcelos's relegation of "the Indian to the mists of a tragic and oblivious past" (Pérez-Torres 6). *Caballero*'s efforts to determine the place of the Mexican in the United States put pressure, therefore, on both the limits of narrative as well as the teleological constraints of Vasconcelos's racial thinking.

Time becomes a problem of form and literary representation in *Caballero*. In positing allegory against trope the authors demonstrate how form conditions knowledge. Angela's and Susanita's marriages do, however, enact Vasconcelos's tasteful eugenics, despite the surreptitious workings of form, which appear to subvert the arguments made by the novel's surface content. But theirs is a gendered desire that thwarts a rational chronology. The novel's privileging of *female* desire, which Vasconcelos does not address, disrupts his eugenics of taste. The women are making choices, *Caballero* argues, not being buffeted about by mystical nature. The irrationality (in terms of its being outside a closed system) of women's desire correlates to the irrationality of history in *Caballero*, and non-heteronormative desire disrupts the utopian project of racial transcendence conceived similarly by both Vasconcelos and LULAC.

LULAC and Vasconcelos imagine a future without race, which arguably can be read as an Anglo future into which Mexican specificity dissipates. For LULAC this takes the form of wrangling over census classifications; for Vasconcelos, progress into this third stage is grounded in a spiritual aesthetics, the free reign of art and desire. This transcendence, for Vasconcelos, revolves around the reproduction of people successively perfected through the mystical eugenics of taste. The truly aesthetic pair in *Caballero*, however, cannot reproduce.

The novel never says definitively whether the two have a sexual relationship, offering only coy suggestions and the explanation that Luis Gonzaga's and Captain Devlin's mutual interest in the visual arts unites them as kindred spirits. When they exchange drawings of Padre Pierre they recognize each other's talents and are "neither Mexican nor Anglo Saxon but artists" (156). Art provides a space where both Devlin and Luis Gonzaga can be together, as lovers, artists, and countrymen, and art, as Vasconcelos reminds us, is "the singular law of the third period, the law of sympathy, refined by the sense of beauty" (31).[27] Luis Gonzaga and Devlin are misfits of a sort: Luis Gonzaga is too effeminate for ranchero culture, and Devlin is a practicing Catholic in a Protestant nation. Associating them so clearly with Vasconcelos's third stage suggests that they herald a new era, one of spiritual, artistic enlightenment with neither race nor nation and with an entirely redefined understanding of sexuality.

Clearly they are meant to suggest such things in their evocation of Vasconcelos, but art is the only thing these two men can produce together. Reproductive desire does not drive their spiritual pairing; they cannot physically make *la raza cósmica*. Yet, these two characters are central to the novel's action, suggesting that despite the utopian vision offered in Angela's and Susanita's stories, *Caballero* is, on some level, resisting the reproductive logic of the state written into Vasconcelos's teleological reading of desire.

The state, as Jacqui Alexander has cogently argued, has a vested interest in heteronormative sexuality, which provides a means of understanding the significance of Luis Gonzaga and Captain Devlin's muted romance. The state, writes Alexander, can be understood as a series of interlocking "processes of heterosexualization" (183) that create a model of "citizenship normativized within the prism of heterosexuality" (181). This heterosexual citizenship unites state and corporate interests, she continues, "in practices of racialization and (hetero)sexualization" that grease the wheels of what Alexander refers to as "the hegemonic financial market time of modernity" (191). In other words, heterosexual reproduction is a vital arm of political and corporate empire, rendering queerness a threat to state security and Luis Gonzaga and Captain Devlin's relationship a narrative act of resistance to the encroachments of Mexican and Anglo-American capitalist nationalism.

Understood in this way, Luis Gonzaga and Captain Devlin operate in tune with Judith Halberstam's configuration of queerness in *In a Queer Time and Place*, where she builds on Foucault's identification of queerness as more of a lifestyle threat than a way of having sex (1). In their pursuit of art and each other, Luis Gonzaga and Captain Devlin refute "the institutions of family, heterosexuality, and reproduction," as Halberstam understands queerness to function. Halberstam expands these notions, however, to a theorization of "queerness as an outcome of strange temporalities" and an explication of "queer uses of time and space" (1). Moving away from more recent understandings of queer time as the performance of HIV and AIDS' "compression and annihilation," Halberstam offers a reading of queer time as "the potentiality of a life unscripted by the conventions of family, inheritance, and child rearing" (2). Most compelling in Halberstam's analysis is the connection of the times of family and inheritance to national time. The time of inheritance, the passing down of generational values according to a putative biological clock that governs the reproduction of citizens, "also connects the family to the historical past of the nation, and glances ahead to connect the family to the future of both familial and national stability" (5). Queer uses of time then, according to Halberstam, undermine the permanence and production of national space.

Their inability to reproduce situates Luis Gonzaga and Captain Devlin within the bounds of a queer temporality that hovers beyond the margins of either model of transnational space and time developed in Susanita's and Angela's stories. Their refutation of heteronormative temporality is also a refutation of the geopolitical borders that irrationally separate Luis Gonzaga and Captain Devlin, as well as the utopian reimagining of those borders in Susanita's and Angela's narrative modes. The logic of the novel, however, writes Luis Gonzaga and Captain Devlin out of the new state that will emerge from Mexican and U.S. political conflict. The state, as Alexander has shown, relies on a heterosexual citizenship that cannot account for the homosexual. Susanita and Angela, who have both reproduced by novel's end, can live in a reconfigured U.S. Texas, but Luis Gonzaga must leave. Queerness has no place in the state, however progressive and inclusive, imagined by the authors of *Caballero*.

The spaces occupied by Luis Gonzaga and Captain Devlin are not accounted for in liberalism's heteronormative logics. Though their presence in the novel raises the possibility of truly revised American space that can incorporate queer citizenship, the novel ultimately cannot see this vision through and excludes them from its concluding hetero-vistas. In *Caballero*, queer citizenship is an oxymoron, and though Luis Gonzaga and Captain Devlin open up countless possibilities, though they rewrite the borders of American time, citizenship, and space, the novel sends them to Europe in the end. Luis Gonzaga and Captain Devlin remain an undeveloped possibility upon which *Caballero* cannot deliver, a possibility resurrected and further explored by queer and feminist writers later in the century, such as Ana Castillo, to whom I turn in the following chapter.

Caballero's failure to deliver is, however, incredibly ambiguous. Luis Gonzaga and Captain Devlin come together over a skeleton, which suggests both the decaying remains of an idea and its foundations. The skeleton is both human beginning and end. Either race and citizenship are dying in *Caballero* or they are being built anew. If the latter, it is in ways that diverge sharply from Vasconcelos's mystical model or LULAC's action plans. This chapter treated Luis Gonzaga's and Captain Devlin's skeleton in the context of early twentieth-century ethnographic and literary approaches to race and culture. That reading takes on even greater heft considering Vasconcelos's reading of race, spirituality, and aesthetic transcendence. González and Raleigh's turn to fiction in *Caballero* suggests that attempts to explain or represent culture are always already problematic. *Caballero*, however, has temporal as well as representational questions at its core. The novel is about the "deaths" of history as much as of race; one can pin down the borders of neither. Race. Nation. History. These things can never be adequately narrated, will always be incompletely explained, for there will always be more life in the skeleton than anyone can see.

PART THREE

American Diasporas

5 /   Ana Castillo's "distinct place in the Americas"

In Chapter 4 I discussed how desire opens a thirdspace in *Caballero*: a place outside time, history, and nation where Captain Devlin and Luis Gonzaga can be together as artists, and where Susanita and Warrener's love can hum along with the rhythms of nature. The full potential of that space is never explored, however, as the novel can neither account for the possibility of Devlin and Luis's queer citizenship nor can it fully inhabit the radically revised America their relationship postulates. This is, however, the transamerican space imagined in the work of Ana Castillo. Her novels, *Sapogonia* (1990) and *The Guardians* (2007) in particular, flesh out the contours of an American imaginary barely glimpsed in *Caballero* and thoroughly rejected by the patriarchal, heteronormative, nationalist narrative that has come to dominate cultural histories of *el movimiento*. Castillo writes in and through the porous boundaries of this American imaginary by dwelling upon the perceived disjunct between experience and representation, and the difficulties of joining cultural production to political action.

A prolific poet, novelist, and cultural critic, Castillo has, since the beginning of her career, been an outspoken advocate for social justice. She has written extensively about the politics of race and gender, both theoretically in *Massacre of the Dreamers* (1994), a collection of essays on Chicana feminism, and in her novels and chapbooks. A consistent topic of Castillo's has been the movement of bodies, both in terms of the artistic individual, like Carmen Santos, the polio-stricken flamenco dancer in *Peel My Love Like an Onion* (2000), but also more pointedly in terms of immigration and the cross-border flow of bodies.

Carmen's family migrated from Mexico to Chicago before she was born, but immigration is the central topic of *Sapogonia* and *The Guardians*, two vastly different novels. *Sapogonia* is driven by ideas less than plot. It comprises a disjointed and non-linear series of chapters following the civil war in Sapogonia, an imaginary South American country, and various characters' relation to it in the United States. In *The Guardians*, Regina, a fifty-year-old Mexican American widow, and her fifteen-year-old nephew Gabo await news of Gabo's father, Regina's brother Rafa, who went missing while crossing the border into New Mexico, where Regina and Gabo live. *The Guardians* progresses succinctly and linearly through a plot motivated by the actions of easily discernible characters. Though these two novels are quite different stylistically, both explore the meaning of "nation." They ask what nations are, who belongs in a nation, and whether the nation constitutes bodies or vice versa. A core concern for both novels is what happens to the nation when bodies move, when, like Max, *Sapogonia*'s dashing antihero, they cross borders seamlessly, or when, like Rafa, they are lost.

The novels take dissimilar approaches to these questions with *Sapogonia* laying the conceptual, theoretical foundations for the grassroots interventions the reader encounters in *The Guardians*. In this sense *The Guardians* is almost the direct opposite of *Sapogonia*, but both novels engage similar questions about the efficacy of art and the politics of representation. The conflict between art and reality resonates across both novels in meditations on citizenship and the state. They each explore *el movimiento* and its legacy by grappling with the tension between the national and the global and refuting individual subjectivity through self-conscious, formal innovations that champion a more communal, transamerican conception of self.

Religion and spirituality are the vehicles both novels use to engage these interpretive questions of space, place, and consciousness. The use of religion is, on one level, paradoxical because Castillo is openly critical of the Catholic Church's "vast history of domination throughout the world," its resistance to liberation theology in Latin America, and its support of the very same patriarchy against which "radical activistas" struggle (*Massacre* 88–89). This position is echoed by many of her characters including Rafa, who, according to Gabo, "liked to quote Marx" about religion being the opiate of the masses, and Regina, who disdains the Church's wealth while "millions of mexicanos among the faithful

[are] living in poverty" (*Guardians* 21). In *Sapogonia*, moreover, Max equates organized religion with colonialism's violent histories (36).

For Castillo personally, and for her fictional characters, organized religion's greatest offense is the creation and dissemination of master narratives that blind people to the reality at hand in favor of harmful deceptions that benefit the Church. Crucita, the ex-wife of Miguel, Regina's love interest in *The Guardians*, for instance, believes herself to be protected in Juárez by the Lord's work she is doing setting up a church, but she is kidnaped and tortured (185); and Gabo's saintliness cannot protect him at the end of the novel when Tiny Tears, the very soul he is trying to save, stabs him to death. Religious and historical narratives are further bound in the figure of Prescott Burke, the pastor with whom Crucita is working to establish a church. Her romantic involvement with him ended her marriage to Miguel, and when she disappears, his own marriage, unknown to Crucita, is revealed (184). Not only is he a deceptive religious figure whose religiosity failed to protect Crucita, but his names echo those of William Prescott, Walter Prescott Webb, and John Gregory Bourke, historians whose work on the United States and Mexico has long been recognized as reflecting U.S. hegemony and Mexican oppression.[1]

Against such historical and religious deceptions Castillo posits a feminist spirituality of her own design. She writes of woman as "the great dual force of life and death" who has the power to create and maintain life ("Extraordinarily" 78). That *curanderismo* (status as a healing person) grounds Castillo's unearthing of "the ways of our Mexic Amerindian ancestors preserved by our mestizo elders." Woman's mystical connection to the past and physical materiality ground the spirituality Castillo describes as born from "Mexica (Nahua) [Aztec] and Christian traditions" and connecting people to the earth and each other (*Massacre* 145). Religion and spirituality play crucial roles in how both *Sapogonia* and *The Guardians* imagine time, space, and human connection. Pastora is the spiritual heart of *Sapogonia* and the novel dwells on her syncretic religious practices wedding Santería to Aztec and Catholic worship and her communion with her spiritual guide, Max's dead, indigenous grandmother.[2]

Sapogonia's abstract profundity is brought down to earth in *The Guardians*, which centers its action on the Catholic Church but resists the abstraction of organized religion's grand narratives. The "guardians" of the title are the Franklin Mountains, which border the small town where the plot unfolds; but the "guardians" are also the four characters who guide the novel's action and share names with biblical archangels:

Rafael, Miguel, Uriel (Regina's best friend), and Gabo (short for Gabriel). These characters all live in and around Cabuche, a fictional town whose name recalls "Capuchin," the progressive order of monks founded in 1525 who preached a literal observance of St. Francis's teaching ("Capuchin"). The Capuchin were made famous in the twentieth century by Padre Pío of Pietrelcina (1887–1968), to whom Gabo directs his letters, the only vehicle through which the reader hears his voice. Padre Pío was revered for his powers of bi-location and healing, but he was most well-known for his visible stigmata, which Gabo, too, develops (64).[3]

Connecting Gabo with the Italian saint—Pío was canonized in 2002—collapses time and space by rendering the twentieth-century priest a contemporary of a twenty-first-century Mexican immigrant in the southwestern United States. That Pío was a Capuchin ensures that these references to the glories of Italy, such as Regina's desire to take Gabo there in order to teach him "a little something about great art" (6), are tinged with historical critiques of the Catholic Church's excess and neglect of the poor.[4] The novel brings these arguments from Italy back to the Americas with Miguel Betancourt, the history teacher at the school where Regina works, who shares a name with San Pedro de San José Betancour, Central America's first saint, canonized in 2003 ("St. Pedro").[5] Connecting Miguel, a die-hard Chicano activist (41), with a Central American saint makes a subtle argument for a transamerican perspective on anti-colonial struggles past and present.

Despite such overt religious allegory, *The Guardians* resists its own sanctification, rebuffs attempts to plumb its interpretive depth. Though the novel is rife with references to reading and interpretation, Castillo undermines her own almost sanctimonious assertions of deeper meaning. Uriel may read "her Tarot cards and pendulums" (119), and Milton, Miguel's blind grandfather, can just barely see Gabo's red hair, which he interprets as a halo, "gold ring y todo," that lets him know that "ese muchacho is with God" (94).[6] Nevertheless, Regina says that Gabo's dog Winnie is "not Lassie. She don't rescue people out of fires" (119); and while the novel's title invites grand, biblical allusion, Milton realizes, "Los Franklins stand guard over history—man's and nature's. That's what they do. But there's nothing inviting about them" (128). Even while the novel invites readers to push beneath the surface to a deeper meaning, it asserts that there is no deeper meaning, a point lost on reviewers who read the novel's biblical allusions as an attempt to elevate border matters to a universal allegory of good and evil (Seaman) or who complain that the novel's focus on current events detracts from "the more far-reaching resonance of her characters' all-too-human experiences" (Camp).

Rather than crafting allegorical morality tales or humanizing her characters into metaphorical abstraction, Castillo asserts that real people, like the characters in her novel, lead real lives conditioned by geopolitical forces beyond their control or ken, in which literature has the potential to make an intervention. In this regard, Gabo's reading of his father's death presents a productive paradox. "It was just our lives," he says, but then retrospectively reads deeper meaning into the events preceding it, such as the dead hawk he finds and Winnie's blinding herself in one eye on a cactus (21). Gabo resists interpretation—"My family's story was not like that of García Márquez's Buendía family—one generation tied to the next in a magical Latino country" (103)[7]—but he reads meaning into the world around him. Stories are not always magical, fantastical, or highly literary, Gabo argues, but that does not mean that readers should pay any less attention to them.

Both *Sapogonia* and *The Guardians* explore story's representational value as well as its ability to suggest that which lies beyond representation. These two things work in concert, arguing that while there is always a humanity that transcends the immediacy of the narrative, that immediacy must not be forgotten. History cannot blend into the architecture of colonialism, as Max notes when he visits Notre Dame (*Sapogonia* 36). Sometimes there is no deeper meaning. Sometimes, as Gabo says, the story is "just our lives" (*The Guardians* 21).

The Global Self in an Imaginary Country

The Guardians generated quite a bit of press upon release, due mainly in part to its timeliness and Castillo's increased fame after *So Far from God* (1993), which was published a few years after and was much more accessible than *Sapogonia*. Unlike *The Guardians*, *Sapogonia* was not widely reviewed and has been all but ignored in Castillo scholarship. Castillo has acknowledged in interviews her own dissatisfactions with the novel (see Milligan), but *Sapogonia*'s scholarly neglect might have more to do with its complexity and not entirely successful formal innovations. Further, the novel is not an objective, easily parsed portrayal of Chicana/o identity. Here, I wed these two critiques—a formal complexity that borders on the incoherent, with vague and complex ethnic identities—in order to make the argument that *Sapogonia* is, in fact, not a Chicana novel, at least not in the way that term has been understood.

Sapogonia revolves around the civil war in Sapogonia, an imaginary country, or as Castillo writes, "a distinct place in the Americas where all mestizos reside, regardless of nationality, individual racial composition, or legal residential status—or perhaps because of all of these" (1).[8] Máximo Madrigal, a young, wealthy Sapogón from a ranching family, travels to North America to make his fortune. He romances many ladies on his way to becoming a famous Chicago-based sculptor, but the novel focuses on his relationship with Pastora Velásquez Aké, a well-known folk singer with indigenous South American roots. The novel traces their on-again-off-again relationship against the war's progression. Their romance is the vehicle for an exploration of wide-ranging political and philosophical problems like immigration, civil war, the value of art, and the meaning of the individual as constituted by these interconnected themes. The narrative is non-linear; past, present, and future interact and interfere with each other. Similarly, characters in the novel traverse the boundaries of space, time, and the self. Pastora and Max, especially, are presented not as individuals but as conglomerate entities supported by spirit guides from the past and the future.

This blurring of geographic, temporal, and personal boundaries is all in the service of retheorizing the novel-form from the genre of bourgeois subjectivity and interiority to one of communal subjectivity. The novel is the genre, historically, of femininity and domesticity, later of interiority and bourgeois subjectivity, the twin ideological constructs of modernity.[9] Castillo turns these conventions inside out, refuting gendered subjectivity as well as individual interiority in favor of communal identity and a global nationalism. This formal intervention happens in four domains: the definitions of nation, history, and time; romance and coupling; purely formal concerns like event sequencing and narrative voice; and finally the relationship between globality and selfhood.

When scholars discuss *Sapogonia* at all, they do so in one of two ways. Either it is a "borderlands" novel about hybrid characters negotiating U.S.-Mexican relations, or it is a novel about gender politics, where Pastora and Max's relationship is a disquisition on Chicana oppression. However, Sapogonia's status as an imaginary country invites a broader context than the United States and Mexico, and the shifting narrative point of view combined with Pastora and Max's multiple locations in space and time suggest that there is more at work in their coupling than anti-machismo diatribe. Through descriptions of Sapogonia's borders, history, conflicts, and citizens Castillo argues for the similarly porous boundaries of concepts like history, time, and nation. The novel is not simply a description of Max and Pastora's long affair, nor is it about the U.S.-Mexico border. *Sapogonia* describes a Chicana/o national imaginary dependent upon, not isolated from, the interconnected histories of Latin American nations.

This is most apparent in how the novel deals with nations, nationalism, and national histories. Competing definitions of "nation" arise in the tension between borders and boundaries, introduced in the prologue, which permeates the entire novel: even though "a history of slavery, genocide, immigration, and civil uprisings [has] left [its] mark" on both the Sapogonian gene map and the "border outline of its territory," the country remains unidentified "by modern boundaries" (1–2). Sapogonia has a border outline but no boundaries. It is allegorical and material, simultaneously subject and resistant to northern forces. At various points in the novel, Sapogonia is a solely economic and political construct, and at other times it is an allegory of indigenous history, a place "where all mestizos reside" (1). The competing pulls are evident also in the international maneuverings of the novel's characters who confront nations as political constructs but also feel primordial connections with them. *Sapogonia* allegorizes Ernst Gellner's distinction between modernist and primordial understandings of the nation, the former represented by the conflicted histories of many Latin American countries, the latter represented by indigenous ways of knowing.[10]

The prologue understands a border to be the result of political maneuverings, while boundaries come from people, their migrations, and their interactions with the land. Sapogonia's boundaries continue to shift because its bodies continue to grow, and yet its political borders are also rooted in the body. Both its citizens' bodies and its border outline are marked by Sapogonia's violent history. While on the one hand the prologue makes a distinction between borders and boundaries as inorganic and organic, respectively, both borders and boundaries are ultimately rooted in the bodies of its citizens. The body politic manifests borders and boundaries differently, however. With the former, the body reflects the scars of past trauma, while the latter is a dynamic process of creating something new.

The tension between border and boundary means that different characters respond to the idea of national divisions in vastly different ways, depending on their socioeconomic status. Max, for example, effortlessly travels around the world on forged papers, struggling to understand his similarities to and differences from other Latin American immigrants.

On his way from New York to Los Angeles, Max "could not decipher one face from the next" (76) at a Chicago bus station. In the midst of such fraternity, however, the novel asserts the borders between us by introducing immigration agents into the scene. Max watches, uncomfortably, as "immigration officials" apprehend men whom he assumes are illegal immigrants (75). Max's initial empathy turns quickly to indifference as he struggles to quell his own immigrant insecurities by asserting his difference from these poor laborers. Max is a member of a global, migrant collective who has increasing difficulty asserting himself as a Sapogón throughout the novel as his political conscience develops.

That conscience develops as his understanding of himself as an historical subject deepens, and his appreciation of history illuminates the distinctions between modern and primordial understandings of the nation. Sapogonia's history can be understood in one of two ways: there is the primordial view of it as the place where all mestizos reside versus its modern history as a unit within the global economy. Max has trouble seeing the latter until he compares Sapogonia's history with France's. Max understands the difference between France and Sapogonia as a feeling rather than an effect of colonial dominance. Sapogonia, with its indigenous past and lingering traces of colonial, Spanish architecture, "was noble with history," he observes. On the other hand, "France went beyond demonstrating before the grandeur of the ages; it was intimate with it" (36). For Max, this is merely an interesting difference, not a call to national defense. France's intimacy with history suggests mutual constitution, an involvement so close that France cannot recognize history as a thing apart from itself. Max experiences this at Notre Dame, where he "sat without being aware of time, as one could only do in such a place" (36). Not being aware of time indicates an inability to recognize time as apart from oneself. Sapogonia, by contrast, does not allow Max these opportunities to blend seamlessly into time and history. Spanish architecture and bodily scars mark Sapogonia; history and Western conceptions of time are forced upon it in ways that do not allow them to disappear. Sapogonia can only demonstrate before history, not become a part of it. To be aware of time is to be aware of one's coloniality, as Max slowly becomes throughout the novel.

Max only feels this temporal difference; he cannot come to know it until the end of the novel, and so in many ways *Sapogonia* is the story of Max's growing knowledge about the difference between France and Sapogonia, about the distinction between modern and primordial definitions of the nation. Other characters in *Sapogonia* must learn these things as well. As they sort through their political and personal relationships, they experience the pulls of history differently. For the individual characters this manifests in, for example, Pastora's work with Sapogonian refugees and her mystical conversations with her spirit guides, including Max's grandmother. The characters struggle to define themselves in relation to time and the past in much the same way that Sapogonia itself struggles under the weight of its colonial history. From the Chicana/o activists Max performs with to the Latina political council Pastora works for, all are engaged in similar battles. In each instance, the characters struggle to transcend themselves, to forge meaningful connections despite the national politics that hold them back.

The most pressing political division in *Sapogonia* is that between the United States and Latin America, and the novel directly takes up the former's intervention in the latter, immigration, and the gender politics of Latina/o communities. Even as the novel works through these political concerns, however, it poses the question of its own efficacy. The role of cultural production in political struggle is the surface manifestation of *Sapogonia*'s exploration of form. Nearly all the characters in the novel are engaged in various kinds of artistic work suggesting the limitations of both the artist and the novel-form. Artistic creation and its philosophical dilemmas in *Sapogonia*, then, serve as a way to theorize political struggle. As characters negotiate their relationship to political and cultural activism, they progress from self-centered individuality to a more communally grounded subjectivity.

Max, for example, slowly comes to appreciate the world outside himself as he makes art inspired by Sapogonia's civil war, which is a conglomeration of the civil strife experienced by many Latin American countries. The novel is less concerned with the particulars of Sapogonia's civil war, however, than with how individual characters respond to it, the absence of liberty it creates, and how that absence translates into the denial of artistic creation and individual subjectivity, a series of ideas revealed through Max's growing realization of the severity of his country's plight. When the Sapogonian military murders the president and clamps down further on civil liberties, Max, lover of adventure and easy living, is finally compelled to claim his country as his own. Feelings of loss, nostalgia, and responsibility provoke him to take a stand with his art by creating sculptures from the wood on his grandfather's land, sculptures later destroyed by the Sapogonian government (265). These absences—of liberty and his ability to create—divest Max of his sense of his own self-importance and cause him to finally view himself as part of the communal, Sapogonian nation, history, and identity.

Though Max comes to understand the world as integrated as he completes his spiritual, artistic journey, *Sapogonia* takes pains to show global division as well by comparing Max's physical journeys around the world with the travels of other immigrants. There are two kinds of migrations in *Sapogonia*: voluntary, like Max's, and involuntary, like the men he sees at the Chicago bus station. While all the characters in *Sapogonia* are portrayed as immigrants of a sort, the two kinds of immigrants, voluntary and involuntary, are separated by class and gender divisions that belie the transamerican vision the novel develops elsewhere.

Max's and Dora's flights from Sapogonia drive home the importance of class and introduce gender into Castillo's analyses of global migrations. While Max is rich, Dora is poor; Max is unburdened while Dora travels with her young child; while Max moves easily around the world on forged papers, Dora hides in produce trucks, fears for her life, and is eventually deported back to Sapogonia. Their stories differ on a deeper, structural level as well. Gender is a component of class in the novel, as men are unencumbered by children and move effortlessly around the globe while women like Pastora, Dora, and Max's mother have their actions, decisions, and movements conditioned by their motherhood. Pastora is actually confined to bed rest during her pregnancy; Dora's decision to return to the United States is predicated on her son's need of medical attention; and Max's unwed mother simply does not have the freedom in her culture to go anywhere without a husband.

Sapogonia sees gender and class as intimately related effects of colonial capital that are equally difficult to transcend, however necessary that transcendence may be. In *Sapogonia*, community is the driving force behind the politics of artistic creation and self-conscious invocations of literary form. While women in the novel have a privileged position in terms of understanding the importance of community, it is difficult to attain and maintain. The domestic idyll of Pastora and her roommate, Perla, eventually comes to an end, and the women in the detention center to which Pastora is later sentenced are openly hostile to each other. Women's inability to form community illustrates Castillo's perception of female sexuality as a classist and sexist construction deployed to control women's laboring bodies.[11] The ability to form sexual, or even close, non-sexual, relationships is economically conditioned. In this context, the women's inability to do so indicates their economic and psychological subjugation, and part of the work of the novel is to imagine ways in which these women can free themselves from this bondage.

This can only happen by forming meaningful and nurturing relationships. The couples in *Sapogonia*, each of whom speaks to an aspect of Pastora and Max's romance, offer a complex analysis of the relationship between the United States and its southern neighbors that engages a gendered critique of history, economics, and art. Pastora and Max must free themselves from colonialist notions of gender; they must learn to form close relationships by redefining subjectivity. Rather than viewing themselves as subjects, they must learn to be objects for each other. Therein lies the theoretical and pedagogical imperative of their romance: it represents the coming together of ancient forces, a combining of the primordial and modern understandings of the nation and rectifying the split forged between the two by the United States.

More than just a romance between two people, the novel uses their story to address questions of art and philosophy, as well as internationalism. The novel suggests that their commitment to each other would ensure mutual destruction. Though other critics, and Castillo herself, have read this as a commentary on machismo, it is also a meditation on the mythical and historical dimensions of nationalism.[12] Pastora and Max's cycle of creation and destruction is both the balance of life and a theory of international relations. Countries need each other to create and produce, but no country wants to be overpowered by another. Pastora and Max enjoy a similar dynamic, a point the novel makes by linking them with mythological figures and associating their interactions with temporal dislocations. It is not until chapter 22, for instance, that the novel gives readers the story of Pastora and Max's first sexual encounter, though Max refers to it several times previously. Furthermore, it is not until both of them are displaced in time and space, crossing paths accidentally in New York, that they can recognize the reality of their relationship. Each had thought of the other as a fantasy, the narrator reveals, "until they had just accidentally crossed time zones and, without notice, found themselves face to face" (169), suggesting that their interactions happen in an entirely different dimension. The narrator's assertions to that effect are supported by the novel's mapping Pastora and Max's interactions onto Aztec myths and religious practices. Max imagines himself as Huitzilopochtli, Aztec god of war, and Pastora alternately as Coatlique, Huitzilopochtli's mother, and Xalaquia, a sacrificial personification of Coatlique (150).

These conflations of time and space suggest that modern nation-states, despite their power and seeming inevitability, are, like Pastora and Max, merely a manifestation of eternal creative and destructive forces existing in all aspects of nature. Pastora and Max, as well as being vehicles for the novel's arguments about nations and historical time, also bolster the novel's theory of cultural production. Nation-states are as transitory as ideologies of gender, the novel argues. The difficulty Max has in appreciating this point is closely tied to his shallow, in Pastora's opinion, artistic practice. Max criticizes Pastora for seemingly sacrificing her music for her family, a sacrifice he reads as a capitulation to her sex (302). Pastora, on the other hand, sees her focus on family as the same as her art: a capitulation to humanity (303).

Despite Max's limited appreciation of Pastora's actions, the narrator argues that Max does "in his own paradoxical way" respect women (193). His inability to plumb gender's surface, to grasp art's human resonance, is tied to a deeper artistic failure to penetrate representational surface. Pastora and Max's differing views on art correspond to the dueling notions of nation—modern and primordial—circulating throughout the novel: there are surface borders but a meaning to the nation that transcends artificial boundaries. There is representation, and there is its transcendent meaning. Similarly, *Sapogonia*'s couples do address gender oppression in Latina/o communities. But they also gesture toward the reconfigured subjectivity integral to the novel's national arguments as well as its theorizations of time and history.

Distinguishing between plot and story, a core narratological strategy, clarifies *Sapogonia*'s connection between gender, subjectivity, nations, and historical time. Though different theorists use different terms—for example, David Lodge's *fabula* and *sjuzhet*, or Gérard Genette's *histoire* and *récit*—Mieke Bal articulates the idea most clearly. She designates three layers of distinction: fabula, story, and text. "A fabula is a series of logically and chronologically related events." A story presents the fabula in a certain manner, be that chronologically, logically, or not. Finally, a narrative text involves the telling of "a story in a particular medium such as language, imagery, sound, buildings, or a combination thereof" (5). Unlike Genette and other earlier narratologists, Bal argues strenuously that cultural and political meaning external to the text can be excavated with the tools of narrative analysis, particularly this distinction between fabula, story, and text. Bal's categories illuminate *Sapogonia*'s formal innovation. While the novel's surface content may be fairly easy to parse, its stylistic devices have received less attention and contributed to *Sapogonia*'s reputation as Castillo's problem novel.

Two related areas of formal argumentation are in play in *Sapogonia*: isolated stylistic experimentation and broader generic arguments about the status of the novel-form. For example, Max is the only character in *Sapogonia* to speak in the first person. While we can read this as a stylistic invocation of machismo, formal choices such as a shifting narrative point of view help *Sapogonia* argue against the primacy of the "I," advocate for the notion of a communal self, and rearticulate a philosophy of nationalism. Furthermore, this undercutting of the "I" calls the entire project of novel writing into question. If the novel is the genre of modernity, of bourgeois subjectivity, then Castillo's attempts to dismantle the "I" in favor of communal notions of identity signal an inversion of the novel, a reclamation of the genre from modernist definitions of the nation and for a more primordial one. I am, of course, not suggesting that all novelists who experiment with point of view are engaged in similar projects, but *Sapogonia*'s constant shifting among first-, second-, and third-person narration signals both an undermining of subjectivity as well as a critique of concepts built upon notions of subjectivity such as linearity, history, and nation.

Shifting narrative points of view privilege multivocality, as do the novel's many extra-literary references to music and musical harmony. While Pastora is waiting for Perla and Saúl to arrive at rehearsal she considers the sound the three of them create, hoping that "the harmonious combination would have appeal to a new, however small, following." Pastora's repertoire of "protest music, never a frivolous song of love and its follies," speaks a multifarious truth best conveyed with a variety of voices, a "we" as opposed to an "I" (120). While the shifting narrative point of view draws attention to the power of narrative to occlude or manipulate facts, the references to musical harmonies in the novel suggest the ways in which a coming together of voices creates new sounds and truths.

In calling attention to the conditions of its production by invoking other artistic media, *Sapogonia* enacts György Lukács's dictum that the very function of the novel is to affirm dissonance. The novel, he argues, always "appears as something in the process of becoming," which is why Lukács's contemporaries considered it to be "the most hazardous genre," especially for those "who equate having a problematic with being problematic" (72–73). *Sapogonia* engages a dialectic between form and content, which is one reason why so many view it as Castillo's problem novel: they equate the generic problems it exploits with its being a problematic novel. Its focus on form, however, grounds its arguments about history, the nation, and subjectivity.

Sapogonia's subtitle, *An Anti-Romance in 3/8 Meter*, further emphasizes the dialectic of narrative form and content. It can be read as anti-love as well as anti-romance in the technical meaning of romance as allegory. The novel itself, however, an allegorical love story about the multiple layers of signification in narrative, contradicts both meanings. Pastora and Max share an intense emotional connection, and the two characters allegorize a host of things in the novel's arguments, from mythical memory to contemporary U.S.-Latin American relations. The attachment of "meter" to the assertion of anti-romance, though, offers several other ways of reading "romance" in the subtitle.

"Meter" points away from narrative toward music, as does the novel's use of multiple points of view and harmonic references. Meter can also refer to poetic rhythm, but the specification "3/8" definitely indicates musical, over linguistic, rhythm. If *Sapogonia* is an anti-romance in musical rhythms, then perhaps anti-romance suggests anti-narrative, or at least a subversion of narrative conventions such as patriarchal, heterosexual romance and easily discernible allegory. The question then becomes one of the relation between musical form and narrative content, or how musical rhythms can convey love and allegory.

The novel's assertion of musical rhythm indicates a rhythm different from language and words, supporting the claim that *Sapogonia* is a novel about the novel-form. Pastora's second album combines jazz with themes of mental revolution (159), and the presence of jazz rhythms helps explain some of the novel's temporal dislocations, the way events seem to happen out of chronological order or repeatedly with slight variation—as when Max's grandmother tells him that "all children are the children of God" (97) and Pastora later tells him that there are no mothers or fathers (304)—much like the recurrence and manipulations of melody lines in jazz compositions and improvisations. These temporal dislocations suggest the inability of linear narrative to convey the truth of history and events, much like modern boundaries are incapable of conveying the true meaning or extent of Sapogonia.

Sapogonia's circuitous narrative path also suggests the fragmentation of characters like Max and Pastora who must work to revise their understandings of subjectivity and the past. Both are engaged in constructing the kind of communal identity the novel argues is essential for liberation and national community. A communal identity is possessed by a global self—the novel's fourth and final interpretive axis—by which I mean to indicate the multiple ways the novel privileges community over individual solipsism. To invoke Lukács again, the novel-form's problematic results from the modern condition, from a lack of totality in the modern world. *Sapogonia*, however, refutes the conditions of modernity in its search for unity and totality as a counter to the divisive forces of modern capital.

Sapogonia's formal innovations are, ultimately, in the service of enacting a "we" that denies individual subjectivity and hence reclaims the novel-form from Lukács's fragmented modernity and for a more primordial, unified whole. This "we," represented by Pastora, Max, their spirit guides, and all the other couples and forces that combine to form their perceived individuality, is analogous to the changing Latina/o communities that the novel invokes. This "we" is also evident when Max first arrives in New York and sees his father in every "immigrant worker in the subway; Asian-faced or East Indian" (60). Max understands that regardless of racial or national differences, lower- and working-class immigrants are united in their shared burden of maltreatment and overwork. When he travels to Los Angeles Max sees that though Latinas/os in the United States come from all over Latin America, once in the United States they share a common bond. As a "migra official" tells Max before deporting him to Tijuana, "Spanish, Mexican . . . It's all the same shit" (82).[13] While this position is certainly offered for criticism, it is also a point of fact: Chicanas/os have been exploited in the United States just as profoundly as the United States has managed to facilitate the exploitation of peoples in most Latin American countries. Max learns to appreciate this shared heritage, and Pastora is able to reference it at a mayoral press conference while also asserting the remarkable diversity of Latina/o communities (311).

Time, history, nations, people, and all manner of cultural production are entwined in *Sapogonia* in the service of staking ambitious claims for Chicana/o literature and Latina/o identity in the Americas. *Sapogonia* argues that nations, like history, cannot function as discrete units. Just as past, present, and future are continually intertwined, nations, national histories, and citizens are constantly crossing borders and shifting shape. Even the individual citizens in the novel are not individuals in the way we commonly understand the term but conglomerate entities supported by spirit guides from the past and the future. While many of *Sapogonia*'s arguments are straightforward descriptions of national and individual conflicts, the novel's most significant claims are achieved through a play of form. Castillo turns novelistic conventions inside out, refuting gendered subjectivity as well as individual interiority in favor of communal identity and a global nationalism.

Guarding the Borders of Narrative

In a 1990 interview with Hector Torres, Castillo explains how her political focus on collectivity manifests itself formally in her poetry. Castillo uses the lowercase (rather than capital) "i" to indicate the first-person singular. This, she says, "came from the fact that [she] did come from that collective consciousness of the Chicana, so [they] use the small letter 'i' because [they] weren't speaking as eminent individuals but as part of a collective experience" (160). In *Sapogonia* that collective experience is represented by the devaluation of the "I" and the veneration of protagonists who are conglomerate entities. Collectivity emerges in rather abstract, formal ways, though the novel does clearly make arguments about *latinidad* and changing U.S. Latina/o identities.

Sapogonia's abstractions are *The Guardians*' concrete realities. In the latter, Castillo rescues "Xicanisma from the suffocating atmosphere of conference rooms, the acrobatics of academic terms and concepts," as she advocates in *Massacre of the Dreamers*, her pioneering collection of essays on Chicana feminism. *The Guardians* grounds collective politics not in theoretical abstraction but in the "work place, social gatherings, kitchens, bedrooms, and society in general" (*Massacre* 11). *The Guardians*' collectivities are not temporal, historical, or even necessarily geopolitical but about characters drawn from the real world, experiencing the same things that countless thousands crossing the U.S.-Mexico border have also experienced.

Though Castillo's characters feel immediate and real, the novel presents them as literary objects and makes clear that their experiences are linguistically mediated. The novel alternates among four distinct narrative voices—Regina's conversational tone, Gabo's letters to Padre Pío, Miguel's historical rants, and *el abuelo* Milton's memoirish ramblings—ensuring the reader's constant awareness of the book as a made thing. The novel does not draw the reader in but rather foregrounds its status as narrative in the service of staking larger claims for narrative's "real world" significance. This point is made through Regina's commentary on the importance of "papers" for immigrant reality. "That's all every immigrant in the world wants, to get her papers in order. To officially become a person," she thinks, remembering her own struggles to obtain legal status in the United States (116). When Regina finally gets her "widow's papers" (179) in order after her husband's death in Vietnam, she becomes "real," instantiated before the law but also in the public imaginary.

But just as *Sapogonia* grapples with its own political efficacy, *The*

Guardians wonders how effective narrative can really be when the forces conditioning that experience are so vast and deeply entrenched in border history. The novel presents the depth and breadth of that historical mosaic through its individual characters. Milton, for example, tells Regina the history of his *barrio*, Chihuahuita, ending with the powerful drug dealers whom he describes as "mafiosos who don't care about nobody or nothing" (69). These mafiosos come to life in the Villanuevas, the cartel that, according to Gabo's gangster friends, is holding Gabo's father hostage (87), and the families with whom Gabo's friends are loosely affiliated, the Palominos and Arrellanos. Besides drugs, the gangs also traffic in women, children, and human organs, which leads to a subplot involving the Juárez femicides when Crucita, Miguel's ex-wife, is kidnaped.[14]

Even though he is personally affected by the near-transcendent horror of border criminality, Miguel believes in narrative's ability to address injustice. Though Regina initially describes Miguel as a man who "just likes to hear himself talk" (48), who sounds like "a book with a quiz at the end of every chapter" (60), she also recognizes that he is a writer whose didacticism is in the service of historical narratives that counter the dominant border narratives alluded to in the character Prescott Burke. Miguel writes for hapless readers like Crucita, who can be seduced by disempowering, imperial narratives like organized religion or like the evening news where, Regina astutely notes, gang violence is juxtaposed with footage of "Bush's war." The fundamental inhumanity of both is obscured by the rhetoric of compassionate conservatism—Cabuche's children are "not just left behind. They're plain abandoned" (58), quips Regina—that blinds people to the conditions of their own oppression.

Miguel writes to make these conditions apparent, to render them real through narrative. He situates border crime in a regional context with global implications, arguing that the United States must shoulder its share of the blame. Preparing for a protest against the Minutemen, he argues that the vigilante group patrolling the border has failed to understand that illegal immigration provides needed cheap labor for many industries that, in fact, do not want legal immigrants as employees. Illegal immigrants' precarious status ensures their compliance and willingness to work for subpar wages (123). The United States all but invites illegal immigrants and creates the conditions forcing them north, fomenting violence within Mexico by training the government operatives who have since abandoned ship to work for the *narcotrafficantes* (150).[15] The novel then connects Miguel's analyses to the long history of imperial capital's pull in the region through repeated references to the Mexican Revolution and Ricardo Flores Magón's anarchist Partido Liberal Mexicano (PLM).[16] "How long can the United States contain what its vices and counterproductive prohibitions have wrought?" Miguel asks rhetorically (151).

Stories like Miguel's can produce liberatory knowledge, but *The Guardians'* social aims are multivalent and somewhat less facile. The realities of daily life have, after all, prevented Miguel from actually writing his book, "*The Dirty Wars of Latin America: Building Drug Empires.* Or something like that" (32). For itself, the novel imagines two sets of readers and delivers to them similar yet distinct political messages. On the one hand, *The Guardians* is geared toward a presumably Anglo, or at least non-Latina/o, readership, offering a basic history of U.S.-Mexican relations and humanizing immigrants through cultural descriptions that put a face to abstract immigration debates. But the novel is also speaking to U.S. Latinas/os whose differing experiences of and with immigration can render them as equally apathetic as some of their Anglo compatriots. Regina's thoughts while watching a group of workers moving through the fields near her home are directed toward both reading communities. She thinks of her own childhood self: both subjectively and objectively "not a girl, but a robot" (116). *The Guardians* is concerned to replace the mechanistic with the humanistic in its characters' and readers' perceptions of themselves and their environment.

In its attempts to address intracommunal tensions within Latina/o communities, to humanize immigrants to each other, the book builds on *Sapogonia's* investigation of U.S. Latina/o identities in the wake of the civil unrest of the 1970s and 1980s. *Sapogonia* poses a conceptual challenge to its readers about nationalism and cultural identity, while *The Guardians* presses those concepts into specific, graphic, and immediate service. *The Guardians* was released on July 31, 2007, mere weeks after the collapse of S. 1639, the U.S. Senate's bill for comprehensive immigration reform, which had included guest worker provisions as well as a "z" visa that would have provided a path to citizenship for current illegal residents. The timing was fortuitous for Castillo's novel, which fills the breach with a searing portrait of immigrant struggles that also criticizes U.S. inaction. Like Miguel, Regina is frustrated by the U.S. denial of its reliance on immigrant labor and imagines a space where color neither conditions character nor delimits the boundaries of the human, where "being a brown woman [does not signal] that you were born poor and ignorant and would probably die poor and ignorant" (29). Regina argues that immigration reform alone cannot instantiate human value, cannot make immigrants *real* to the dominant majority.

The Guardians seeks multiple ways to make its characters resonate across a diverse readership. It does this by representing the immigrant experience and presenting immigration as a force of nature that transcends modernity's national boundaries. "From the beginning of time," Regina opines, "the human being, just like all nature, has migrated to where it could survive. Trying to stop it means one thing only for the species: death." People, like water, are unstoppable, and these people put themselves in grave danger. The novel's descriptions of this danger make immigrants more *real* to an uninformed readership, not just with affecting detail but by making everyone vulnerable. Accounts of the danger are presented either in the second person, as in Regina's description "you're at the mercy of not just 'your' coyote but all coyotes, all traffickers prowling out there for the victims of poverty and laws against nature" (118), or they are framed with repeated assertions, like Milton's, that "it could happen to anybody. . . . Not just to los mojados perdidos" (lost wetbacks; 143), "it" being death in the desert and bodily decomposition, which he witnesses at the morgue in Juárez. And though, when identifying Rafa's body, Regina says, "It could have been any undocumented man caught up in the evils of border crossings" (207), the novel has clearly argued that documents alone cannot save one from the unforgiving desert and its lawless violence.

Regina provides coherence to the narrative, and on the one hand her assertions of paper's importance—as the thing every immigrant wants to get in order, and as that which might stave off death—offer one way to read the novel: as a political intervention that might affect real change. Characters like Milton, however, who claim that nothing can stave off desert danger, and Miguel, the amateur historian who wants to write a book but cannot synthesize history's horrors into narrative, undercut Regina's celebration of paper's potential. In this sense *The Guardians* echoes *Sapogonia*'s anxieties about its own artistic efficacy. Unlike the latter, *The Guardians* dwells much more on concrete political realities, offering a murkier and less optimistic future vision.

When Gabo, proselytizing in Capuchin vestments he finds at church, declares to the crowded school cafeteria, "No darker hour could we be living in than this one, when a great nation sets upon declaring wars in the name of peace" (165), *The Guardians* begins to truly wear its politics on its sleeve. Coupled with Regina's connection of the U.S. war in Iraq to the domestic war on drugs and subsequent abandonment of the border's children (58), the novel presents its vision of patriarchal imperialism as a cornerstone of racial and sexual oppression on the border, linking regional concerns to global flows of capital. These forceful political arguments led some reviewers to criticize what they perceived as a sanctimonious preachiness.[17] But when such reviewers opine that *The Guardians* politics are too awkwardly obvious, or depressing, they largely miss Castillo's point.

Writing for the *Rocky Mountain News*, for example, reviewer Jennie Camp complains that Castillo's audience is unclear and that this subsequently muddles the novel's message. *The Guardians* does not have one specific audience, however; rather, it has set itself the project of having disparate audiences "feel compassion for these characters" (Willis). This is of particular importance for Castillo with regard to primarily Latina/o audiences. As Pastora reminds the mayor in *Sapogonia* and as Castillo herself notes, "we can't talk about Latinos as a homogeneous group. We never could." Education and issues of political representation have, in the past, served as communal rallying points, but even these have faded in significance, according to Castillo, for twenty-first-century Latinas/os, among whom she sees a pointed lack of "enthusiasm" and a fair amount of "quiet resignation, an apolitical attitude, if you will," where the "American dream" has become "all about you—making it for you and your family, and after that, you know, good luck everybody" (Willis). *The Guardians* seeks to forge common bonds "between someone who has a social consciousness and someone who wants social justice to be done for their own behalf," a difference that underpins the deep "internal frictions" in Latina/o communities that coalesce around immigration issues.

The ties that bind young Latinas/os as a group are, today, "not necessarily about their heritage, or their parents' struggles to establish themselves here, or their U.S. Latina/o parents who were very active in their community," Castillo observes (Willis). As Castillo and Pastora note, U.S. Latinas/os are wildly heterogeneous and carry the marks of multiple national histories, so the bond *The Guardians* tries to forge is not necessarily a specific, cultural bond. It is a human bond, woven through the novel's narrative structure. The novel brings conflicting and distinct voices together synchronically across class and diachronically across generations into one multifaceted and compassionate view of immigrant struggles, and it tries to put these struggles into a global context: it, however the reader defines "it," could happen to you. Here again *The Guardians* echoes *Sapogonia*; both novels argue that individual people are, to a large extent, the product of forces beyond their local control, that the self is in many ways beyond one's reach, despite the fact that one experiences the self in visceral, immediate ways. In *Sapogonia* this

becomes an argument about genre as the novel's formal experimentation explores the implications of the self and tries to reclaim the novel
from individuality as a communal form. *The Guardians* pushes this line
of inquiry by asking how a formal rejection of identity translates into a
world of action.

The Guardians raises, but has difficulty answering, this question. Rafa,
the present absence at the heart of the novel, is the lost self that provides
occasion for such philosophic meditation and forces the characters to
read him as exemplary. Gabo vacillates between seeing his father's death
as either profoundly significant or empty of meaning. "Like crumbs of
bread, bits of [Rafa's] soul had been leaving traces for days" in various
signs of death like the hawk Gabo finds and Winnie's lost eye. Despite his
poetic rendering, however, Gabo concludes that "nothing . . . was more
than what it was. It was just our lives" (21). Rafa's death still resonates,
however. It means something, and he is mourned, just as Regina mourns
Gabo when he is killed at the end of the novel. In order to carry on, the
characters have to find ways to transcend the self and its particular locations while still finding value and taking comfort in aspects of its specificity, as when Regina reads the book of Matthew to be close to Gabo.
"Sometimes I just like to feel the pages like I'm reading Braille. I feel
my sobrino there . . . Gabo talking to me through Matthew" (210). The
novel must—and challenges its characters to—strike a balance between
interpretation and direct experience, between the immediacy of the self
and the future of social consciousness.

Miguel glosses "Chicano" as the subject position that allows for this
transcendence. Despite his sometimes macho, *movimiento* posturing, he
emerges as the most ethical, socially conscious character. "I'm one of the
few people around here who still calls himself Chicano," he thinks, in
one of his monologues. "A lot of people don't like that word. They don't
get it. They think it means gangbanging. It's like one of those outdated
labels that most people never understood and now everybody hates and
has no use for. Like *feminist*. Half the women I know don't like that
word, either, but when you ask them what it means they say they don't
really know" (41). Notably Miguel does not directly define "Chicano"; he
only alludes to its similarity with "feminist," a word that suggests gender equity but resonates across a range of social issues. One can articulate feminism in multiple ways, as with Chicano; and, as with the self,
Chicano retains affective value for its ability to signify beyond its own
specificity. With Miguel as bellwether, *The Guardians* defines Chicano
not in terms of border location or *movimiento* politics. He was, by his

own description, born "too late" for those things (31). Instead, Chicano emerges, via Miguel, as affect, as compassion, as social engagement, as acknowledging one's flaws but striving always to better oneself. It has no specific place; it has no specific politics. Chicano means being human in the world.

Both *Sapogonia* and *The Guardians* explore the multiplicity of U.S. Latina/o identity while developing a model of *chicanismo* as global consciousness, a politics that retains geopolitical specificity while also remaining attuned to the world. This is a difficult position to occupy, as Castillo's many flawed characters attest. But it is the process of grappling with the challenge that grounds *chicanismo* in a capacious humanity.

6 /   Border Patrol as Global Surveillance: Post-9/11 Chicana/o Detective Fiction

The peregrinations of Ana Castillo's characters in the previous chapter illustrate just how much notions of national space and subjects have shifted since the mid-nineteenth century. Writers like Domingo Sarmiento, Lorenzo de Zavala, and Vicente Pérez Rosales traced the emergence of race as an organizing principle of space. As national economies have become increasingly interdependent and global, the clear borders of the nation-state, which came into focus for the writers in Chapter 1, have become less functions of state and geographic boundaries, as our Latin American travelers would have experienced them, and constituted more, as political geographers Louis Amoore, Stephen Marmura, and Mark Salter argue, by interstate information exchanges, biometrics, and broad enclosure zones (96). The fuzziness of borders has become even more marked since the September 11, 2001, attacks.

Since 9/11, the difficulty of policing and demarcating borders has become a topic of much public debate and, as the political philosopher Willem de Lint describes, performance. While contemporary security practices that have proliferated in the wake of 9/11, like intensified airport screenings, have their roots in liberal, nineteenth-century borders, their spectacular performances of security are meant more to manipulate a vulnerable polity than to achieve real security aims (de Lint 174). Like 9/11 itself, the post-9/11 border poses a conceptual difficulty unimagined by Sarmiento, Zavala, or Pérez Rosales.[1] They narrated the rise of American borders that construed an emerging Latino collectivity as alien. The four novels discussed in this chapter, on the other hand, narrate a moment of "surveillance creep" or "border spread" (de Lint 173) that gives the appearance of more permeable global borders while in fact solidifying the territorial integrity and sovereignty of the nation-state. Borders and national space, in other words, are more important than ever, all appearances, global flows of capital, and people notwithstanding.

This paradox is entirely familiar to Latina/o immigrants in the United States, upon whose inexpensive labor local economies depend but who are nevertheless subject to paranoid legislation and increasingly inhumane deportation practices at the beginning of the twenty-first century. How, then, to imagine the place of Chicanas/os and Latinas/os in the U.S. national imaginary? Post-9/11 Chicana/o detective fiction takes up this question. The novels treated here chart a course through the shifting spaces of Chicana/o literature and provide a discursive map of its global engagement. In the first two—Alicia Gaspar de Alba's *Desert Blood* (2005) and Martín Limón's *The Door to Bitterness* (2005)—characters frequently do not know where they are or find themselves searching for unstable places, mobile sites, or unmapped territories. The last two novels—Mario Acevedo's *The Nymphos of Rocky Flats* (2006) and *The Undead Kama Sutra* (2008)—repudiate spatial knowledge altogether in their allegorizations of U.S. political debate as intergalactic conflict. Taken together these novels map a journey from the U.S.-Mexico border, to Korea, and finally to outer space, where U.S. xenophobia and paranoia are satirized for a primarily U.S. readership.

Gaspar de Alba, Limón, and Acevedo do not just represent immigrant or Chicana/o experiences but attempt to parse the meaning of locating one's brown body in U.S. national space and to challenge hierarchies of space in the Americas. The spatial progression found in their novels charts an expanding arena for Chicana/o racial and ethnic identity, showing no one place as epicenter, arguing instead for a definition of *chicanismo* as a critical mode of engaging with U.S. power. Chicana/o space thus emerges in post-9/11 Chicana/o detective fiction as an expansive and abstract terrain that hearkens back to the transamerican visions espoused by the Latin American travelers of Chapter 1.

Sarmiento's, Zavala's, and Pérez Rosales's American cartographies show the advent of spatial hierarchies and make plain the claim of Edward Soja and the Los Angeles school of urban geographers that space is a mutable construct. Chicana/o studies scholars have built on these observations to argue further that spatial processes are fraught with racial ideologies,[2] an idea that lies at the heart of this book's assertion that representations of the nation in Chicana/o literature are part of a long history of transamerican spatial imaginaries. The Chicana/o detective fiction considered here responds to the post-9/11 reorganization of national space in ways that reinforce and expand the literary genealogy of the Chicana/o national imaginary I have been tracing thus far. Gaspar de Alba, Limón, and Acevedo are concerned less with spatial description, however, and more with spatial phenomenology, with the human experience of place.[3] The spatial experiences and transformations their novels enact are part of what Fredric Jameson describes as the "unfold[ing] historicity" of 9/11 (301). The historical significance of 9/11 lies—for Chicana/o and American literature more broadly—in how Gaspar de Alba, Limón, and Acevedo imagine and experience U.S. space before, during, and after 9/11 and the ensuing War on Terror.

As a genre, detective fiction is well suited to an investigation of spatial meaning. The movements of the hardboiled detective in the United States demarcate national space and highlight its racial organization. Scholars have noted the centrality of "spatial categories" to the hardboiled genre where "relations between outside and inside, and between depth and surface interact with the primary dialectic of truth and tension" (Kennedy 227). The hardboiled detective's skill is determined in part by how well he (and "he" is usually a he) negotiates social spaces that are often in conflict with each other. This skill distinguishes him from his more genteel predecessors, marking hardboiled detective fiction as uniquely situated in U.S. space.[4] Unlike the refined protagonists of British detective fiction, the hardboiled hero is a déclassé, hard-drinking, foul-mouthed outsider attuned to gritty, urban realities.

Despite his location outside the mainstream, the classic hardboiled hero still reflects dominant, mainstream values. Maureen Reddy, for example, notes that white, heterosexual men occupy the center of hardboiled fiction, projecting a white subjectivity that defines all else as its other (9). In *Gumshoe America*, Sean McCann concurs with Reddy but reads the genre's misogyny, racism, and violence as "core features" of hardboiled writers' response to the social anxieties and class divisions produced by New Deal, American liberalism during the 1930s (308). Halfhearted apologists, like McCann, and vocal critics, such as Reddy, agree nevertheless on the racial identity of the classic, hardboiled detective and that he negotiates regimes of power from a relatively privileged position. These facts make the rise, in the 1980s and 1990s, of "ethnic" detective fiction all the more compelling. If hardboiled fiction embodies white subjectivity, then what difference does the detective of color make?

For the most part, scholars have read ethnic detective fiction as a celebration of otherness.[5] As Andrew Pepper notes, however, the hard-boiled detective is both inside and outside, self and other (7). This social conundrum produces angst and self-loathing in the classic hardboiled detective and complicates a reading of ethnic detective fiction as a celebration of difference, per se. Rather than focusing on the particularities of racial identity, therefore, in the analyses that follow I investigate *why*, not *how*, the Chicana/o detective is different from the white detective and how that difference is written. Focusing on the *otherness* of the Chicana/o detective locates the detective within the hardboiled hero's spatial matrix, while the detectives discussed here challenge that organizing logic by becoming lost in space, refuting spatial logic, and thus undermining the nation's racial contours.

Vivian Sobchack analyzes the condition of being lost in terms of feminine, rather than racial, experiences of space. She notes the difference between a Euclidean perception of space as ordered by maps and other landmarks and what she calls a "hyperbolic" experience of space based on physical perception. In the absence of Euclidean markers, solely perceiving space can, she argues, "be disorienting, unsettling, even perilous" (21). Women, according to Sobchack, experience spatial disorientation differently from men since their experiences of being objectified in their daily lives generates a spatial knowledge predicated on their sense of themselves as objects within, rather than subjects capable of transcending, space. Women are thus likely to find maps and other finding aids arbitrary in relation to their own bodies, whereas men are more apt to appreciate maps as "potential and future extensions of a bodily being" (34), as logical extensions of their physical presence.

Sobchack's analysis applies equally well to racial as to gendered subjects. Her analyses of the perceived dangers in being lost are, she admits, grounded in a white subjectivity (27), suggesting that people of color might perceive themselves as objects in immanent space, as do white women, rather than as transcendent subjects, like white men do. Applying Sobchack's gendered analysis of lost-ness to racial subjects allows us to understand Sarmiento's, Zavala's, and Pérez Rosales's knowing appreciation of maps and spatial self-assurance as marking them, in many ways, as white. By contrast, the spatial dislocations of the wandering detectives explored here can be seen as an index of their racialization within the nation-state.

The nation-state, however, has increasingly indeterminate borders. For example, when George Sueño, in *The Door to Bitterness*, is led through the alleys of Itaewon, Seoul's red-light district, to a rendezvous with a key suspect, he feels out of his element. These alleys "cannot be plotted on a grid" and are controlled by the *jo-sans* (business girls) who lead American GIs to and from their rooms (220). The United States might project power over the region, but there are still spaces that elude military control, though their black market economies are the direct result of the U.S. presence in Korea. Sueño's disorientation in these uncharted territories, coupled with his own double-consciousness as a Chicana/o soldier of a dominant military force, combine in a highly sophisticated reading of race as a product of U.S. force abroad.

Likewise, each author treated here refashions the racial dimensions of national space. They engage the contradiction between U.S. dependence on border economies and the post-9/11 culture of paranoia and increased border surveillance. And they turn their gazes away from the border to ask how spaces are made and transformed, and how these transformations affect racialized subjects in the United States. In their sketches of national space post-9/11, these novels ask what borders mean and how the War on Terror has affected the relationship between race and nation. Here I explore the novels' tentative answers to these open-ended questions, moving, in conclusion, to ask how a long history of Chicana/o literature grounds these shifts in national space.

Lost in the Border

Each novel discussed in this chapter is concerned with the intersections of space with not only race but also gender and sexuality, which become key indices of the social hierarchies the novels negotiate. Gaspar de Alba, Limón, and Acevedo all deploy spatial organization as an index of other social organizations such as race and gender. Both occupy structural positions of negotiated difference; that is, both are functions of economic power. Perhaps no other book addresses this issue so directly as *Desert Blood*, Alicia Gaspar de Alba's fictional account of the serial murders of women in Ciudad Juárez, Mexico.[6] In the novel, Ivon Villa, a visiting professor of women's studies, is struggling to finish her dissertation while traveling to El Paso, her hometown, to adopt a child from a poor Mexican teenager. On arrival she learns of the murders, and when her sister Irene is kidnaped Ivon desperately tries to find her and solve the larger crime. Along the way, she grapples with her family history, destroys an Internet porn ring, and saves her sister from being the next victim in a live, Web-streaming snuff film.

Scholarship on *Desert Blood* tends to focus on its correlation to the real-life crimes and literature's ability, in Rachel Adams's words, "to intervene in the social problems it represents" ("At the Borders" 265). *Desert Blood* is certainly invested in "the particular role that novels can play in galvanizing public sentiment" ("At the Borders" 267), and Gaspar de Alba has been very active in publicizing the crimes through her teaching, research, and speaking engagements around the country. In 2003 Gaspar de Alba organized an international conference—"The Maquiladora Murders, Or, Who Is Killing the Women of Juárez?"—cosponsored by Amnesty International, at the University of California, Los Angeles, where she teaches. There has been very little work on the novel as a literary object or, besides Adams's article, on its generic status as detective fiction.

Desert Blood metaphorizes academic research as a form of detecting crime, and Ivon, as a Chicana lesbian academic, ontologically refutes the classic, hardboiled hero. Her subjectivity and experience are of primary importance to the novel's plot. Ivon shares with Sam Spade and Phillip Marlowe a love for women and liquor, and like those two detectives, Ivon is a maverick, an independent outsider relying on instinct and iconoclasm. The novel's focus on Ivon, coupled with its attempts to individualize the crimes by giving victims a narrative voice, at times conflicts with its parallel desire to show the murders as part of a larger criminal network in the U.S.-Mexico border region. The novel wants to portray the crimes as open-ended and without solution while also offering a tidy resolution to Irene's disappearance. The reader is meant to understand the exceptionality of Irene's case in contrast to the unsolved murders, a contrast requiring the novel to focalize through Ivon, who interprets most of the novel's action and imagery for the reader. *Desert Blood* is most interesting, though, when Ivon is confused or lost. The novel is most effective when it disables its own protagonist.

Desert Blood makes plain that Ivon's stubbornness restricts her access to certain information, as when her cousin, Ximena, withholds the details of her car crash (181) or the detective working on Irene's case declines to tell Ivon where she can buy a new battery for Irene's El Camino (230). More interesting, however, is the difficulty Ivon has making sense out of the information she *does* have: video footage from a Juárez TV show, fliers advertising pornographic Web sites, the sites themselves, newspaper articles, books, and her own experience. Ivon cannot connect the dots: "The star reminded her of something, but she couldn't place it" (181); "Something flickered in her memory. . . . Where had she seen that before?" (208); "What was it about those pennies?" (252); "A part of her already knew" (284). Her investigation coalesces around this recurring failure.

Ivon's subpar memory is a narrative strategy meant to create suspense, but it is also a nod to the detective's historic fallibility; that the investigator is, after all, only human is a key feature of the hardboiled genre in both its classic and contemporary permutations. Ivon's inability to remember also recalls Stefano Tani's "anti-detective." Tani, whose influence Gaspar de Alba acknowledges directly (343), defines anti-detective fiction as that which "tantalizes its readers by disappointing common detective-novel expectations" such as resolution (Tani xv). Irene's rescue and return subvert *Desert Blood*'s goal of being an "anti-detective" novel, a goal it works toward in its presentation of the complex web of international finance and crime radiating from the U.S.-Mexico border. The difficulty Ivon has making sense out of her situation reflects the region's pervasive corruption and impunity, qualities Gaspar de Alba has noted in her scholarly work on the Juárez femicides.[7] But just as Irene's kidnaping is easily solved, the novel explains this criminal miasma by falling back on a vaguely defined "globalization," depicted largely as U.S. capital, that simplifies the subject's relation to the state. The individual, mostly Ivon, is of primary importance in this novel that wants to leave open ends while simultaneously controlling the reading experience.

Desert Blood interprets its own metaphors, which are rooted in a relatively simple view of border economics that belies Gaspar de Alba's other scholarship. In the "Disclaimer" with which *Desert Blood* opens Gaspar de Alba lets her readers know that she has "added a metaphorical dimension to the story, using the image of American coins, particularly pennies, to signify the value of the victims in the corporate machine" (v). Within the novel, Ivon replaces Gaspar de Alba as the reader's guide. Ivon's theory of the *maquila* system's responsibility for the murders evolves in tandem with the plot and, because she focalizes the novel's action, becomes the structure through which the reader is meant to appreciate the murders. The women boarding buses outside a Juárez factory look like clones of each other to Ivon, and she meditates on the "irony of . . . an assembly worker disassembled in the desert" (255). A young boy tries to sell her recycled, seductively dressed Barbie dolls. "Maqui-locas . . . Muy cheap!" he says, punning on the Spanish words for "factory" and "crazy" (43). The novel makes very clear its understanding that the murdered *maquila* workers—"Muy cheap!"—are the "price of free trade" (332) and that industry turns a profit from their bodies by extracting labor, controlling their reproduction, and killing them for sport.

Maquilas embody industry in the novel, and they signal recent, rapid changes in the border economy. *Desert Blood* does not, however, explain the establishment of the "twin plant" industry in Mexico in the late 1960s. Nor does the novel inform readers that the United States is not the only country to operate *maquilas* on the industrialized border.[8] *Desert Blood* blames the Juárez murders on the rise of *maquilas*, but the *maquilas* are just one facet of a cancerous system of human devaluation, the surface of which *Desert Blood* scratches but which Diana Valdez has documented compellingly in *The Killing Fields* (2006), which chronicles her years of investigative journalism about the Juárez murders. She traces the roots of the crimes to Mexico's "dirty war" against communists in the 1960s, when an elite paramilitary group known as the White Brigade carried out clandestine operations including the infiltration of student groups, community raids, and kidnapings (188).[9] Many of these government-trained operatives, Valdez asserts, eventually left government service to work for the burgeoning drug cartels that operate with impunity throughout Mexico (190).

The connection between fatal violence against women and drug cartels is not, however, limited to Mexico, as Valdez shows with data on feminicide throughout Mexico and the Americas. Serial murders of women occurred throughout the late 1990s and early 2000s in areas protecting the Carrillo Fuentes cartel like Chile, Guatemala, Argentina, and Columbia (283).[10] Rosa Linda Fregoso echoes Valdez's call to "de-Juárezify feminicide" (110), citing 1,780 murders in Guatemala, 462 in Honduras, 117 in Costa Rica, and 5 per month in El Salvador between 2001 and 2005 (109). Fregoso argues against a reading of feminicide, such as that found in *Desert Blood*, as the direct result of economic liberalization. Rather, Fregoso contends that a "necropolitical" (109) order of power is emerging in the borderlands and that this necropolitics, rather than "globalization," bears more of the burden of blame for the feminicide in Juárez and elsewhere.

Desert Blood is not unsympathetic to Fregoso's analysis. It does mention alternate theories of the crimes. Passing references are made to "the Egyptian," Abdel Latif Sharif Sharif, a chemist arrested in 1995 for the murders, whom the leader of the snuff film ring refers to as "not my problem" (196). Additionally, the detective handling Irene's disappearance also investigates El Paso's status as "the largest dumping ground of sex offenders in the country" (234). Though these ideas are mentioned, Ivon does not give them her full attention, and her attention is the reader's entrée into the novel's action. Two key moments in which action is focalized elsewhere—the gripping murder scenes of Cecilia (1) and Mireya (147), told from the victims' perspectives—serve mainly as occasions for Ivon's further self-reflection: Cecilia is the mother of the unborn child Ivon wants to adopt (the fetus is killed as well), and Ivon is part of a group of volunteers who find Mireya's decomposed body in the desert. Further, the theory of the crimes Ivon develops stems from the central dramas of her own life: her homosexuality becomes an allegory for what is happening to the *maquila* workers. Gangsters and lesbians are Americanized women "spoiled by first world liberties and behaviors" (134); and the women of Juárez, according to volunteer coordinator Father Frank, "are being sacrificed to redeem the men for their inability to provide for their families, their social emasculation, if you will, at the hands of these American corporations" (252). For Ivon, the murders come to represent a particular kind of Mexican response to the more flexible gender dynamics in the United States.

Though *Desert Blood* wants to depict a broad criminal network, its scope remains limited to Ivon's theory of the crimes, which is focused through the clarity and trajectory of Irene's case, even though this clarity is often asserted as exceptional. The novel is torn between its desire to foreground a Chicana lesbian subjectivity that perceives a particular what, where, and why of border economies and its desire to produce ambiguity in the detective form. That ambiguity takes the shape of social commentary on the internecine criminal networks of the border region, but the novel does not place these networks in the broader, global contexts toward which it gestures.

If, however, the U.S.-Mexico border is not the final and defining border of these crimes, as Valdez, Fregoso, and the novel itself all argue, then what are, or are there any? Is there a way to explain the multinational, multidimensional violence without recourse to easy metaphors and caricatures of villainy? *Desert Blood* is limited by the consciousness of its protagonist. It achieves its aims as a novel by accident in the moments when Ivon is disabled as a rational actor, when she is confused or lost. The depth of the corruption, the geographical breadth of the financial networks, and the intricacies of international law that allow these criminals to operate with impunity manifest elliptically in the novel as Ivon's recurring inability to know where she is. The ways in which spaces are foreign and familiar, recognizable but unintelligible, make plain the deep interconnections that enable the ongoing violence in the hemisphere. *Desert Blood* is most interesting and makes its most innovative social commentary in its presentation of Ivon's relation to space.

Fregoso argues for a retheorization of the border as "more than the edge between two nations, [as] a dispersed hemispheric and global terrain" (110) in which local regions are unthinkable outside a broad hemispheric context. Even though *Desert Blood* makes a self-aware critique of a particular border economy, Ivon's peripatetic and dislocated travels across, through, and within the border suggest a level of complexity beyond the simple analysis Ivon offers as she writes her dissertation and finds her sister.

Desert Blood depicts the irrationality of border space with characters who develop a sense-certainty about place rooted in their own bodies and perceptions of their spatial locations. For example, Ivon's sister Irene resists the ways in which public perception of her body is conditioned by the border. At the fair in Juárez she "felt like everyone was staring at her" because even though her body "looked like [theirs], same color of skin, same Mexican features," her clothes and mannerisms suggest she is "from the other side" and therefore a "sell-out" (104). Place, then, both is and is not rooted in the body. Even though Irene's body is perceived as different, it is, as she notes, the same as the Mexican bodies in Juárez. Irene's objective relation to border space is supplanted by Ivon's own subjective relation, when she is able to locate herself at the ASARCO smelter through memories of her grandfather (294). While Irene dislocates herself from a specific place, Ivon uses her personal history of caring for her grandfather to root herself in space and to chart an escape plan for herself and Irene from the set of the snuff film where Irene is being held captive.

This spatial certainty follows, however, on the heels of a series of spatial confusions. When Ivon visits her ex-girlfriend's house in Juárez, she momentarily wonders if she is in the right place. The place feels the same, but all the houses have been completely, and inconsistently, renovated, making it look entirely different. The diversity of architectural styles "was like a miniature version of embassy row in Washington DC. It could only mean one thing: drug money" (260). Inside, Raquel's house is "even more conspicuous" (261), but the ostentation is less interesting than the external diversity. The area still feels familiar but is now—literally and figuratively—foreign. Ivon is confused by seemingly new but clearly old houses that have been internationally transformed with Swiss, French, Spanish, and Victorian British exteriors. Time and space contract in this neighborhood that stands as a microcosm of the influx of foreign capital and influence into Mexico.

The spatial confusion occasioned by Raquel's neighborhood devolves into the utterly surreal when Ivon leaves Raquel's house in Irene's re-covered car and manages to lose herself in the winding streets of a new industrial park at the city's edge, the Elysian Fields, where, unbeknownst to Ivon, one of the snuff partners has his office (221). Ivon has never seen this area "with its fake gas lamps and wrought-iron benches, its poplars and weeping willows and pristine stretches of verdant grass, [that] could easily have been transplanted from Paris." A sign in the park advertising the businesses operating in the Elysian Fields trumpets their mission—*"To promote and expand world trade and tourism"*—but the park also looks "like simulated reality, and for a second she felt like she'd driven into a movie set" (269). The Elysian Fields stands as testament to foreign capital's creation of totally new Mexican spaces; world tourism will be encouraged not just through foreign investment but by making Mexico over into a subdivision of European capitals, taking not just resources but land itself away from the Mexican people. Here, Ivon is not just dis-oriented but thrust into a completely new transnational imaginary. If she had a sense of U.S.-Mexican interconnection before the Elysian Fields, traveling through this space transforms that vision into a confusing, global panorama.

Moving through the Elysian Fields, Ivon sees that the border she thought she knew does not exist; an alternate reality lurks beneath it, shifting the emotional and physical terrain. As she tries to make her way out of the park, frustrated by her inability to find her sister thus far, Ivon "wished Ivon didn't even exist" (270). Referring to herself in the third person, in the middle of this disorienting space, indicates the depth of connection between space and the self. So much of Ivon's identity is rooted in her conception of the border that as that space drifts away, she begins to lose a sense of herself; that decentering of Ivon's self informs the final instance of the border's transformation in *Desert Blood* from fixed locale to mobile, geopolitical node.

The holy grail of Ivon's quest for her sister is a bar called the Casa Colorada, which, unbeknownst to Ivon, is really two places: one is an actual gay bar on the outskirts of Juárez's red-light district; the other, Casa Roja, which Ivon assumes is the same place (*colorada* and *roja* both mean "red" in Spanish), is a room that, as Irene finally realizes, "wasn't a room at all, but a converted bus" (291). Pounding the streets of Juárez looking for Irene, Ivon asks people if they know where Casa Colorada is. She gets varying responses, from raised eyebrows and questions about her interest in "something different" (206) to narrowed eyes and ques-tions about her intentions (207). It is clear that the people she speaks to know about the place but are reluctant to talk. One transvestite who does drop hints later winds up dead in the desert with her mouth stapled shut (256). When one man explains that Casa Colorada and Casa Roja are "the same color but not the same place," Ivon pays no attention to the distinction (209).

When, finally at the snuff film site, Ivon sees the same red bus that earlier had almost run her off the road, Gaspar de Alba leaves it to the reader to make the final connection. Ivon's goal is to find her sister. Once that goal is accomplished her theorizing ends, and she ceases to think about the Casa Roja. Even though *Desert Blood* focuses on Ivon's movement through space and her reading of the bars and buses, the Casa Roja does show the border transformed and traversed, whether or not Ivon wants to incorporate that into her dissertation chapter. Irene finally recognizes that she is in a red bus, not a red room, and that the bus repeatedly crosses the border.

As one of several crime scenes, the bus is a node whose movements trace the constantly changing shape of power. The Casa Roja moves along a political rhizome; it is a flashpoint that transgresses and reshapes the meaning of the border, whose coordinates at any given time are difficult to map. The Casa Roja kneads space, compacting and stretching it, bringing Ivon alternately closer to and farther from its truth. The changing graffiti in one of the bars Ivon visits tells this same story: "Poor Juárez, so close to hell, so far from Jesus" (98); and "Poor Juárez, so far from the truth, so close to Jesus" (186). To be far from Jesus, in a metaphorical sense, is in one reading to be far from the truth; to be close to Jesus is to be close to truth but also close to the ASARCO smelter, which lies in the shadow of a large statue of Jesus. Ivon cannot understand what the graffiti means, even after someone explains it to her, because she is searching for too abstract a meaning and cannot recognize the significance of the border's changing space, that the ground is shifting beneath her and all the characters in the novel.

With descriptions of Ivon's movement through space, *Desert Blood* makes several significant observations about the changing nature of power in the U.S.-Mexico border region and the ways in which these shifts geopolitically reconfigure the area. Just as the Casa Roja moves throughout the border, the maps of crime are constantly being redrawn or jettisoned entirely. Grassroots groups of volunteers pore over ignored, unmapped spaces looking for bodies, and even the detective's map of sex offenders and crimes of El Paso seems superfluous at novel's end. With the snuff ring destroyed, the Casa Roja can drive off into the sunset of an uncertain future.

The Border's Traveling Expansiveness

The border's unfolding historicity is reflected in the criminal networks, which *Desert Blood*, despite itself, does manage to leave open at novel's end. Martín Limón's *The Door to Bitterness* further develops the indeterminacy of the border depicted in Ivon's spatial disorientation. Limón's novel plays with space similarly, with a protagonist whose geopolitical awareness coincides with a keen perception of his own outsider status. *The Door to Bitterness* turns the detective's historic location both inside and outside communities under investigation to an investigation of the racial unease of its protagonist, Sueño. In the novel, Sueño, a Chicano from East Los Angeles, and his white partner, Ernie Bascom, both military detectives, act as unwitting agents of U.S. power, the domestic failings of which the novel is able to critique by depicting the United States in a foreign setting. In this way Limón's novel shows the "border" to be not just between the United States and Mexico but rather, as Fregoso theorizes it, a global racial and economic dynamic. The novel is part of a series featuring military detectives Sueño and Bascom that has been widely and favorably reviewed. The first, *Jade Lady Burning* (1992), was a *New York Times* "Notable Book of the Year," as was *The Door to Bitterness*. In the novels, descriptions of U.S. military actions in South Korea serve as an allegory for U.S. racial relations, which the reader appreciates only elliptically as Sueño parses Korea's complex, postwar social hierarchies. *The Door to Bitterness* is the first in the series to explicitly take up the racial and gendered hierarchies that have lain in the background of the other novels.

The Door to Bitterness complicates national space by analyzing the United States through its Korean permutations. It similarly complicates the classic hardboiled hero whose generic function was, in the 1920s and 1930s, to demarcate racial and national space. Sueño and Bascom function in the hardboiled mode as outside operators conflicted by their complicity with the system. Sueño calls the military police a "pack of cowboys" who would "get somebody killed" before they could ameliorate a situation (257), and he mocks his superiors' idiosyncrasies (81). When, at the beginning of the novel, Sueño awakes in an alley to find his weapon and military identification card gone, he describes his holster "as empty as a GI's heart" (2), an emptiness further exemplified in his saying that the ultimate betrayal of his assistant and occasional lover, Suk-ja, "didn't matter" (260). But Sueño works against this mold, too, in moments that contradict his macho assertion of having an "empty heart." He sees young American GIs as similar to Korean prostitutes in their naïveté (51); he comforts battered women (71); and he identifies with the motherless, outcast murderers at the center of the plot (275). Sueño's aptitude for human connection suggests the novel is trying to do something more with this character than reiterate, or spice up, the conventional hardboiled persona.

Far from being an uncomplicated caricature, Sueño's persona is in a state of flux. Lost and cast adrift abroad, he must find his way to a metaphorical home through the intricacies of a culture not his own. His name suggests as much. "Sueño" means "dream" in Spanish, and the novel is structured around his alternating waking and dream states. The novel begins with him waking up in an addled state, wondering if his disordered memories are bits of a dream (2). He often drifts off into his own world, mid-conversation, prompting his partner, Bascom, to ask, "Sueño . . . You still with us?" (216). He even describes himself as being in "what psychologists might call a dream state" (224) after a rendezvous with one of the murderers he is pursuing. Sueño's mental state corresponds to his physical state, his location. He is a sojourner in Korea trying to find his way home, and the novel is rife with allusions to Odysseus. Pursuing a suspect on foot, Sueño is waylaid and viciously stabbed by a group of drunken Greek sailors, and the first murder occurs at the Olympos Hotel and Casino (15). Like Odysseus, Sueño is a quick and clever study. The knowledge he gains from his research into Korean language and culture ultimately helps him solve the crimes. As he learns more about Chusok, the Korean harvest festival at which one honors one's ancestors, he comes to understand that the murders follow the pattern of the *sei-bei* ceremonies of ancestor worship (252). Recognizing Ai-ja and her brother Kong's attempts to honor their mother by killing those who have betrayed her allows Sueño to reclaim his own mother and sense of self by proxy.

Sueño's interactions with Ai-ja and Kong allow him to perceive and understand his own racial alienation. When he bows to their mother's picture and says, "On behalf of my countrymen, I apologize. We were wrong. . . . We should have taken care of you. It was our responsibility, but we didn't live up to our responsibility. For that I shall always be ashamed" (275), he shoulders the blame for a country that has alienated him as much as it has created the conditions of Ai-ja and Kong's alienation from contemporary Korea. GI sexual activity created the mixed-race population of which Ai-ja and Kong are a part: the half-*Miguks* (*Miguk* is Korean slang for American GI) who proliferated in the wake of the Korean War and are kept far down on the social and economic ladder in the Seoul that Limón portrays. The half-*Miguks* are untouchable and invisible in a Korea that sees "all GIs [as] part of one race: foreigners" (45). Sueño is frustrated when Korean witnesses to the Olympos shooting are unable to describe or racially identify the shooter but then realizes that this blindness to racial complexity characterizes Anglo-Americans as well. Two white U.S. soldiers cannot fully describe Kong or name his race. "I wasn't surprised," says Sueño, whose military ID Kong is using. "He could've been Korean, an American. He could've been a lot of things" (130). Kong falls beyond the pale of Korean racial schema, as does Sueño in the United States. While Kong impersonates Sueño, Sueño, in thinking about Korean racial politics, feels his own distance from a U.S. racial center even more keenly.

While Sueño feels the effects of his own racialization, as when he wants "to lean across the gear shift and punch [Bascom] flush upside his Anglo-Saxon head" (30), he does not know much about his racial history or identity. Sueño does not hit Bascom; he holds his anger in, which is "a trait, part of Mexican-American culture, [he's] told, to become very quiet when confronted or angry" (30). He has to be told that reticence is a part of his culture. In many ways, Sueño is as blind as the Koreans and Anglo soldiers he criticizes, and the novel traces his growing understanding of that fact, his arousal from his apathetic, dream state. Through his investigation of Ai-ja and Kong, Sueño comes to his own understanding of what his race means to him. He comes to terms with his mother's early death and being raised in the Los Angeles foster system. Motherless, like Kong and Ai-ja, Sueño is also left to navigate his way to adulthood across a stormy sea of racial prejudice where he "felt alone in a strange country . . . too" (88). Sueño has difficulty forming meaningful relationships, but because of his absent parents and amorphous feelings of societal rejection he is able to connect with Ai-ja and Kong.

All three are on the outside looking in, but Sueño's perceptions of space convey a deep desire to be on the inside. His cityscapes all have "winding" (68) streets that "curved and then curved again" (91), a confusing and endless circling around an inaccessible center. Moving through a train station, Bascom asks Sueño if he is lost when Sueño bypasses the restricted U.S. zone inside the terminal. Sueño thinks, "somehow I couldn't bring myself to enter. . . . It would be too much like leaving Korea. Ernie was right. I was lost. As lost as a little half-American girl who'd grown up in this indifferent city" (75). In Korea Sueño feels more at home in his foreignness than he ever did in Los Angeles, but his investigation of

Ai-ja and Kong forces him to face the pain of his alienation in the United States, which is supposed to be his home.

Sueño's outsider status lends him an almost panoptic vision of both places, however. Sorting through a street photographer's pictures of Korean *jo-sans* and their American GI clients, Sueño remembers a childhood trip "to the scenic grandeur of Griffith Park Observatory." His school had taken "a busload of us Chicano kids" there, where they enjoyed a "panoramic view of the Los Angeles basin." As the lights dimmed, "the entire star-studded universe erupted from the darkness" (171). His status as socially marginalized yet possessed, in that instance, of an all-seeing eye, is mirrored in the copious collection of Jimmy, the photographer. Jimmy has spent "years wandering from bar to bar with a camera [chronicling] a way of life" (171). Marginal to the power structures transforming his country, Jimmy also has an all-seeing eye, a camera, that projects a panorama for Sueño's appreciative gaze. Both observers enjoy an encompassing angle on their respective communities. Jimmy's perspective and ensuing vision provide occasion for Sueño to remember his powerful, accidental view of Los Angeles. Sueño's position in the United States, incomprehensible to him as a child, becomes clear in the context of Jimmy's incisive photographic array.

This marginal spatial perception is in conflict with the maps, cardinal directions, relative locations, and geographic features the novel foregrounds. Jimmy's photographs capture what cannot be mapped, not "for security reasons" like Camp Stanley (144) but because, like Itaewon's alleys, they "cannot be plotted on a grid" (220); the military cannot impose its own order upon these interstitial spaces. At the same time that the novel asserts that some things cannot be mapped, however, it provocatively conflates military with geographic reality. The Demilitarized Zone (DMZ) splits North from South Korea "like a burrowing python" (112) but so does the Han River estuary (261). Conflating the military with the natural, in the form of snakes and rivers, exposes the novel's discomfort with liminality and Sueño's burgeoning racial consciousness, even as it questions the government's ability to impose a spatial will over natural, human and geographic, inclination.

The mapped and the uncharted, like racial majorities and margins, do not exist in stark opposition. There is always, as the classic hard-boiled detective will tell his readers, a dual capitulation and resistance to hegemony, a point *The Door to Bitterness* asserts in its title (there are not bitter and sweet places, only doors between them) but also in descriptions of gray markets in Itaewon and the Yellow House, Inchon's red-light district (50). The main trade in both places is prostitution, and while the governments try to control it through spatial constraint, these zones also breed empowerment and subversion. Sueño has difficulty seeing this, however, caught up as he is in a gloomy, condescending empathy with the prostitutes he encounters. He imagines their humiliation at having to register at health clinics for prostitution licenses (12) and feels complicit in a system that takes advantage of vulnerable women (6). His sentiment is made possible through his own patriarchal privilege, which Suk-ja points out when she takes Sueño and Bascom to task for ignoring Ai-ja's perspective. "What about woman?" she asks. "She no have no plan? She no say nothing? . . . Maybe she smarter than man. . . . Take all money, go" (215). Their sergeant, likewise, suggests that perhaps "[t]hat nutty broad [Ai-ja] is smarter than [Sueño] and Bascom put together" (255). The novel thus depicts Sueño's pity as a defense mechanism against appreciating his own conflicted position both inside and outside the master's house.

As a result of not fully appreciating his own discomfort at being a marginalized colonizer, Sueño does not fully appreciate the complexity of the various power structures he encounters. For example, Suk-ja uses Sueño's interest in her to negotiate her way out of her contract with her *mama-san* and into a position as a double agent aiding Sueño; and Ai-ja manipulates Kong's patriarchal rage into a plan to honor their mother. Prostitutes and female black marketeers dominate the spaces that constrain them, as Sueño notes when being led to a late-night rendezvous with Ai-ja (220). Similarly, anytime Sueño is in danger he "felt that [his] mother was near. Walking beside [him]" (263). With his unknown mother to guard his personal space and the internecine alleys of South Korea's red-light districts patrolled by legions of working girls, space, in Sueño's descriptions of these uncharted territories, becomes fluid. Space has shifting, temporal borders conditioned more by Sueño's marginality than by the transience of its military configurations.

The novel critiques this governmental construction of space when Ai-ja and Kong manage to escape government's spatial confines. At the end of *The Door to Bitterness* they avoid certain death at the hands of the Korean National Police by jumping off a cliff into the churning waters of the Yellow Sea. Having completed the Chusok ceremonies and laid their mother's ashes to rest, they finally reject the bounds of the nation that has rejected them. They embrace Korea's shifting, fluid borders that Sueño conflates with the DMZ. Ai-ja and Kong's mother had tied them to Korea, but Korea was unable to accept them as full citizens. Ultimately, in the novel's analysis, women and mothers connect citizens to the meta-phorical space of the nation. With those ties cut, Sueño, Ai-ja, and Kong are cast adrift, outside the nation's material borders. On the one hand, this feels like an empty critique: a saccharine celebration of mother love from a military man guided through Korea's red-light districts by his own lust. But Sueño's honoring of Ai-ja and Kong's mother, when they force him to bow to her photo (275), and his memories of his own mother and Los Angeles serve not just to codify women's place in the immaterial, hence irrelevant and ineffective, realm but also to critique the construction of that ephemeral space.

U.S. military action exacerbates Korea's extant gendered economies and creates an entire population of mixed-race children whose very bodies indicate the gendered dimensions of military power. In its attempts to regulate the health of Korean prostitutes, the United States winds up destroying the very families it has helped create as sick mothers are placed in sanatoriums away from American GIs and their own children. This, the reader learns, is what happens to Ai-ja and Kong, who watch their mother die of tuberculosis, having made her way back to them after escaping from a sanatorium (208). Imposing its own agenda, the United States elevates Anglo well-being at Korean expense and cuts the bonds between mother and child. A resentful Korea is unwilling to care for these mixed-race children, who go on to follow a life of crime. Sueño's mother also dies, and he too is cast out from the center of his country's culture. Sueño feels Ai-ja and Kong's pain over losing their mother and understands the further pain and isolation of being a racial minority.

Sueño, Kong, and Ai-ja are all controlled by a border whose presence none can fathom. As Sueño, the dreamer, conflates the Han River estuary and the DMZ, the reader also wonders about these borders: are they real, are they materially grounded, or are they entirely artificial? The borders created by the Korean Civil War take a human toll on children like Ai-ja and Kong, just as the U.S.-Mexico border takes a human toll on Sueño in Los Angeles and Korea. In this sense, *The Door to Bitterness* is not just about Ai-ja and Kong, but their similarities with Sueño. Their individual tragedy is not as crucial to the novel's argument as the broader story of the spatial regulation of gender and race, and the sense of social strife as a geopolitical effect. The novel enacts the kind of progressive border analysis Fregoso calls for, in that it is not about an individual drama but about the ways in which spatial demarcation is an articulation of racial and gendered hierarchies. Disparate characters in the novel cannot locate themselves properly; there is no place they belong. Like Sueño at the train station, they are all lost (75), dislocated by structurally similar processes in Korea and the United States.

Intergalactic Allegories of Border Space

These processes are represented by the transformative "doors" through which Limón's characters are passing. In *The Door to Bitterness* military aggression and global flows of capital push people, like Sueño, into liminal spaces while simultaneously creating marginal spaces, like the Half-Half Club (Limón 148), for people like Ai-ja and her brother Kong. Mario Acevedo's *The Nymphos of Rocky Flats* and *The Undead Kama Sutra* give readers transformation of a different sort. The novels depict the effects of similar geopolitical forces on a very different community: the international network of the undead—vampires—governed by the Araneum, Latin for spider web, "an appropriate name" according to Felix Gomez, the series' Chicano protagonist (*Nymphos* 42).

Acevedo's novels offer new types of marginal characters with unique, scathingly sardonic perspectives on national space and racial politics. While both *Desert Blood* and *The Door to Bitterness* place the question of national territory and borders at the center of their analyses, Felix sees human, territorial conflict as almost irrelevant to the galactic discord with which he and his fellow vampires are challenged. People are "but dots on a miserable speck of rock tucked into an insignificant corner of the galaxy," he muses (*Nymphos* 329). Felix's and his fellow vampires' engagements with aliens from outer space and their wrangling over Earth, which one alien refers to as the "forbidden jewel" (*Undead* 278), employ biting satire and political allegory to comment on the restructurings of post-9/11 national space and the racial conflicts thus engendered.

Both novels focus on the adventures of Felix Gomez, a Chicano private detective who was turned into a vampire while serving as a U.S. soldier in Iraq during Operation Iraqi Freedom (2003). In The *Nymphos of Rocky Flats*, Felix travels to Denver at the request of his friend Gilbert, who wants Felix to help investigate an outbreak of nymphomania at the Rocky Flats Environmental Technology Site, where he works for the U.S. Department of Energy. During the course of his investigation Felix is drawn into Denver's local vampire politics. The community there is plagued by *vânätori*, vampire hunters, drawn to Denver by the nymphomania, which they attribute to the vampires. Felix discovers, however, that the nymphomania has been caused by alien artifacts from the 1947 crash, in Roswell, New Mexico, of an unidentified flying object.[11] Gilbert turns out to be an alien imposter, and, after killing the *vânätori*, Felix destroys the equipment Gilbert wants him to retrieve.

Gilbert and Felix reach an uneasy truce at the end of *Nymphos*, and in *The Undead Kama Sutra*, Gilbert enlists Felix's help once more. In this installment, Felix travels to Key West to see Carmen Arellano, his friend and leader of the Denver vampire community. She has been researching an ancient manuscript called "The Undead Kama Sutra," which promises to help vampires achieve spiritual transcendence through sex. After being shot by an alien blaster, Gilbert dies, but not before telling Felix to "save the Earth women" (6). A complicated plot ensues in which members of an alien mafia convince the U.S. government to sell them Earth women, who are then resold as high-priced, outer space pets. The aliens have enlisted the government's help by giving big pharmaceutical companies formulas for breast enhancing and for hair-removing medications that generate significant revenue. Felix and Carmen bust the plot, but Carmen is captured and sent into outer space at novel's end.

Acevedo's novels are quite serious, despite the rather silly trappings of their plots. They combine humor with the conventions of classic vampire and detective fiction to draw weighty observations from the sublimely ridiculous. The vampire has long been a vehicle for social analysis. From the unambiguous monstrosity of Bram Stoker's *Dracula* (1897) to the domesticated moroseness of Anne Rice's undead, vampires reflect a society's unconscious fears and desires, according to Joan Gordon and Veronica Hollinger (2). As Deborah Overstreet catalogs, vampires have always signaled sex and its dangers, and though they can be read as class predators, draining the life of the laboring classes, "vampirism can also be a metaphor for alienation" (9). On this point the vampire coincides neatly with the detective who also feels alternately compelled by and alienated from different worlds. Acevedo's Felix Gomez, while domesticated and sympathetic, is triply alienated: a detective who derides his human clients; a monster and an "alien" in the public imagination; a Mexican American in the United States. His status as a vampire detective allows the novel to speak indirectly of xenophobia, and the introduction of aliens from outer space, rather than Mexico, turns U.S. immigration debates of the early 2000s on their head.

In interviews, Acevedo asserts that he was never a fan of science fiction, fantasy, or horror. His early, unpublished novels, rather, were "big, political pot-boilers thick with crap about 'important' issues. The stories bored even me," he asserts. He credits his writing group with helping him write to his "low-brow smart-ass" strengths and "to comment in an oblique way on social and cultural issues" (M. Ramos). Though he may call his assessments oblique, *Nymphos'* stance on 9/11 and the ensuing war in Iraq are quite clear. Acevedo, himself a veteran of Operation Desert Storm (1991), narrates combat in such evocative terms as to make the reader's heart break along with Felix's when he mistakes a young girl and her family for Iraqi insurgents, precipitating his vampiric transformation when he wanders confusedly into a vampire's house begging for punishment (13). "I was a murderer," Felix thinks, "I knew what I had seen through the goggles. How could I have been so wrong?" (10). He extends this self-criticism to the larger war, stating flatly, "our great cause was a sham. I didn't want anything more to do with this stupid war" (12). The war itself becomes a play of surfaces, illusion, a theme several characters echo stateside. "It's the illusion of vigilance that comforts them," Gilbert tells Felix, referring to the excessive security measures at Rocky Flats, explaining that "any act of paranoia is justified" after 9/11 (23). Another, less critical military man, Rocky Flats' manager Herbert Hoover Merriweather, tells Felix that to question one's loyalties means "you're thinking too much. In this post-9/11 world, none of us has [that] luxury. . . . Leave the thinking to the government" (147). Juxtaposing Gilbert and Merriweather against Felix's own bitter suspicions, the novel asks what the United States sees through its goggles and if it understands the human toll Operation Iraqi Freedom is taking.

Felix's vampiric transformation proves the inhumanity of war; the only way he can countenance it is to leave his humanity behind. Though he is being evasive when he deflects people's curiosity about his appearance by attributing it to "Gulf War Syndrome" (*Nymphos* 23, 81), the war in Iraq has, literally, made Felix inhuman. On the one hand, this borders dangerously close to orientalism, to making "the East" a land of mysterious and exotic things like vampires. The location of Felix's office "on the second floor of the Oriental Theater in Denver, Colorado" (*Undead* 364) further places inhumanity in "the East." On the other hand, we learn of the Araneum's worldwide reach and the existence of vibrant vampire communities around the world.

In the same way that the Araneum's global presence resists the exotic, Felix's anti-hardboiled heroism makes it impossible to read vampirism as his racial other. Though Gilbert expressly identifies Felix as "an outsider" and the novel begins with Felix's crisp understatement, "I don't like what Operation Iraqi Freedom has done to me" (1), the similarities with Marlowe and Spade end there. Felix is emotionally fragile and still processing his guilt over killing the Iraqi family. This psychic wound

prevents him from drinking human blood, an asceticism that diminish-
es his vampire powers (44). No womanizer he, Felix is very shy about his
crush on Wendy, his dryad love interest (171), and far from lording his
patriarchal privilege about, he turns to Wendy for help because he knows
she is smarter than he is (159). Women, in fact, overwhelm Felix in both
novels. The nymphomaniacs resist his vampire powers of mind control
and Wendy saves him from certain death in *The Nymphos of Rocky Flats*.
In *The Undead Kama Sutra*, Felix is only able to move forward with his
case once he overcomes his fear of Carmen's sexuality.

The plots of both novels turn on the idea that men are insecure and
thus undervalue women; however, Gomez still retains patriarchal notions of himself, and the novels do rely on racial hierarchies of a sort.
Felix may be a failed hero at the end of *The Undead Kama Sutra* because
of his inability to save Carmen, but he still wants to be a hero. Similarly,
racial hierarchies, in the form of "auras," lie at the heart of both novels;
but the novels deploy their own species distinctions as a means of mocking paranoid racial discourse and are thus particularly useful for thinking about what Chicana/o literature means for the twenty-first century.

In *The Nymphos of Rocky Flats*, references to *chicanismo* are relatively
cosmetic: Felix's landlord is Mexican (34); Felix professes a love of beer
and tacos (72); a mariachi band performs at the local vampire hangout
(154); and Carmen, who wears Aztec calendars as earrings, decorates her
car with Frida Khalo miniatures (258). References to race in *The Undead
Kama Sutra* are more direct and fairly substantive. In the novel's climax
Felix must infiltrate the grounds of a highly secure resort from which he
hopes to rescue Carmen. In order to sneak past the many guards, Felix
attaches himself to a maintenance crew composed of Mexican and Nicaraguan immigrants. "Weeds and dirty toilets don't take care of themselves," Felix quips (312). He uses the metaphorical invisibility of Latinos
to his advantage when a guard is momentarily suspicious of his being
new on the job. Felix responds to his English with Spanish and gives him
a "simple-minded grin" (314). That this mollifies the guard suggests the
true invisibility of Latina/o labor; the guard sees what he wants to see:
an insignificant, "simple-minded" Spanish speaker, expectations Felix
disrupts by being a vampire secret agent.

The resort Felix infiltrates is the base for the U.S. government's alien
trade in women and pharmaceuticals, a confluence of elements that
comments satirically on anti-immigrant xenophobia. Arguments for
strengthening the U.S.-Mexico border invoke "security"; a porous border invites terrorist threat, which, while real, is often exaggerated for

xenophobic ends.[12] Felix is an actual "terrorist" seeking to disrupt U.S. activities. But the scenarios in both novels force readers to ask why they should be concerned with terrorists when their own government constantly deceives and means them actual harm. Furthermore, Felix is not an immigrant, so the guard's acceptance of him as part of the crew invokes the tendency to see all Latinas/os as part of one, undifferentiated, potentially threatening mass. The true brilliance of the satire at play here, however, lies in the total inversion of immigration paranoia as the novels move from human to intergalactic concerns.

Earth, so focused on patrolling its own borders, is completely unaware of its own quarantine by the Galactic Union (*Nymphos* 340). The shift from Earth to outer space redraws the spatial contours of race and ethnicity that emerge with Sarmiento, Zavala, and Pérez Rosales and strengthen throughout the twentieth century. Space, in Acevedo, takes on entirely new dimensions, and his novels become not so much about Chicana/o experience as they are about the structures, or psychology, of human difference. The novels may be about vampires and aliens, but the interspecies conflicts they recount are structurally similar to the racial hierarchies conditioning Chicana/o experience. Thus, even though Felix may be triply alienated as a Chicana/o vampire detective, he comes to understand that no identification authorizes his own bigotry.

At the beginning of *Nymphos*, Felix complacently dismisses his initial fear of a group of humans he believes may be following him. "I was dealing with humans," he thinks. "What could go wrong?" (38). Sure of his own superiority, Felix cannot believe in a human threat until later in the novel when he is undeniably confronted with it and his own arrogance. Felix disdains humans, but *Nymphos* tells the story of how he comes to recognize the misleading and limiting effect of hierarchies of difference. Wendy's explanation of the different auras, which she calls chakras, allows the novel to treat human racial prejudice allegorically as interspecies or intergalactic conflict with Felix serving as an unlikely Everyman. Auras, in the novels, separate and organize beings, serving much the same function as race for humans, and Felix is unwilling to give up the power to see them. "We vampires use our knowledge of psychic energy to manipulate humans," he says, explaining why he destroys the Psychotronic Device Gilbert hired him to find (*Nymphos* 345). The device would have allowed aliens to detect auras too, but "Earth's vampires didn't need competition from extraterrestrials" (*Nymphos* 345). Felix does not trust the aliens to use the power to see auras responsibly.

Felix agrees with Gilbert that humans are "violent and dangerous"

(*Nymphos* 341) and with Clayborn, who sees them as "violent and treacherous" (*Undead* 278), but not entirely. Felix knows that humans can be evil, but this does not translate into trusting aliens like Gilbert or Clayborn. *Nymphos* and *Undead* depict Felix's growing humanistic compassion and his maintenance of hope for the species. Many non-human characters in *Nymphos* see humans as the source of true depravity. "Look at the real evil in history," one vampire tells him. "The Inquisition, the Holocaust. Vampires didn't hijack airplanes and crash them into buildings" (*Nymphos* 51). This same vampire is also very critical of Felix's decision to abstain from human blood because of his guilt over killing the Iraqi family. "Why must it bother you?" he asks. "Do you think the real perpetrators of the war—Saddam Hussein, President Bush, the oil barons, the arms merchants—lose any sleep over what they've done?" (*Nymphos* 44). Both aliens and his fellow vampires depict evil as a human trait that humans project onto the unknown.

"We fill a need for humans," a vampire tells Felix, explaining that the "terror of being preyed upon" is both exciting and a way for humans to project their own predatory tendencies (*Nymphos* 49). Felix persists, however, in taking human responsibility for his actions. He understands that U.S. military power has changed him completely, and *Nymphos* is unequivocal in its critique of the War on Terror and the belief that the U.S. military, not vampires, is the real blood-sucking beast. Yet Felix resists easy absolution. It is easy to read, in the novels' description of the United States' uneasy collusion with and desperate fear of aliens from outer space, an allegory of early twenty-first-century immigration paranoia. But in having Felix maintain personal, human responsibility for his actions, the novel resists a knee-jerk vilification of humanity or government. Felix does not buy the aliens' argument about humanity's evil; to him it is just as wrongheaded as the U.S. fear of "aliens," both in politics and science fiction. In taking responsibility for his actions, Felix holds out hope for human goodness and morality, which allows *Nymphos* and *Undead* to read as defenses of humanity as much as of earthly aliens.

Positive and Negative Freedoms post-9/11

Of the four analyzed here, Acevedo's novels are most explicitly about 9/11 and the War on Terror, but *Desert Blood* and *The Door to Bitterness* do also each take up aspects of the global that underpin Acevedo's hopeful social commentary. Each author is concerned with economic globalization, superstructures' conditioning of human value, and the subsequent creation of marginalized communities. Their characters have very little opportunity for self-determination. In *Desert Blood*, laboring women are confined to factory space while Mexico's political terrain constantly transforms itself. Martin Limón's characters operate within an underground economy tolerated and moderated by South Korean and U.S. military authorities, while Acevedo's vampires, aliens, and women are buffeted about by not just an international but an intergalactic profit motive. However, these global gestures resonate beyond the U.S.-Mexico border and Mexican American racialization.

Though we will likely never be able to say with certainty what 9/11 *meant*, it is possible to think about how it has changed the relationship between national and global imaginaries in Chicana/o literature. In their descriptions of the racialization of experience by global, economic forces, Gaspar de Alba, Limón, and Acevedo are also attempting to sort the continuing relevance of the nation. Can a nation be held to account for the Juárez murders? Is there an entity called the United States that can be blamed for Felix Gomez's inhumanity? Who is responsible for Ai-ja and her brother Kong? Though the nation-state has shaped these forces, it is paradoxically absent from any imagined solution.

At the same time that Gaspar de Alba, Limón, and Acevedo describe the state's declining influence, they continue to express the profound importance of the nation as a means of grounding progressive action. This tricky dance is negotiated textually in each novel's deployment of space as a plot device. Sueño's consumption and dissection of Korean space counters U.S. disaffection through his empathy with racialized, Korean subjects. Acevedo and Gaspar de Alba similarly try to write outside the boundaries of U.S. territory as well as Chicana/o affect. Their deconstruction of Catholic iconography offers one lens through which we might see the future of Chicana/o literature.

Desert Blood's action is dominated by El Cristo Rey, a 42.5-foot statue of Christ on the cross overlooking El Paso, and at the end of *The Undead Kama Sutra*, Felix meets with Araneum vampires at the Mother Cabrini shrine, a 22-foot statue of Jesus on the outskirts of Denver. The statues stand almost as a counter to the democratizing rhetoric of global markets that both novels reference: the promises of NAFTA and the borderless humanity of pharmaceutical corporations. The statues seem to suggest that though the borders of the nation may be porous, fluid, almost imperceptible to capital, people are still rooted in place and community. People, the church's ostensible concern, do not necessarily move in the same direction as money. Yet both novels are highly critical of the

FIGURE 6.1 El Cristo Rey statue in El Paso. Courtesy of Miguel Unzueta.

Catholic Church, which they argue can no longer account for Chicana/o reality, even as it demarcates Chicana/o space. Characters in both novels move beyond these putatively ineffectual icons' scopes. If Chicana/o space cannot be mapped in traditional ways—territorial or spiritual— then ironizing the statues destabilizes the nation, it forces the question of where the nation is, what it means, and who "belongs" to it. Such a critique undermines the notion of a libratory third space, so central to Chicana/o studies. People do not move in the same way as capital, but traditional invocations of the people as inhabiting an in-between space, be it actual church sanctuary or theoretical, hybrid, border zones, are also unable to address the real-life concerns of Chicanas/os and Latinas/os in the United States. People do move, and communities change, though not always in progressive ways. Hence, the monuments are both meaningful and profoundly meaningless.

Humanists, argues the anthropologist Aihwa Ong, want to read the mass migrations of labor around the world as a potentially libratory,

FIGURE 6.2 Mother Cabrini shrine. Courtesy of Sarah Bailey Felsen.

cosmopolitan, global citizenship.[13] Such readings do not take into account that, like the factory workers in *Desert Blood*, the country prostitutes who populate Limón's Seoul, or the abducted women in *The Undead
Kama Sutra*, the great majority of migrant labor in the world is forced
and hardly fertile ground for progressive, jet-setting politics. These novels force readers to wonder whether diaspora is every truly postnational,
if citizenship can ever be global or cosmopolitan.[14]

Globalization is primarily a theory of markets, not culture, resulting,
for the most part, in cosmopolitanism without a human rights agenda.
Neoliberal economic models transform citizenship from a guarantee of
rights to the individual's obligation to act in self-interest. Within these
models, globalization potentially dismantles the progressive aspects of
nations as guarantors of freedom, substituting self-interested freedom in
its stead. This dynamic is painfully evident in the four novels discussed
here, but these texts are trying to create a global conscience that also
believes in the nation. Felix Gomez believes in humanity; George Sueño
takes responsibility, on behalf of his country, for Ai-ja and Kong's mother; Ivon's mission is to educate and activate in order to foster transnational cooperation on behalf of the murdered women. Ultimately each of
these novels asserts an ethical citizenship that recognizes a transnational
humanity. They understand the global imbrications of the United States,
but they do not exploit the transnational at the expense of the national.
They hold out hope for a progressive nation-state that can encompass
their hybrid national imaginaries.

Desert Blood, The Door to Bitterness, The Nymphos of Rocky Flats, and
The Undead Kama Sutra recognize that calls to transnationalism or glo-
balism are thinly veiled assertions of colonial power in the same way
that nineteenth-century articulations of Pan-Americanism supported
U.S. dominance in the hemisphere. The postnation, border zone, and
hybrid thirdspace ultimately codify state power and reify racial hierarchies. The stakes are higher, however, post-9/11 when the effects of that
power, of U.S. global, economic dominance, are felt tragically on such
a broad scale and are changing so rapidly. The United States will never
be the same; we will never again be blind to how U.S. force has created
a wide-ranging global underclass of racialized others, a point that will
be continually made plain as the global south rises in economic importance. Chicanas/os, likewise, are fundamentally altered. September 11
made clear that Chicana/o concerns are global concerns. The Cabrini
shrine and El Cristo Rey are icons of both an outdated ethnic identity
and promises for the future. Chicanas/os can no longer be so tightly

circumscribed by the Church, or the Southwest, but, as the statues also suggest, we must stand with arms outstretched to the world. Borders are breaking down all around us, even as they are being built up. We must, these novels argue, take personal responsibility for our fellow humans and for our actions, both within and without the state.

Conclusion: " . . . Walking in the Dark Forest of the Twenty-First Century"

That is how, in March 2002, Mexican-born, San Francisco–based performance artist Guillermo Gómez-Peña, in conversation with Lisa Wolford, described what it felt like for him to make art after September 11, 2001 (*ethno-techno* 282). Parsing the events of the early 2000s one can easily understand why. In November 2005, the administration of then president George W. Bush announced the Secure Border Initiative. SBINet, through a contract awarded to Boeing, was not only to increase guards and expand the physical wall along the two-thousand-mile U.S.-Mexico border but also to wire it for the new millennium with a technology-rich array of cameras, sensors, and radar that would precisely pinpoint people crossing into the United States illegally (Archibold). This heightened security was part of the long history of the U.S.-Mexico border's militarization, but it was also given impetus by the increasing paranoia in the United States after 9/11 about the porosity of U.S. borders and the ease with which terrorists might infiltrate the country. In the years immediately following the 9/11 attacks, collective anxieties about terror were quickly and easily cathected onto longstanding uneasiness with perceived others, and the global War on Terror came also to serve, as Mario Acevedo's campy, detective fiction asserts, as justifiable allegory of racial and ethnic discrimination.

The 2008 election of Barack Obama as the first African American president of the United States was thought by many to indicate a turning point in the national conversation about race, immigration, and national borders. Deportations increased by 5 percent, however, in 2009, signaling a continuation rather than a reversal of Bush-era xenophobia (Kaye). It remains to be seen how much effect, if any, the hundreds of thousands of activists who crowded the National Mall on March 21, 2010, in frustration over stalled immigration reform will have. Joe Arpaio, known nationally for his aggressive anti-immigrant tactics, is still sheriff of Maricopa County, Arizona, suggesting that national space still, in many ways, correlates quite strongly to a national race, despite our brief moment of electoral reconciliation. Alex Rivera makes this same point in his film *Sleep Dealer* (2008), a futuristic dystopia depicting a world connected by technology yet divided by geopolitical borders, in which Mexican workers sell their labor by connecting their bodies, over the Internet, to robots on *el otro lado* (the other side).

Sleep Dealer has a hopeful, if not happy, ending, however, with protagonists destroying a major dam controlling the regional water supply and vowing to continue the struggle against multinational capital. And, on March 16, 2010, Homeland Security secretary Janet Napolitano, who battled Arpaio when she served as Arizona's governor, announced that her department would be pulling $50 million in funding for SBINet. To be sure, Secretary Napolitano is not advocating open borders; those funds will be redirected toward proven technologies that can be implemented immediately, such as heat sensors and night-vision goggles. We appear, though, on the cusp of this second decade of the twenty-first century, to be at a virtual crossroads at once promising and problematic. The border remains, but the irrational anxieties fueling SBINet have somewhat subsided; divisions exist, but perhaps we are moving toward more reasonable and effective means of reconciling them.

In his landmark speech on U.S. racial relations, delivered during the presidential campaign in March 2008 in Philadelphia, Barack Obama made an argument about race that resonates with the argument about national space suggested by Napolitano's 2010 announcement about SBINet. The historical legacy of race is real and divisive. Today's disparities, he said, "can be directly traced to inequalities passed on from an earlier generation that suffered under the brutal legacy of slavery and Jim Crow" (4). We must, he argued, direct our energies not toward anger at past inequality but toward redressing today's income and achievement gaps, and ending the "cycle of violence . . . that continues to haunt us" (5). The only way to do this, however, is not by ignoring our past but by confronting the historical truth of racism so that "together we can move beyond some of our old racial wounds" (6). Not transcend race but move beyond "racial wounds." We must "[embrace] the burdens of our past without becoming victims of our past," acknowledge history in order to move into the future and find what binds us together as a people (6).

This struggle to move forward that Obama describes is also the Chicana/o struggle, the American struggle, the global struggle to simultaneously assert particularity and commonality. It was the struggle articulated by the mid-twentieth-century *movimiento* poet Alurista through his controversial and experimental poetics. Alurista connected the transgression of geopolitical borders with the elision of borders between peoples, the interconnection of creative forces. Individuals, he believed, cannot be truly free until they recognize the interconnection of all humanity, and Chicanas/os cannot be truly free until they recognize that the struggle in the United States is intricately bound with the anti-imperialist struggle in other countries. "Porque la soberanía nacional de los pueblos chicanos no se puede concebir . . . independiente, aislada, separada de la soberanía nacional de los pueblos centro y sudamericanos" ("Because Chicano national sovereignty cannot be understood . . . apart from the national sovereignty of the Central and South American people"), claims Alurista (Ruffinelli 31).

Many of his contemporaries thought Alurista's belief in poetry's ability to unify self with other as inextricable from international struggles against imperial capitalism idealistic and impractical, just as many voters doubted Obama. Both men argue that we must know the particularity of our history in order to move beyond it into the future of race and space in the Americas. The struggle against racism and injustice is a global, historical struggle, and we are all—Chicanas/os, Anglos, world citizens—imbricated in a global network within which we feel the tug and pull of these small battles that are all the more visible and pressing post-9/11.

The last chapters of this book make that same argument. Ana Castillo, Alicia Gaspar de Alba, Martin Limón, and Mario Acevedo each explore the ways in which the racialization of Latinas/os and the spaces they move within have altered with the advent of the War on Terror. The insight of these authors to connect U.S. interventions in the Middle East with domestic racial politics illuminates a global theory of race in which the particularity of the Chicana/o experience has a historical value that is nevertheless transcended by its place in a world geopolitical system. But their insights are not novel, as I have been at pains to show throughout *Chicano Nations*. They resonate with the long history of Chicana/o literature, with Domingo Sarmiento's early transamericanism, Lorenzo de Zavala's correlation of race with disease and the racism of liberalism,

FIGURE 7.1. Typical Arab chola. Photo by James McCaffery. Courtesy of La Pocha Nostra.

and Vicente Pérez Rosales's theorizations of the racial state. Mariano Vallejo's compromised hemispherism demonstrates the codification of race concomitant with state formation in the Americas; and María Mena, Daniel Venegas, Jovita González, Eve Raleigh, and José Vasconcelos all show, in their writing, how the formation of a Mexican American and Latina/o collectivity in the United States is in dialogue with hemispheric and global politics.

Since its inception, then, Chicana/o literature's national imaginary has been inseparable from a global and hemispheric perspective. What some refer to as postnationalism, or transnationalism, is thus not a contemporary phenomenon germane to twentieth-century articulations of *chicanismo* but part of the warp and woof of Chicana/o literary history. Though this perspective may not be contemporary, it has its perhaps most compelling articulation in the work of La Pocha Nostra, whose various performance pieces post-9/11 rearticulate, in visual form, the arguments about race and space made by the authors in *Chicano Nations*. La Pocha Nostra is a transnational, multi-ethnic artists' "laboratory," organized by Guillermo Gómez-Peña, that describes itself as a "trans-disciplinary arts organization [that aims] to cross and erase dangerous borders including those between art and politics, practice and theory . . . to dissolve borders and myths of purity." Its mission is reflected in its name, loosely translated as "our impurities" or "the cartel of cultural bastards" ("Manifesto").

In all its projects, La Pocha Nostra works "to build more open, fluid, and tolerant communities defying dysfunctional or dated notions of identity, nationality, language and art making" (Manifesto). Two interactive, evolving, photo-performance pieces speak to this transgressive process with specific regard to Chicanas/os, Arab Americans, Arabs, and post-9/11 politics of race and space. "The New Barbarians" is an expanding collection of fashion photographs that seek to capture the dimensions of the mercurial other in the post-9/11 U.S. cultural imaginary. The photographs, which have appeared in places ranging from academic journals to gallery installations, highlight the titillation and terror evoked by a combination of Mexican and Muslim iconography, filtered through the objectifying, abstracting lens of fashion photography. The project began in 2003 in response to Operation Iraqi Freedom with the goal of "map[ping] out a new territory in terms of 'we' and 'them'," we being "the migrants, exiles, nomads, & wetbacks in permanent process of voluntary deportation . . . the transient orphans of dying nation-states la

FIGURE 7.2. La Pocha Nostra. Courtesy of Zach Gross.

otra America . . . the citizens of the outer limits and crevasses of 'Western Civilization'" (Gómez-Peña, "The New Barbarians" 1). "They," according to the New Barbarians' declaration, are "the Lords of fear & Intolerance," "The Lords of censorship" (2), "those up there who make dangerous decisions for mankind," "those who are as afraid of us as we are of them" (3), "the share holders of mono-culture" (4), and "the masters and apologists of war" (5). "We" speak back to "them" in "The New Barbarians" in a collective voice in hopes of humanizing art and war.

"The Chica-Iranian Project: Orientalism Gone Wrong in Aztlán" takes up a similar project in an on-line, interactive experiment. Coordinated by Gómez-Peña and Ali Dagdar, the project brings together Iranian and Chicana/o artists who create ethnic personas embodying a cross-fertilization of Arab and Mexican culture. The viewer is shown a random selection of photographs and asked to identify the name of the artist pictured. The piece, meant to highlight the viewer's subconscious and reflexive ethnic profiling, comments also on the fetishization and vilification of otherness in a nativist climate.

Both collaborative endeavors—"The Chica-Iranian Project" and "The New Barbarians"—refute such objectification; they resist ossified narratives of identity and place by forging a collectivity out of abjection. The force of their visual arguments lies in their pinpointing interconnected processes of racialization while also playing with the tropological typification the projects are meant to undermine. That is, they work because of a visual irony in which the hijab, for example, signals an inassimilable, frightening Arab-ness, the veil through which the Anglo-American majority is unable to obtain a clear view of the Middle East, and a mark of resistance to the enforced cultural homogenization of post-9/11 "censorship, intolerance, and paranoid nationalism" ("Manifesto").

La Pocha Nostra's performance pieces echo Ali and Ali's cynicism in Guillermo Verdecchia's play *The Adventures of Ali and Ali and the Axes of Evil*, which I discussed in the introduction to this book. While the audience leaves Ali and Ali savoring Ali Ababwa's optimistic, dreamlike vision of the future, La Pocha Nostra refuses to deliver such succor to its viewers. La Pocha Nostra walks with the writers discussed in *Chicano Nations*, into "the dark forest of the twenty-first century" (*ethno-techno* 282). Those who witness its performances must take responsibility for their own hermeticism, their own ethnic profiling, their own borders. Just as the character Verdecchia tells his audience, in *Fronteras Americanas*, that they "still have time [to] go forwards. Towards the centre, towards the border" (78), La Pocha Nostra challenges its witnesses to move beyond themselves.

So does Domingo Sarmiento. And Lorenzo de Zavala, and Vicente Pérez Rosales. So do Mariano Vallejo, María Mena, Daniel Venegas, Jovita González, Eve Raleigh, and José Vasconcelos. So does Ana Castillo. And Alicia Gaspar de Alba, Martín Limón, and Mario Acevedo. They challenge us to plumb their depths, to read beneath their surfaces, to transgress the mental borders that might keep us from appreciating them as part of Chicana/o literary history. For if history teaches us nothing else, La Pocha Nostra reminds us that we determine the value of our own history. Race, space, place, and nation are all states of mind. They are rooted in geopolitical realities, certainly, but we must be willing to move across the borders they represent, beyond the dark forest, into the future.

NOTES

Introduction

1. In Mexica (Aztec) mythology Aztlán is the homeland from which the Mexica migrated south to Tenochtitlan, present-day Mexico City, in the Valley of Mexico. Many Chicana/o activists have either assumed Aztlán to be the southwestern United States (because surviving Mexica codices note that the Mexica migrated south) or adopt the rhetoric of Aztlán as shorthand for the ignoble confiscation of Mexican lands in the region by the United States (the work of Reies López Tijerina and the Alianza Federal de Mercedes on behalf of New Mexican land claimants in the 1960s is an excellent example of this type of activism). As Daniel Cooper Alarcón has noted in *The Aztec Palimpsest* (1997), however, the exact location of Aztlán is unclear and researchers have formulated credible theories placing it as far north as Wisconsin (see, for example, the work of Roberto Rodriguez and Patricia Gonzales in their Aztlanahuac Project). Furthermore, as Alarcón's work suggests, it is unclear whether the Mexica actually migrated south or invented a migration myth to justify their conquest of the Valley of Mexico. For these reasons, scholars and cultural workers in the twenty-first century, such as the writer Gloria Anzaldúa and the performance artist Guillermo Gomez-Peña, are less apt to dwell on the exact geographical location of Aztlán and more likely to use Aztlán to signify a combination of the materiality of the U.S.-Mexico border and the psychological effects of being torn between two countries, as many Chicanas/os feel themselves to be.

2. "El Plan," a founding document of Chicana/o nationalism, defines nationalism as "the common denominator that all members of La Raza can agree upon." It is "the key to organization," which includes "economic control of our lives and our communities," "community control of our schools," "restitution for past economic slavery," an assurance that artists "produce literature and art that is appealing to our people and relates to our revolutionary culture," "self-defense against the occupying forces of the oppressors," and the "creation of an independent local, regional, and national political

party." Nationalism, according to "El Plan," included the organization of all Chicana/os within the rubric of "El Plan," which its drafters saw as "the plan of liberation" (2–5).

3. For a wonderfully rich, documentary overview of this process, see Alma García's edited collection *Chicana Feminist Thought*.

4. López's study of *movimiento* poet Ricardo Sánchez seeks to put Sánchez's work in a broad philosophical and literary context rather than read him in the context of *movimiento* political debate. He reads Sánchez in the context of José Vasconcelos and Antonio Caso, as well as Henri Bergson, to argue that the art of *el movimiento* represents one part of a long process of questioning modernity and progress.

5. Gregorio Cortez is the real-life hero of a popular Mexican American *corrido* (border ballad), which was the subject of Américo Paredes' *With His Pistol in His Hand* (1958). In 1901, after a sheriff shot his brother, Cortez shot the sheriff, fled, and evaded capture for several days. The Mexican Army considered it a provocation to attack when Taylor's forces, under secret orders from President James Polk, crossed the Nueces River into disputed territory in March 1846.

6. See note 2.

7. "History of Aztlán" is a prose poem that traces the history of Mexican Americans from the time of the Toltecs through the 1969 Denver Youth Conference where "El Plan de Aztlán" was drafted. Copyright restrictions prohibit quoting from the poem at this time; however, the original manuscript may be found among Alurista's papers at the University of Texas's Benson Collection in Austin.

8. The Ouroboros, or serpent eating its own tail, is an image common to many cultures, including those of ancient Mexico (Charlesworth 40). It typically symbolizes the cyclic nature of history and the body, as well as rebirth and regeneration. The image is iterated in the statue of Coatlique—mother of Huitzilopochtli, Aztec god of war—on display at the National Museum of Anthropology in Mexico City. The statue depicts Coatlique with two serpents, rather than a head, sprouting from her neck.

9. Three key studies in this vein whose methodological models *Chicano Nations* is heavily influenced by are: Kirsten Gruesz's exemplary *Ambassadors of Culture* (2002), which traces lines of literary influence between nineteenth-century U.S. and Latin American writers; Anna Brickhouse's *Transamerican Literary Relations and the Nineteenth Century Public Sphere* (2004), which rereads the "American Renaissance" from the vantage point of Latin American nation making in the same period; and Michelle Stephens's *Black Empire* (2005), which theorizes transnational blackness and U.S. cultural production.

10. This is my translation of the original Spanish, which reads: "Llamaremos bolivarismo al ideal hispanoamericano de crear una federación con todos los pueblos de cultura española. Llameremos monroísmo al ideal anglosajón de incorporar las veinte naciones hispánicas al Imperio nórdico, mediante la political del panamericanismo."

11. Paula Moya and Ramón Saldívar make much the same point in their introduction to the special issue of *Modern Fiction Studies* they edited, "Fictions of the Trans-American Imaginary." It is, they argue, "quite clear that the end of the era of nationalism is not remotely in sight." Nevertheless, scholarship such as the type included in their special issue must incorporate "a hemispheric framework into our analyses" (4). Such an approach is crucial, they claim, to the "development of alternative critical and *comparative* paradigms through which American national identity and literature can be understood" (3).

12. In *The Borderlands of Culture* (2006) and *Migrant Imaginaries* (2008), for example, Ramón Saldívar and Alicia Schmidt Camacho, respectively, explore the transnational and global dimensions of Chicana/o culture. Their work theorizes this transnationality as an effect of contemporary economic conditions traceable to the mid-nineteenth century and affecting primarily the laboring classes.

13. "Agrabah" is also the name of the fictional Middle Eastern land in which the Disney movie *Aladdin* (1992) is set, and Ali Ababwa is the name Aladdin uses when he adopts the disguise of a rich prince in order to win Princess Jasmine's hand in marriage.

14. A "testimonio" is a generally oral narrative written by a subjugated or oppressed minority who has usually suffered some kind of political trauma. "Testimonio" is the accepted generic classification used to denote the narratives of Mexican Californians collected by Bancroft and his staff.

1 / *Latinidad* Abroad

1. Bolívar wrote "The Jamaica Letter" in response to inquiries by Henry Cullen, a British resident of the island, after the fall of Venezuela's second republic. Though the letter was addressed to Cullen it speaks to the larger Jamaican British community and was translated into English during Bolívar's exile there (Bushnell 220).

2. "*refugium peccatorum* para peruanos y para argentinos" (292); English citations from Pérez Rosales come from John Polt's translation, edited and introduced by Loveman. Spanish citations come from Casa de las Américas's 1972 edition of *Recuerdos del Pasado*. Page references with two numbers refer first to Loveman's edition then to Casa de Las Américas's edition.

3. "por el desplante y la desfachatada arrogancia"; "en un español barbarizado cuanto disparate se [le] venía al pico de la pluma" (294).

4. "que era desatino estudiar la lengua castellana, porque el castellano era un idioma muerto para la civilización . . . tratónos de entendimientos bobos; nos dijo que, mientras que las musas acarician festivas a los Varela y Echevarría en Buenos Aires, solo se ocupaban en roncar en pierna suelta en Chile" (294–95).

5. Josefina Ludmer makes this argument about Sarmiento and other writers in her study of the "gauchesque" tradition in Argentine literature.

6. An advocate of simplified spelling, Sarmiento often uses his own iconoclastic "i" in place of the standard "y" for "and" and replaces the letter "y" with "i" as the mood strikes.

7. English citations are from Michael Rockland's translation. The Spanish citations are from the version of *Viajes por . . . América* included in *Obras*. Page references with two numbers refer first to the English edition then the Spanish edition.

8. "una descripción ordenada de los Estados Unidos"; "otro camino" (335).

9. "La palabra pasaporte es desconocida en los Estados" (365).

10. "Si la Francia hubiese abolido el pasaporte, habría hecho mas progresos en la libertad que no los ha hecho con medio siglo de revoluciones i sus avanzadas teorías sociales, i en los Estados-Unidos pueden estudiarse los efectos" (367).

11. "conciencia política" (380).

12. "la moral" (381).

13. "Hai un fenómeno que se realiza en los Estados-Unidos [que] no ha sido hasta hoi de una manera precisa establecido" (381).

14. "la asociación, la moral en grande, obrando sobre millones de hombres, entre familias, ciudades, estados I naciones, completada mas tarde por las leyes de humanidad entera" (382).

15. Modeled on the laws of the Iowa territory, the Oregon laws, passed in 1843 and amended in 1845, established the provisional government of the territory. They emerged from a series of public meetings held around communal issues such as the death of one settler without a will and the effects of predatory animals on livestock—hence the name "organic" because the laws developed in response to the needs of the settlers (Dary 110).

16. "Tan llena de expansión i actividad" (443).

17. "parejas de jóvenes de veinte años, abrazados, reposándose el uno en el seno del otro" (349).

18. "Atribuyo a aquellos amores ambulantes . . . la manía de viajar que distingue al yankee" (350).

19. "la Unión fue inundada por millones de mapas de Méjico" (350).

20. "los Yankees"; "*a la hora de ésta*"; "con el dedo puesto en el mapa"; "la topografía , producciones i ventajas del pais" (350).

21. "Yo creo que los Yankees están celosos de las cascada i que la han de ocupar, como ocupan i pueblan los bosques" (436).

22. "Traiame arrobado de dos días atrás la contemplación de la naturaleza, i a veces sorprendía en el fondo de mi corazón un sentimiento extraño, que no habia experimentado" (437).

23. "Enseñar, o escribir qué? Con este idioma que nadie necesita saber!" (437).

24. "El vapor o el convoi del ferrocarril atraviesan bosques primitivos" (346).

25. Crowley offers a fine overview of Sarmiento's political life, though Rockland's introduction is far more analytical. Both are geared toward North American audiences.

26. "los animalitos mas inciviles que llevan fraque o paletó debajo del sol" (359).

27. Nearly twenty years after the publication of *Viajes por . . . América*, while serving as Argentine ambassador to the United States, Sarmiento openly critiqued U.S. expansion. In an 1865 speech to the Rhode Island Historical Society titled "North and South America," Sarmiento asserted that the Monroe Doctrine had "lost its sanctity and ceased to be a protective barrier of separation to become in itself a threat." He saw the United States casting "shadows" of itself across the globe rather than working in true partnership with the South, West, North, and Europe (in Rockland 43).

28. "La libertad emigrada al nórte da al hombre que llega alas para volar; ruedan torrentes humanos por entre las selvas primitivas, i la palabra pasa muda por sobre sus cabezas en hilos de hierro, para ir a activar a lo léjos aquella invasión del hombre sobre el suelo que le estaba reservado" (340).

29. "aburrirse santamente en el hogar doméstico. La mujer ha dicho adiós para siempre al mundo de cuyos placeres gozó tanto tiempo con entera libertad. . . . En adelante, el cerrado asilo doméstico es su penitenciaria perpetua; el ROASTBEEF su acusador eterno; el hormiguero de chiquillos rubios i retozones, su torcedor continuo" (349).

30. "Las mujeres norte-americanas pertenecen todas a una misma clase, con tipos de fisonomía que por lo general honran a la especie humana" (351).

31. "la llaga profunda i la fístula incurable que amenaza gangrenar el cuerpo robusto de la Union" (490).

32. "bosques primitivos" (346).

33. "el alma de la sociedad que la esplota" (490).

34. "como el agua frotando las superficies angulosas de diversas piedras conforma los guijarros cual si fueran una familia de hermanos" (340).

35. "que ni los cadáveres entrega de sus víctimas" (432).

36. "descollando blanquecino" (431).

37. See John-Michael Rivera for more on Zavala's journalism (33) and early education (32).

38. "¡Oh Niágara! . . . yo veía en ti la representación más melancólica de nuestras desastrosas revoluciones. Yo leía en la sucesión de tus olas, las generaciones que corren a la eternidad; y en las cataratas que preceden a tu abismo, los esfuerzos de unos hombres que impelen a los otros para sucederlos en sus lugares" (256). Unless otherwise noted, all English citations come from Wallace Woolsey's 2005 translation of Zavala's *Viajes*, included in Arte Público's bilingual edition, and will be cited parenthetically. Spanish citations come from this same edition. Page references with two numbers refer first to the English edition and then to the Spanish version.

39. "Muy débil barrera es el Niágara y los lagos para evitar que el Canadá sea un día parte de los Estados Unidos del Norte" (255).

40. "En la primera murió hace poco, un maniático llamado Sam Patch, que se entretenía en saltar cataratas. . . . Me acuerdo haber oído de un tal Rodríguez, igualmente maniático de Mérida de Yucatán, que andaba continuamente en las torres de las iglesias y en los más elevados edificios, saltando con admirable agilidad, y que murió en una de sus empresas" (342).

41. "En ningún pueblo del globo hay tan grande cantidad de periódicos proporcionalmente a la población, que en los Estados Unidos del Norte . . . en donde los que pretenden dirigir los negocios públicos. . . . procuran mantener el monopolio del pensamiento, y oponen obstáculos al progreso intelectual de sus conciudadanos" (270).

42. "perturbar la paz" (220).

43. "legislador filósofo" (336).

44. My translation; "la prostitución de la religión en usos de la política secular ha producido muchos prejuicios" (271).

45. Here Zavala responds directly to public praise of the United States by his contemporaries, which Rivera describes (38).

46. "El modelo era sublime; pero inimitable . . . jamás se llegan a igualar aquellas sublimes concepciones." "Los artistas originales no copian . . . inventan" (390).

47. Mexal offers a thought-provoking discussion of Zavala's grappling with "liberalism's ambivalence towards itself" (89).

48. "Esta situación es poco natural en un país donde se profesan los principios de la más amplia libertad" (287).

49. "Y qué diremos de las de los indios en Chalma, en Guadalupe y en los otros santuarios. . . . ¡Ah! la pluma se cae de la mano para no exponer a la vista del mundo civilizado, una turba de idólatras . . . que vienen a entregar en manos de frailes holgazanes el fruto de sus trabajos anuales" (234).

50. "estigmas naturales" (339). Zavala refers to neither Finley nor the ACS directly, writing only of "the famous society founded about thirty years ago with the

philosophical object of redeeming slaves and sending them to Liberia, the name given to a colony established on the coast of Africa to receive these unfortunate beings" (141; "la célebre sociedad establecida hace cerca de treinta años, cuyo objeto filosófica es redimir esclavos y envirarlos a *Liveria*, nombre dado a una colonia establecida en la costa de África para recibir estos seres desgraciados" [338]).

51. "noble y belicoso"; "el aguardiente y la pólvora"; "El cristianismo es el solo beneficio que los indios han recibido de los blancos"; "sublime"; "pero los pobres indios deben desconfiar de un don de que viene de tales gentes" (261).

52. "colores muy buenos, ojos vivaces y grandes, manos y pies bien formados" (278).

53. "una fisonomía muy espiritual" (309).

54. "respetable anciano" (238).

55. "carácter tan frío y circunspecto" (350). As a representative of the Mexican government, Zavala had personal, social, and convivial interactions with these three men, all of whom who entertained Zavala in their homes.

56. Citations with two page numbers refer first to the English translation, then to the original Spanish.

57. "en la enorme distancia que existe entre las capacidades materiales y mentales de ambos países" (336).

58. "*Campos Meetings*" (231).

59. "Muriate de sosa, carbonate de sosa, carbonate de cal, carbonate de magnesia, y carbonate de hierro" (263).

60. "Qué cosa al parecer más racional y útil que el establecimiento de sociedades, cuyo objeto sea el predicar y dar ejemplos de sobriedad y templanza?" (340).

61. "Muy frecuentes son las muertes repentinas todos los médicos convienen en que mezcladas con un poco de aguardiente no causan tan funestos efectos" (341).

62. "Generalmente, son pálidos y no representan una salud muy lozana. Parece que así debe ser contrariando la más fuerte inclinación de la naturaleza humana" (346). The Shakers were a millenarian group that established communal farms as well as a distinctive style of visual and performance folk art in the United States beginning in the eighteenth century. Their popularity peaked during the 1840s but steadily declined in the latter half of the nineteenth century due to a variety of factors, not the least among which was their insistence on celibacy and opposition to childbearing.

63. "No es cierto que mezcladas las castas jamás desaparecerían sus estigmas naturales" (339).

64. Though science has since disproved the miasmic theory, its proponents did create the idea of public health and public sanitation in urban centers. For more on this, see Mary Poovey and Martin Melosi.

65. "Desgraciadamente Nueva-Orleans es incurablemente enferma"; "mata a los que no huyen del seno de la cuidad"; "contajio" (492).

66. "los individuos acomodados"; "calor . . . excesivo" (222).

67. "Una vegetación parásita que la colonización inglesa ha dejado pegada al árbol frondoso de las libertades americanas" (491).

68. "una nación negra atrasada i vil, al lado de otra blanca" (491).

69. "un joven indio de la tribu de los crecks, llamado Moniac, ocupaba un lugar distinguido entre los estudiantes" (382).

70. George Luis Leclerc, Compte de Buffon, was a French naturalist, best known for his multivolume *Histoire naturelle* (1749–1809), in which he asserted that New World

versions of transatlantic mammals were both smaller and weaker than their European counterparts. In 1785 Thomas Jefferson replied to Buffon with *Notes on the State of Virginia*, a compendium of political, natural, and ethnographic history designed to refute Buffon's claims of American inferiority.

71. "una generación nueva"; "enteramente heterogénea"; "un engaño, una ilusión, sino una realidad" (276).

72. "por los otros Estados hacia el sudoeste, y los de Tamaulipas; Nuevo León, San Luís, Chihuahua, Durango, Jalisco, Zacatecas" (276).

73. David Montejano's is the classic historical study in the field, upon which José Limón and Leticia Garza-Falcón have built considerably in cultural studies with *Dancing with the Devil* and *Gente Decente,* respectively.

74. Pérez Rosales responds primarily to the Foreign Miners Tax Law of 1850, but similar legislation passed throughout the decade, including series of anti-vagrancy acts, known popularly as the "Greaser Laws" for their targeting of specifically Mexican and Latin American customs such as bull fighting, cockfighting, and bear baiting. For more on the Greaser Laws, see Pitt (198).

75. "Por fortuna, a un señor Prendergast se le ocurrió, como medio de recoger otro sin moverse de San Francisco. . . . No sé dónde pudo hacerse de un mapa antiguo del virreinato mexicano, y dando a la sección de la Alta California proporciones sin proporción, inundó la cuidad con croquis que, aunque mal hechos y reducidos a cuartillas de papel de fumar, alcanzaron a venderse a veinticinco pesos cada uno" (392).

76. As historian Hubert Bancroft notes in volume 2 of his *History of California*, the Russians had been trying to establish a trading presence in Northern California since the early nineteenth century and were consistently rebuffed by the Mexican government. The Russians established their Fort Ross near Bodega Bay in 1812 and proceeded to poach extensively and trade with native groups in the region. Bancroft argues that though this practice angered the Californios it most likely kept native violence in check (2:299). Governor Echeandía had granted otter-hunting contracts to the Russians in the 1820s, but by the 1830s Governor Victoría was refusing to renew those contracts and Russia was threatening to shift its grain purchasing from California to Chile (Bancroft 4:162).

77. "desastrosa" (350).

78. Ralph Bauer offers an excellent and succinct discussion of these in "Hemispheric Racial Genealogies."

79. Spanish and then Mexican Californians originally used the term "greaser" to refer to English and American tallow and hide merchants. Bancroft traces the moniker's origin to traders who, knowing little Spanish, would often ask for tallow by saying, "Señor, mi quiere grease." The English-speaking traders soon returned the moniker to the Californians who sold the grease to them (Bancroft, *California Pastoral*, 290). Platon Vallejo, son of Mexican military commandant Mariano Vallejo, corroborates with a slightly different story: Watchmen along the shore, posted to alert citizens to approaching pirate ships, would call out "Mantequero" upon determining the ship to be a trading vessel. "English-speaking visitors easily coined an equivalent, 'greaser,' which became one of great dignity and honor. To be a 'greaser' meant to be a prosperous, well-inclined, peaceable person, a substantial trader and all-around good fellow. . . . It is somewhat curious how the use of that word has been transposed," he writes (21).

80. "Sonoran" or "Sonoranian" was a term widely used in Northern California at the time to refer to persons from the northwestern Mexican states of Sonora and Sinaloa (Pitt 53). The original Spanish read: "En éste, como en mis anteriores encuentros con sonoreños y con californeses españoles, tuve ocasión de maravillarme del candor con que discurren estas pobres gentes, cuando se trata de la invasión y dominio de los yanquis en su patria. Creen que ellos no pueden expulsar a los que hasta ahora califican con justicia de tiranos; pero también creen, y a puño cerrado, que, vista le enérgica resistencia de los chilenos, si quisieron, podían expulsarlos" (481).

81. Wealthy, white-identified Mexican Californians referred to themselves as *californios*.

82. "Un chileno veterano de los diggings, en esas alturas era el símbolo de la seguridad individual, el espantajo de las tropelías del yanqui y el hermano a quien debíase siempre tender la mano" (484).

83. Both Faugsted (33) and Giacobbi (20) corroborate Pérez Rosales's assertions of Chilean status, as well as their superior mining skills (Faugsted 24; Giacobbi 19).

84. "ese descendiente de africano, como llamaban los yanquis a los chileno y a los españoles" (374).

85. The Hounds were a makeshift police force composed of the "most unsavory elements" of a disbanded group of New York volunteers brought to California during the Mexican-American War (Bancroft, *Popular Tribunals* 78).

86. Members of the Hounds, who had by this time begun to refer to themselves as the Society of Regulators—though Bancroft notes that a more appropriate title might have been "Society for the Promotion of Vice" or "Hell-fire Club" (*Popular Tribunals* 90)—were tried by a citizens' court on charges of aggravated assault and destruction of property. Most were found guilty and either fined or banished from San Francisco (Giacobbi 37).

87. "Vino a poner el colmo a los desafueros que se cometieron contra los pacíficos e indefensos chilenos. . . . Hacíanse un argumento sencillo y concluyente: el chileno era hijo español, el español tenía sangre mora, luego el chileno debía ser por lo menos hotentote, o, muy piadosamente hablando, algo de muy semejante al humillado y tímido californés" (457).

88. "El amo jetudo"; "nieto de africana" (478).

89. "el número de los asociados para la mutua defensa o de la superioridad de las armas que cargaba el agredido" (447).

90. See note 74.

91. "los mamarrachos más positivos" (489).

92. "de taparse cuidadosamente la boca con el pañuelo de embozo al aspirar el humo, y de descubrirla al arrojarlo" (486).

93. "broceadas éstas para los de afuera" (462).

94. "nadie se fijaba que lo que valía ciento en el interior, casi se regalaba en San Francisco" (463).

95. "fingió no conocerme, ni aun conocer el español" (465).

96. "que no sólo la embarcación era pura sangre, sino que hasta su mismo nombre lo era, porque en vez de decir *Infatigable*, como los bárbaros mexicanos que no saben el inglés la pronunciaban, debía decirse *Impermeable*" (466).

97. "Y el bribón decía . . . que habia estado poco tiempo en Chile, cuando habia encanecido en él" (466); "el cartelón de su casa" (465).

98. "el bueno Decano" (441).

99. "Quien hubiera recorrido las pampa argentinas, metido de repente en un rancho californés, creería sin duda que se encontraba mudando caballos en una de las postas de aquel desierto" (413).

100. "un país semibárbaro a causa de su vida excepcional" (443).

101. "signo de civilización" (451).

102. "Heroico sacrificio" (438).

103. "Los intrusos extranjeros que no les dejaban quietud en parte alguna" (436).

104. Vallejo refers to the bulk of unsavory characters immigrating to California as "Chileans" (V. 178/222), reflecting *californio* animosity toward Chile over Russia's use of Chile as leverage in the negotiations over otter contracts (see note 76). But Vallejo also succumbs to the general vilification of Chileans as vessels of vice and immorality.

105. In *Divergent Modernities*, Julio Ramos describes the *letrado* who inhabited a republic of letters in which literature and law were intimately related, both creating and patrolling national borders. *Modernismo*, on the other hand, led in Ramos's analysis by Cuban exile José Martí, sought to undermine the *letrados'* homogenizing project. Ramos is not the first to argue that *modernismo* emerges in response to social modernization, urbanization, and Latin America's entrance into world markets; but Ramos asserts that Martí located literature's authority in its position outside the political sphere (Ramos xix).

106. Darío is the acknowledged leader of the *modernista* movement. See Ramos for more on Martí as a *modernista* writer.

2 / *Mexicanidad* at Home

1. These epigraphs come from the Madie Brown Empáran Papers, held at Sonoma State Historic Park. Empáran served on the California State Parks Commission and oversaw the acquisition of fifty-two state parks as well as the designation of the Vallejo home, which she curated, as a state historic landmark. In 1965, at the age of seventy-six, Empáran married Mariano Vallejo's grandson Ricardo. Together, the Empárans catalogued, transcribed, and translated hundreds of family letters into fifty-seven dated binders that now form part of Empáran's papers. The original letters are difficult to track as the researcher must rely on Empáran's relatively thorough, but often incomplete, bibliographic style. Where possible I have included the original Spanish, but in most cases I rely on Empáran's translations.

2. Vallejo donated all of his official correspondence and documents to Bancroft's library but kept a large portion of his personal papers for himself, a collection that grew until his death twenty years after his donation. This collection is housed in the Sonoma Barracks, which Vallejo and his men built, along with the Mission Solano, around what later became Sonoma's central plaza. It is currently maintained and curated by the California State Department of Parks and Recreation.

3. For example, in a letter to his wife, Francisca, dated March 20, 1865, from the Fifth Avenue hotel, Vallejo writes: "This city of New York is a town in which everyone walks, goes and comes in the streets without recognizing or talking to one another; and the hubbub and confusion is such and the noise so great that one talks in shouts to be heard."

4. Prieto (1818–97) was a Mexican Romantic writer, journalist, politician, and co-founder, in 1836, of the Academia Letrán, a forum for romantic writers.

5. Vallejo to Platon, March 19, 1879: "Hoy en Méjico muy poca gentes de nuestras, los españoles que allí existen los ven." (Today in Mexico you see very few of our people, the Spaniards, though they do live here.)

6. Vallejo to Francisca, August 20, 1877: "La ciudad de Méjico contiene trescientos mil habitantes y de esas mismas hay doscientos sesenta mil indios, que infestan las calles." (Three hundred thousand people live in Mexico City; 260,000 of them are Indians who infest the streets.)

7. Hippolyte Bouchard was a French ex-patriot sailing under the Argentine flag. He landed his ships at Monterey in 1818 with the aim of convincing, by force if necessary, the *californios* to join in revolt against Spain. Vallejo, then eleven years old, was evacuated along with his mother and siblings to Mission Soledad, returning after a week to find their homes looted and destroyed (Rosenus, 6–7).

8. Supplies from Mexico were inconsistent as well as insufficient for the troops in Alta California. After a long dry spell in 1829 soldiers became restless; they had not been paid for several months, their uniforms were in tatters, and they were hungry. A group of rebels took Vallejo, Juan Alvarado, José Castro, and several other officers hostage until Governor Echeandía intervened. The event was formative for Vallejo not only in terms of strengthening his views on Mexico's poor administration; Echeandía sent him to San Diego until tensions could blow over, and on this mission Vallejo met his future wife, Francisca Carillo (Comstock, 35–37).

9. In 1866, Vallejo, along with Victor Castro and Augustin Alvarado, gave money, arms, and a ship to Placido Vega, who had been appointed special commissioner by the Mexican government to secure foreign aid in defense of Mexico against the French, who had installed Emperor Maximilian in Mexico City in 1864 (Castro 2). In August 1866 their ship landed in Sinaloa, and Vallejo's son Uladislao marched with Vega six hundred miles inland to personally deliver the weapons to exiled President Benito Juárez (Castro 6). Mexico had granted Castro, Alvarado, and Vallejo a large tract of land on the eastern shore of the Gulf of California. When Mexico failed to survey said land, or ratify the grant, the Californians sued unsuccessfully for its dollar value.

10. A letter to his daughter Adela dated August 30, 1877, from Mexico City illustrates this: "Now I will tell you something of this city, so celebrated amongst lovers of our history. The ancient Spaniards, our true ancestors, founded it 356 years ago, and the years passed until 1821 [Mexican independence from Spain], a date commemorated with great, monumental buildings; [but] since 1821 nothing has been done to improve those buildings." ("Ahora te diré algo de ésta ciudad tan famosa en los amantes de nuestra historia. Los antiguos españoles, nuestros verdaderos progenitores, la fundaron hace ya 356 años, y siguieron los años hasta 1821 edificándola, con grandes edificios monumentales [pero] desde [1821] nada nada había mejorado sus edificios"; my translation.)

11. Jay Cooke, an American financier who invented war bonds during the U.S. Civil War, was also heavily invested in railroads. His holdings were overextended, and his financial collapse caused a domino effect to ripple through U.S. industries as companies reliant upon his capital folded in his wake.

12. This letter well exemplifies the pitfalls of working with Empáran's papers. Though she includes a large section of this letter in her book (139), a history of the Vallejos told through chapters devoted to the letters of each member of the immediate family, she leaves out Vallejo's pretended insanity. The book includes no index, and I

have been unable to locate the original letter, though this translation was cataloged in Empáran's binders.

13. To a Mexican reporter from the *Monitor Republican*, a Mexican paper, interviewing Vallejo about his seeking rail concessions from Mexican president Porfirio Díaz, Vallejo has this to say about his identity: "I am an American because the treaty of Guadalupe placed me on the other side of the line, dividing the two nations, but I was born a Mexican; my ancestors were Mexican and I have always maintained with my sword the honor of Mexico. I have both Mexican and American children and I desire for my native land all the prosperity and progress enjoyed by the country of some of my children and mine by adoption" (in Empáran 141).

14. Drawing on John Beverley's work, Sánchez defines *testimonio* as a "first-person narration of a marginalized individual . . . who . . . participates in some significant historical experience. [They tell their story with] a certain urgency, [from a] collective and marginal [perspective, and the resulting text is] the collaborative product of an informant and a professional interviewer" (11). According to Sánchez, the dependent construction of the *californio testimonios* distinguishes them from autobiography, particularly because they were constructed within the dominant power relationships of Anglo interviewers and Mexican informants (8).

15. The Treaty of Guadalupe-Hidalgo, which ended the Mexican-American War in 1848, secured land titles granted by the Spanish and Mexican governments. In 1850 California was admitted to the United States as a state, and in 1851 the U.S. Congress passed the California Land Act. Historians are near unanimous in their opinion that this law—which required claimants to prove their titles before the Board of U.S. Land Commissioners and set up arcane and complicated rules for doing so—flagrantly defied the treaty and was a legalistic ruse to wrest land out of Mexican and into Anglo hands. The act required claimants to prove their title before the board with suitable documentation, which was hard to do since many Spanish and Mexican titles were vaguely worded, or not worded at all, having been passed down orally from generation to generation. The board—after a lengthy deliberation often lasting years, during which time Mexican owners were still required to pay taxes on their land and land improvements performed by squatters illegally occupying their land—would then pass judgment on the title and the claimant could choose to pursue the claim further. Many Mexican Californian families, including the Vallejos, lost their lands to the board and their fortunes to lawyers who often charged outrageous fees to help the Mexicans navigate the complicated laws of the United States. Bancroft concludes in *History of California* that "seven-eighths of all the claimants before the commission were virtually robbed by the government. . . . As a rule, they lost nearly all their possessions in the struggle before successive tribunals. . . . The lawyers took immense fees in land and cattle, often for slight services or none at all. . . . The estates passed for the most part into the hands of speculators who were shrewd enough and rich enough to keep them" (VI:576). Mexicans in Arizona, New Mexico, and Texas were subjected to similar treatment. The families having lost their fortunes, the sons and daughters of the once wealthy, powerful, and respected *californios* were left to fend for themselves and so entered the labor force in increasingly proletarian and menial jobs. The effects of the Land Commission are described in excruciating detail in Maria Amparo Ruiz de Burton's 1885 novel *The Squatter and the Don*, the main character of which—Don Mariano—was based on Vallejo. A thorough account of the Land Commission can

be found in volume 6 of Bancroft's *History of California*, Leonard Pitt's *Decline of the Californios* (1966), and Tómas Almaguer's *Racial Fault Lines* (1994).

16. Alan Rosenus's excellent biography *General Vallejo and the Advent of the Americans* provides multiple examples of this view of Vallejo, including Vallejo's dispute with his nephew Juan Alvarado, governor of California in 1841 during the negotiations with Russia over the fate of Fort Ross. Vallejo, going against the wishes of Mexico's president Bustamente, wanted permission to purchase the fort in order to prevent the Russians from dealing with the Americans. Alvarado felt his uncle was merely trying to consolidate his own power and refused to grant permission (26).

17. For a detailed discussion of these changes see Almaguer, chapter 1, "'We Desire Only a White Population in California': The Transformation of Mexican California in Historical-Sociological Perspective," and Leonard Pitt's *Decline of the Californios*, specifically chapter 14, "Upheavals—Political and Natural, 1860–1864." For a consideration of California and the West in the broader context of U.S. history, see Robert Cook's *Civil War America: Making a Nation 1848–1877*, especially chapter 8, "The Land of Gold: The Far West in the Mid-Nineteenth Century."

18. Here I am deeply influenced by the work of Michael Omi, Howard Winant, Tomás Almaguer, and Evelyn Nakano Glenn. Their theorizations of race and nation with a U.S. focus have emphasized the symbiotic relationship between economic institutions and ideological concepts such as freedom and citizenship, which has in turn informed notions of race since the country's founding. Michael Omi and Howard Winant's groundbreaking 1986 study *Racial Formation in the United States* argues powerfully that race and racism are historical constructs that change over time. They are not only fundamental external structures that shape our identities but also integral parts of U.S. institutions. Building on their work, in *Racial Faultlines* (1994) Tomás Almaguer shows how post-1848 westward migration "forged a new pattern of racialized relationships between conquerors, conquered, and the numerous immigrants that settled in the newly acquired territory" (1). Combining the theoretical revelations of both these studies, Evelyn Nakano Glenn's *Unequal Freedom: How Race and Gender Shaped American Citizenship and Labor* (2002) demonstrates how citizenship is the necessary outgrowth of the tension between universalism and exclusion contained within philosophies of race, gender, and labor, topoi that Nakano Glenn argues cannot be considered in isolation.

19. The *Historical Works* pamphlet goes on to describe this division of labor, as do Bancroft in *Literary Industries*, Oak in *Literary Industries in a New Light*, Sánchez in *Telling Identities*, and countless articles in contemporary journals of Bancroft's day.

20. "Es muy possible que el Sr. Bancroft encuentre 'que los datos que U. le ha enviado estan en choque con cuanto han escrito otras personas'; pero ¿que hacer amigo mio? Todo cuanto he informado á U. estoy dispuesto á probarlo con documentos fehacientes y autógrafos que corroboren mis asertos. Se trata de la historia de este país (Alta California) y es necesario ser verídico é imparcial, haciendome ésto recordas las palabras de Ciceron que decía: 'la historia es el testigo de los tiempos, la vista de la memoria, la luz de la verdad, el mensajero de la antigüedad.'" (Unless otherwise noted, all translations are my own; all misspellings appear in the original Spanish.)

21. Henry Oak, Bancroft's head librarian, describes the various controversies that plagued Bancroft and his *Works* in his memoir *"Literary Industries" in a New Light: A Statement of the Authorship of Bancroft's Native Races and History of the Pacific States* (12–18).

22. In his biography *Hubert Howe Bancroft: Historian of the West*, James Caughey gives a full account of these claims (266–70). Caughey recounts how Frances Fuller Victor took out notices in Oregon and Utah papers asserting that she was responsible for Bancroft's volumes on the region. At the San Francisco Winter Fair of 1893 Victor displayed four volumes of the work with her name inserted on the title page as author. Similarly, Henry Oak donated ten volumes of the *Works* with his name inserted in the preface to the library at Dartmouth, his alma mater. Oak's memoir, *"Literary Industries" in a New Light*, deals with these claims at length (33–55). Rosaura Sánchez describes these controversies as well (17–20).

23. The Society of California Pioneers launched a very public, aggressive campaign against Bancroft, ultimately revoking his honorary membership in the society. In its proceedings for November 1893, the society writes, "Bancroft, in his so-called 'History of California' has, within the personal knowledge and recollection of many of the old pioneers here present, distorted the facts and truths of such history, and maligned the memory of many of the men most conspicuous as participants in these early events" (6). At issue is Bancroft's portrayal of Frémont as "a 'filibuster,' whose almost every act in California was a wrong from beginning to end" (7). The society claims that Bancroft's portrait of Frémont is both unsupported and evidence of his "apologetic efforts to present the case in the strongest possible pro-Mexican and anti-American spirit" (15).

24. "pues el dice que la historia debe escribirse despacio y no a la yankee sentado sobre el caballo."

25. "yo ni he tenido, ni tengo la intencion ni el deseo de deviarme de la verdad."

26. "Mas yo no me propongo otro fin si no legar á la posteridad una historia exacta de los hechos tales cuales han acontecido, y en que cada actor, cada pueblo, y cada ciudad figuren segun sus proprios meritos." The translation in the text is Hewitt's; all citations from the *Recuerdos* will read as follows: volume:manuscript page/typescript translation page.

27. "compendio de la verdadura historia de California" (Hewitt translation).

28. "que la historia debe ser tal cual Ciceron la pintó 'lux veritatis, atque testigo temporum.'"

29. "es el reflejo de los hechos, modo de pensar y costumbres regian entre nosotros en 1815."

30. "[E]staba reservado á los norte Americanos cambiar el nombre de ese lugar y llamar á la 'punta de Quintín' '*punta de San Quintín*'; qual sea el motivo que haya inducido á los norte Americanos efectuar tal cambio, lo desconosco, pero creo que puede atribuirse al hecho que habiendo gran numero de ellos llegado á California con la creencia de que los habitantes de este país eran sumamente católicos, con el fin de congraciarse con ellos añadian 'san' á los nombres de los pueblos ó aldeas que visitaban. Recuerdo haber en distintos occasiones oidecir 'Santa Sonoma,' 'San Monterey,' y 'San Branciforte' y guiados por esa costumbre le añadieron el *San* al nombre de Quintín; sobre esa conducta no hago comentaría, pues admito el dicho latino 'de gustibus non est disputandum.' Si 'punta de San Quintín' les agrada mas que el simple 'punta de Quintín' que se queden con su fantasma y su santo, seguro que yo no se los envidio."

31. "Tengo aun presente el brindis del señor Echeandía, y creo oportuno reproducarlo, pues aunque desde entonces han transcurrido cuarenta y tres años todavia lo recuerdo con placer" (Hewitt translation).

32. "Los décimas son pesimas, no tienen ningun merito literario pero á Buelna le acarrearon tranquilidad politica y doméstica; esta prueba lo bien fundado que era el antiguo refrán latino 'parva saepe neglecta scintilla magnum excitavit incendium'" (Hewitt translation).

33. "ha sido causa de tres cuartas de las revoluciones que durante los últimos cinquenta años han asolado Méjico y las demas repúblicas de Sur y Centro América."

34. "Estando el cautivo, relegó al olvido sus gloriosos antecedents, reconocío la independencia de Tejas, y á mayor mengua de la República Mexicana se humiló al gobierno de los Estados Unidos que en despecho de los tratados existents con una república hermana habian azuzado la rebellion de una parte de sus ciudadanos contra el jefe de la República."

35. "[P]odrian juzgar de la manera como ese documento haya influido en el bien estar de la república mexicana, que durante el transcuro de los últimos cuarente y siete años ha sido tantas veces juguete de los muras ambiciosas de algunos hijos rénegados que sordos al grito de angustia . . . hicieron sin cesar y sin piedad las entrañas de la madre patria que á ellos debe sus angustias y quebrantos todos."

36. "estudiamente se mantenia en la barabrria é ignorancia."

37. "todo el fervor de [su] alma repúblicana . . . hacen alarde publicamente de su desenfreno y desprecío de la buena opinion de las personas virtuosas." Governor Chico, according to Vallejo, had left his wife in Mexico and was living with a "mujer libertina" (a libertine) whom Vallejo admits is very beautiful. Though he feels sympathy for those "que sucumben á los ataques de Venus" (succumb to Venusian attacks), Vallejo feels such behavior is unacceptable in a public official.

38. "llevan impreso mas bien el sello de la locura que lo del patriotismo."

39. "Pero eso no debe causar admiración pues sabido es que los Presidentes de la República Mexicana solo se acordaban de California cuando algunos los visitaban personalmente ó bien por conducto de nuestro disputado haciamos llegar a sus manos alguna carta ó regalo."

40. "en su mayor parte, sujetos desnudos de toda clase de atributos que tienen tendencia á enoblecer á los mandatarios."

41. "California es libre, y cortará todas sus relaciones con Mejico hasta que deja de ser oprimido por la actual faccion dominante titulada gobierno central" (Hewitt translation).

42. "como escritor imparcial me incumbe descorrer el velo de los motibos que indujieron al erudito pero mal inencionado poeta á calumniar a los vencendores de Guttiérrez" (Hewitt translation).

43. The contradictions of liberalism evident in Zavala (Mexal).

44. "Californio nacido en este bello país que pertenecía á la República Mejicana."

45. See note 13, for example.

46. Sánchez discusses the Hijar-Padrés colony at length and reads the conflict as hinging on a struggle for political power. In her analysis, the *californios* were threatened by possible usurpation on the part of the colonists (131). While this was indeed true for some, Vallejo's problems with the colony run deeper, torn as he is between a vestigial patriotism and a desire for economic development. Further, such a reading as Sánchez's privileges local concerns over Vallejo's global aspirations for Alta California.

47. "La llegada de tanta gente forastera llenó de contento á nosotros los arribeños,

que veiamos con sumo agrado que desde el otro lado de la Sierra Nevada vineron á sentar sus reales entre nosotros numerosas companias de gente industriosa."

48. "Que lindo hubiese sido, si la decantada ilustracíon que los Americanos del norte han traido á California no hubiese pervertido nuestros patriarcales costumbres, y relajado la moralidad de la joventud."

49. "un pueblo esencialmente fanfarron [que tienen] el ser palanzana [como] su segunda naturaleza y [por quien] es muy difficil que en pais estranjero olviden las costumbres de su patria que son tan distintas de los de los démas pueblos."

50. "instrumentos de una politica estranjera" (Hewitt translation).

51. "la civilizacíon europea á pasos agigantados se [los] estaba viniendo encima" (Hewitt translation).

52. "En el breve transcuro de tiempo en que la Alta California permanecío separada del gobierno de la madre patria que tanto nos habia oprimido . . . brindose . . . á los ciudadanos del universo un campo extenso para prosperar á la sombra de leyes sabias y previsoras."

53. "los que sentimos mas immediamente estos males nos empreñemos en el remedia si es que estamos animado de un vivo deseo por la prosperidad nacional y tenemos cuenta asi mismo con nuestros particulares intereses."

54. "No hacer la felicidad de las naciones las muchas leguas de estension, pero si la hacen la población y el orden; . . . son mas utiles á los Estados los sabios establecimientos que la conquista y . . . el formetno es el alma se la subsistencia y no el regimen coactivo."

55. "se hubiese llevado á debido efecto hubiese dado al Puerto de Monterey gran importancia maritima" (Hewitt translation).

56. Article clipped from the December 12, 1877, edition (Empáran Papers).

3 / Racialized Bodies and the Limits of the Abstract

1. Both Polk and Roosevelt made these assertions during their annual messages to Congress, Polk in 1845, and Roosevelt in 1904, in what has since come to be known as the Roosevelt Corollary to the Monroe Doctrine, characterizing his aggressive, "Big Stick" approach to Latin America.

2. Antonio de León y Gama discovered this statue, now on display at the Museo Nacional de Antropología in Mexico City, in 1790.

3. Tiffany Ana López, for example, places Mena in a position similar to that of the Mexicanos viewed from a train window in an ad for the Santa Fe railway that ran in the November 1912 issue of *The Century,* a year before Mena began publishing there. The ad emphasizes the train's service, and López connects this idea of customer service to "what the Mexicano will *naturally* provide" (28) in the hierarchy of race and class. López notes that "Mena herself was implicated in this system of service for the pleasure of Anglo viewers in her role as a commissioned 'authentic' Mexican voice" (28), pointing out that Mena is producing these images of Mexico for the same customers who will presumably purchase the train tickets advertised.

4. Doña Rita reads about Alegría's death in *El Imparcial,* the same Mexico City paper Turner mentions as publishing a picture of the Sonoran governor Rafael Ysabel laughing over a pile of hands chopped from Yaqui arms during a removal in 1902 (Turner 31).

5. Both Julio Moreno, in *Yankee Don't Go Home!* and Helen Delpar, in *The*

Enormous Vogue of Things Mexican, discuss this flourishing cross-border economic and cultural exchange.

6. Gabriela Ventura offers a comprehensive overview and history of *cronista* misogyny, as well as a literary history of female *cronistas* such as María Luisa Garza and Catalina Escalante.

7. My translation from the original Spanish, which reads: "deben ponerse con su agrupación al frente de las demás sociedades mexicanas, como guiadores hacia un porvenir de activa solidaridad y verdadero patriotismo para todos los exilados" (in Kanellos, "Introducción" xv).

8. My translation from the original Spanish, which reads: "también los periodistas son trabajadores" (in Kanellos, "Introducción" xv).

9. "allí lo tenéis, gozando de la primera humillación que los gringos obligan a sufrir a los emigrantes mexicanos" (27). Unless otherwise noted, English citations from *Don Chipote* come from Arte Público's 2000 edition, translated by Ethriam Brammer; Spanish citations come from the same press's 1998 release.

10. My translation. "y don Chipote no daba más señales de vida que los acordes de bajo mi bemol que dejaba escapar por la boca y uno que otro por el conductor privado" (28).

11. "no era de muy bien calidad" (16).

12. "¡Si vieras que demonios son los gringos! Por acá hay unas cosas que hasta Sufrelambre se queda con la boca abierta!" (69).

13. References with two page numbers refer first to the Spanish then to the English edition.

14. "un apodo muy chistoso que yo no entiendo bien, creo que es 'gaideme' 'sanabagan'" (69).

15. "El que esto escribe que, en época no muy lejana, al igual que la mayoría de los que vienen de México, tuvo que meterle al famoso traque, se dio cuenta exacta de los abusos que los mayordomos cometen con las trabajadores" (64).

16. "aquel mayordomo nos hizo sacar la lengua, trabajándanos a lo desesperado" (64).

17. "de estos Pitacios están llenos los estados unidos" (20).

18. "la chicanada . . . y es por eso, más que por las malas condiciones en que la revolución he puesto al país, por lo que cada día se despuebla más y más" (20).

19. "¿Podrá haber más maldad que la de estos malditos que por pasar por gringos, se niegan a hablar su proprio idioma renegando hasta del país donde nacieron? . . . De estos renegados . . . es de donde salen los más duros epítetos para nosotros" (43–44).

20. "cholo"; "zurumato"; "cosas suyas para zaherir a los recién llegados de México" (44). "Zurumato" is Mexican slang for "stupid"; "cholo" has taken on slang connotations in the twenty-first-century United States, referring to working-class Mexican Americans who are not necessarily but often assumed to be gangsters. Throughout the Americas "cholo" is used in its original capacity as an indicator of mixed (Anglo and native) race.

21. "la peor astilla para el bracero mexicano" (42).

22. "dark-skinned gringo" (52); see note 20 for the etymology of "cholo."

23. "una pelona que sirve las mesas en el mismo restaurante" (122); a "pelona" is, literally, a bald person and refers here to the flapper's bobbed hair.

24. "al que por lo general acude toda la palomilla chicanesca" (147).

25. "los mexicanos harán ricos en Estados Unidos: CUANDO LOS PERICOS MAMEN" (159).

26. "una gargantilla casi en cueros menores" (111). Venegas's use of "gargantilla"— literally a necklace, or choker—instead of "cantante" (singer) implies that the woman is a poor singer. "Gargantilla" is related to the English "gargle" ("hacer gárgaras" in Spanish), which shares a root with "gargoyle" ("gárgola"). The singer here is both ugly and untalented.

27. "era algo del otro mundo" (112).

28. "la chicanada se pone de puntas cuando le ponen por enfrente algo que le recuerde su santa nopalera" (113).

29. "chorros de atole" (112); *atole* is a traditional Mexican drink made primarily from cornmeal, cinnamon, and sugar.

4 / More Life in the Skeleton

1. Though González went by González de Mireles after her marriage, and Eve Raleigh is a pseudonym for Margaret Eimer, I refer to the two as González and Raleigh because they used those names on their manuscript's title page.

2. As Limón notes in his introduction to *Caballero*, very little is known about Eimer. Extensive archival research has turned up little documentary evidence pertaining to her, save for one, uninformative letter she wrote to González in 1946 (Limón xviii). Scholarship on *Caballero* has dwelt mostly on González, at times treating the novel as a single-authored text, in part because González was already a known quantity in Chicana/o studies but also because of the paucity of information regarding Eimer. Though I discuss the novel as jointly authored, I have no light to shed on the Margaret Eimer/Eve Raleigh mystery.

3. Texas A&M University Press published this thesis, edited by María Cotera, as *Life Along the Border: A Landmark Tejana Thesis*, in 2006.

4. For in-depth information about González's biography, see Leticia Garza-Falcón's *Gente Decente* and José Limón's *Dancing with the Devil*.

5. There are, however, important distinctions to be made between González's and Hurston's ethnographic turn. As María Cotera notes in *Native Speakers*, a compelling examination of the connections between the Harlem Renaissance and González's work, Franz Boas, the father of modern anthropology under whom Hurston studied, was significantly more invested in scientific method and anthropological rigor than was Dobie, who freely blurred the boundaries between himself and his subjects and took broad liberties with his ethnographic data. Hurston's turn from Boas to fiction is easier to parse than González's novelistic turn away from what could be arguably described as novelistic ethnography.

6. Daphne Lamothe describes the New Negro artists as modernists who grapple with the changeability of racial knowledge and thus reflect "the larger sense of instability and uncertainty that characterizes U.S. society in the interwar years" (3). They take issue with the idea of an objective anthropology and instead show truth to be "multiply unfolding and composed of a constellation of interconnected concepts and experiences" (3).

7. *Lotería* is a Mexican game of chance, similar to bingo, its U.S. counterpart. Unlike the lettered and numbered squares used in bingo, *lotería* boards have pictures of iconic figures like *La Sirena* (the mermaid), *La Muerte* (death), and *El Marinero* (the

sailor), whose cards are drawn by a caller, just as lettered and numbered markers are drawn in bingo. *Lotería* cards can also be used, like tarot cards, to tell fortunes.

8. For example, though its official motto is "La unión hace la fuerza" (Unity is strength), the U.S.-based student organization Movimiento Estudiantil Chicano de Aztlán (MEChA), which promotes higher education and progressive social action, has adopted as its unofficial slogan a version of the motto Vasconcelos decreed for Mexico's National University in 1921. Vasconcelos's motto reads "Por mi raza hablará el espiritu" (Through my race the spirit shall speak; Marentes 75), while MEChA uses "Por mi raza habla el espiritu" (The spirit speaks through my race).

9. See, for example, José Limón's introduction to the published novel and Garza-Falcón's *Gente Decente*.

10. All "La raza cósmica" citations come from Didier T. Jaén's bilingual edition. References with two page numbers refer first to the Spanish then to the English edition.

11. "troncos: el negro, el indio, el mogol y el blanco" (49).

12. "Pugna de latinidad contra sajonismo ha llegado a ser, sigue siendo, nuestra época; pugna de instituciones, de propósitos y de ideales" (50).

13. "misión transcendental" (49).

14. "en la puerilidad de la descripción de los utensilios y de los indices cefálicos" (48).

15. "hipótesis transcendentales" (48).

16. "la pueril satisfacción de crear nacionitas y soberanías de principado" (55).

17. "reincorporación del mundo rojo" (49).

18. "Ninguna raza vuelve" (56).

19. "reincorporación del mundo rojo" (49).

20. Don Chipote experiences fumigation and delousing (35/27) in *The Adventures of Don Chipote*, as I discuss in Chapter 3.

21. "que el vigor se renueva con los injertos y que el alma misma busco lo disímil para enriquecer la monotonía de su propio contenido" (73).

22. "una obra de arte"; "la belleza y la alegría regirán la elección de parejas, con el resultado infinitamente superior al de esa eugénica fundada en la razón cientifica que nunca mira más que la porción menos importante del suceso amoroso" (70).

23. "nos ufanamos cada uno de nuestro humilde trapo" (51).

24. "sentimiento creador y belleza que convence" (69).

25. See Chapter 1 for more on France's role in spurring Latin American independence movements. Napoleon's invasion and imprisonment of King Ferdinand VII of Spain created a leadership vacuum in the viceregal governance that Latin American patriots exploited.

26. "eugénica misteriosa del gusto estético"; "passion iluminada" (70).

27. "la ley singular del tercer período, la ley de simpatía, refinada por el sentido de la belleza" (71).

5 / Ana Castillo's "Distinct Place in the Americas"

1. William Prescott (1796–1859) was a New England historian of the Spanish empire whose work has been criticized for its romanticization of native populations. Walter Prescott Webb (no relation to William, 1888–1963) was a Texan historian of the

Great Plains and the American West, as well as director of the Texas State Historical Association (1939–46); his writing "reflects the prejudices of his times against a native population dominated not only by the victors but also by historical representations of those events which had vanquished the former" (Garza-Falcón 25). Likewise, Captain John Gregory Bourke of the U.S. Army was an early border ethnographer whose observations of the 1890s were, according to José Saldívar, an essential part of U.S. imperialism's legitimizing project (161).

2. See Sandoval for more on Santería, a syncretic religious practice emerging from West African, Yoruban slaves brought to the Caribbean.

3. See Gigliozzi and McCaffery for more on Padre Pío, who was beatified in 1999 and canonized in 2002.

4. Matteo da Bascio (figured in the novel as Father Juan Bosco, Gabo's priest) founded the Capuchin in 1525 in protest of Church excess. The Capuchin lived ascetic, hermetic lives grounded in aiding the poor and were named for the hood (*capuchin*, in Italian) attached to their rough-hewn robes ("Capuchin").

5. San Pedro lived and died in colonial Guatemala in the 1600s. After leaving the Jesuit seminary in Antigua before taking formal orders, he joined the secular Franciscan order and founded his own social-service mission loosely affiliated with the Church ("St. Pedro").

6. His blindness, name, and angelic visions connect Milton to the English poet John Milton (1608–74), who, also blind, wrote the epic poem *Paradise Lost* in 1667 and was, like Abuelo Milton, a fiercely outspoken, political critic. The name also pays homage to Rolando Hinojosa's *Partners in Crime* (1985). That novel, part of Hinojosa's *Klail City* cycle, deals with drug violence and corruption along the U.S.-Mexico border and is a pioneering work of Chicano detective fiction. John Milton Crossland is a blind African American sharecropper who finds the first of many corpses in the novel but passes away before the mystery is unraveled.

7. Gabo refers here to the Columbian novelist Gabriel García Márquez's *Cien años de soledad* (1967), which chronicles the Buendía family history and that of the fictional town, Macondo, where they live.

8. All references to *Sapogonia* are to the 1994 Anchor reprint edition.

9. Michael McKeon's *Theory of the Novel* remains an excellent source for the novel's history as well as an overview of theoretical approaches to the genre.

10. In *Nationalism*, Ernst Gellner succinctly identifies two competing definitions of nation. In the first, which he calls modernist, the nation is seen as a nineteenth-century, capitalist construct; in the second, primordialist, the nation is understood as a diachronic community of shared ethnicity, land, and history. *Sapogonia's* vacillation between these two poles might be read as simply a sign of the novel's own inconsistencies. According to Castillo, when she learned Bilingual Press intended to publish *Sapogonia* without giving her the chance to edit and revise, she attempted, unsuccessfully, to pull it and consequently always "felt uncomfortable about that edition." When Doubleday bought the book from Bilingual Press and decided to republish it in 1994, Castillo was able to perform some minor edits, which she describes as "liposuction and a facelift," but she still sees the book as her "middle child . . . the most neglected," which she "would not have published . . . as it was" (26). The 1994 edits *are* minor and do not significantly change the story, yet the

novel's slippery definitions of nation cannot be attributed to that alone and deserve close attention.

11. In a 1987 lecture Castillo speaks of female sexuality as "tied into the economic system of the GNP figures of the countries of the world" ("In My Country" 4).

12. In an interview with Hector Torres, for example, Castillo defines *Sapogonia* as primarily an exploration of male consciousness. She says, "I think that he [Máximo] is a representative, in many ways, of a particular time in our history. . . . [C]oming from the early Chicano/Latino Movement, which was dominated by men, I was compelled to understand this individual" (183).

13. "Migra" is Mexican Spanish for "immigration police."

14. See Chapter 6, especially note 6, for more on the serial murders of women in Ciudad Juárez, Mexico, which have been occurring since 1993, and which Miguel, in *The Guardians*, links to the increasing violence along the border and the fact that criminals operate there with virtual impunity.

15. See Chapter 6, especially note 9, for more on the White Brigade of government-trained operatives who, it is alleged, now put their training toward criminal ends.

16. See Chapter 3 for more on the Mexican Revolution's internal power struggles and Flores Magón's anarchist platform.

17. See, for example, Camp, who argues that *The Guardians* reads "like a newspaper editorial" that detracts from "her characters' all-too-human experiences" (36), and Ciolkowski, who sees Regina's "utopian musings" as expressions of "anger and frustration" more than "hope for the future" (8C).

6 / Border Patrol as Global Surveillance

1. Many scholars have written about the difficulty of representing 9/11 in fiction. Ann Keniston and Jeanne Quinn begin their anthology, *Literature After 9/11*, with a meditation on how difficult it has been to adequately memorialize the fallen towers. "[N]o one wants 9/11 to be misrepresented" (1), they write, and yet, the full meaning of the towers' absence is impossible to represent. Similarly, W. J. T. Mitchell, writing in October 2001, opines, "There is nothing quite so irritating at a moment like this as the pose of critical certainty" (570). While the former comfortably inhabit the space of not knowing, Mitchell holds out the promise of, if not knowledge, then at least "new ways of thinking" (571). Fredric Jameson, also writing shortly after the attacks, warns, like Mitchell, against a too-easy reading of 9/11. He urges the importance of remembering that historical events do not happen just once "but extend into a before and after of historical time that only gradually unfolds, to disclose the full dimensions of the historicity of the event" (301). We cannot fix meaning to 9/11, not because meaning is elusive or because our desire to know supersedes the content of the event but because meaning emerges and shifts over time.

2. Soja's *Postmodern Geographies* (1989), with its assertion that "space more than time hides consequences from us" (1), inaugurated a school of critical geography that investigated affective constructions of space and place. Working directly from Soja's insights, in *Barrio-Logos* Raúl Villa illuminates Chicana/os' cultural and political engagements with spatial colonization. Writing specifically about Chicanas and the production of space, Mary Pat Brady concurs that "places are processes, not static locales" (12) and that these processes depend on ideologies of race.

3. I am indebted here to Yi-Fu Tuan's work on space as a product of human

interactions; he defines places as nodes of security like home, school, or work, the movement between which gives subjects a psychological sense of space. As our repertoire of places diversifies, the scope of our emotional geography broadens (6). Movement through space transforms locations into places to which we feel attached, and that continual movement imparts a temporality to space such that it corresponds to our own histories within it (119).

4. Many early writers of detective fiction followed in the footsteps Edgar Allan Poe's C. Auguste Dupin, who combines the rational and irrational with his comforting exercises in ratiocination. These relatively conservative writers set their stories in bourgeois communities, where outside threats are resolved and contained in an ingenious bout of puzzle solving. Their novels never achieved as great a readership in the United States as they did in Britain. The turn to dime novels in the United States in the 1880s was, in part, a rejection of the British tradition and gave rise to a new group of U.S. writers responding directly to British fiction's inability to treat the realities of the postwar United States in the 1920s and 1930s. "Hardboiled" private detectives like Sam Spade (who first appeared in 1930 in Dashiell Hammett's *The Maltese Flacon*) and Phillip Marlowe (who debuted in 1939 in Raymond Chandler's *The Big Sleep*) inhabit a world where "American city wastelands replace the idyllic countryside settings of the British detective novel" (Tani 22). These detectives are not solving intellectual riddles, as was Dupin, but grappling with "a quest for truth" in a morally complex world, devoid of spirituality, light years away from Britain (Tani 23).

5. Ralph Rodriguez, for example, reads Chicana/o detective fiction as a tool that Chicana/o writers have used "to understand the shifting political, social, cultural, and identitarian terrain of the post-nationalist [civil rights] period" (5). Rodriguez reads Chicana/o detective fiction as an "identity project" (8) that, as Dorothea Fisher-Hornung and Monika Mueller assert, combines epistemologies of crime with epistemologies of self (320).

6. Since 1993 hundreds of women have been found dead, mutilated, and with stark evidence of torture in Ciudad Juárez and its environs. Though arrests have been made and theories abound, the crimes continue and remain unsolved. The victims have all had similar physical features, and most have been employed in the *maquilas* (factories) along the El Paso–Ciudad Juárez border.

7. See, for example, "The Maquiladora Murders, 1993–2003." There, Gaspar de Alba traces multiple theories of the crimes and correlates the criminal uncertainty to the confusion among NGOs that are, problematically, aiding victims and their families while simultaneously profiting financially from the global attention Juárez has received since the early 2000s.

8. *Maquilas* (or *maquiladoras*) are foreign-owned factories, located primarily in Mexican border towns, which import material duty-free with the caveat that all finished products be exported from Mexico. With Mexico's establishment in 1965 of the Border Industrialization Program, *maquilas* emerged as a solution to high Mexican unemployment, but they ultimately benefit foreign corporations, including, but not limited to, those based in the United States, much more than the Mexican people. Their appeal lies in low wages, lack of labor or environmental regulations, and extremely low taxes.

9. The Mexican government denied for decades that there was ever such a "dirty war," claiming, much as they would later about the Juárez murders, that the White

Brigade was a myth. Denial was impossible after a draft of a secret report called *The White Book* was leaked to the international press in 2006. In it, the special prosecutor appointed by the Mexican government documented the human rights abuses committed by the Institutional Revolutionary Party (PRI), which ruled Mexico for nearly seventy years (Thompson). *The White Book* alleged that in 1970, as part of Mexico's dirty war, President Luis Echevarría and defense minister Hermenegildo Díaz ordered a comprehensive anti-insurgency campaign involving rape, torture, and looting (Valdez 194).

10. The Carrillo Fuentes family heads the Juárez Cartel, which controls one of the primary routes for narcotics into the United States.

11. Much debate surrounds this crash. The U.S. government maintains the recovered wreckage was of a high-altitude surveillance balloon, while UFO theorists contend the government is keeping alien spacecraft and bodies under wraps. The crash has received significant cinematic, television, and literary treatment, and a festival is held each July at the crash site.

12. For example, the Border Protection, Anti-terrorism, and Illegal Immigration Control Act (H.R. 4437, also known as the "Sensenbrenner Bill"), which Wisconsin representative James Sensenbrenner introduced in the U.S. House in 2005, passed (239 to 182), only to fail in the Senate. Among the many draconian provisions in the bill was a prohibition against providing assistance to the undocumented.

13. Arjun Appadurai's *Modernity at Large* (1996) is still the classic example of this approach. Appadurai argues that the new world order will be characterized by diasporic public spheres that will redirect the public focus from consumers and producers, surpluses and deficits, or the push-pull of migration theory toward a vision of the global economy as a series of intersecting "scapes" of people, media, technology, finance, and ideas.

14. In her article "Experiments with Freedom," Ong argues against the possibility of global citizenship, primarily because the "neoliberal ethical regime" that creates the idea of the cosmopolitical relies on a construction of citizenship as an ethics of the self rather than of community (237). She asserts further that "Humanists continue to uphold human rights as a global ideal, but they should not thereby develop willful blindspots to actually existing transnational politics," including selfish pursuits of freedom, money, and the violent realization of exclusivist identities (242).

Bibliography

Archival Materials

Alurista. "History of Aztlán." Alurista Papers, Benson Latin American Collection, General Libraries, University of Texas at Austin.

Article about Vallejo in Mexico. Empáran's typed notes from article published in City of Mexico *Monitor Republican*. June 27, 1877. Empáran Papers.

Bancroft, Hubert Howe. Letter to Platon Vallejo. November 12, 1915. Hubert Howe Bancroft Papers: Additions. BANC MSS 73/37 c. Bancroft Library. University of California, Berkeley.

Bolívar, Simón. Letter to José Antonio Paes. September 26, 1822. Vallejo Family Papers, Sonoma.

Castillo, Ana. "In My Country: The Writer-in-Progress." Ana Castillo Papers, CEMA 2, Special Collections, University of California, Santa Barbara.

Castro, Victor. *Memorial of Victor Castro, Augustin Alvarado, and M. G. Vallejo to American and Mexican Joint Commission*. Vallejo Family Papers, Berkeley.

Cerruti, Enrique. Letter to H. H. Bancroft. March 3, 1874. Bancroft: Records of the Library. Bancroft Library, University of California, Berkeley.

———. "Ramblings in California." BANC MSS C-E 115. Bancroft Library, University of California, Berkeley.

Hubert Howe Bancroft: Records of the Library and Publishing Companies 1864–1910. BANC MSS B-C 7. Bancroft Library, University of California, Berkeley.

Invitación a una fiesta en commemoracion de la independencia de Chile. Vallejo Family Papers, Sonoma.

"Letter from Washington: Unpublished History of the Mexican War." Empáran's typed notes from article published in *Daily Evening Post*, December 22, 1877. Empáran Papers.

Madie Brown Empáran Papers. Sonoma State Historic Park, California State Parks, Sonoma.

Vallejo Family Papers. Sonoma State Historic Park, California State Parks, Sonoma.

Vallejo Family Papers 1832–89. BANC MSS C-B 441. Bancroft Library, University of California, Berkeley.

Vallejo, Mariano Guadalupe. *Historical and Personal Memoirs Relating to Alta California*. Vols. 1–5. Trans. Earl Hewitt. TS. BANC MSS CD 17–21. Bancroft Library, University of California, Berkeley.

——. Letters to Francisca Vallejo. March 20, 1865, April 30, 1865. Empáran Papers.

——. Letter to Enrique Cerruti. April 21, 1875. Bancroft: Records of the Library.

——. Letter to Platon Vallejo. October 10, 1876. Empáran Papers.

——. Letter to Francisca Vallejo. August 20, 1877. Vallejo Family Papers, Berkeley.

——. Letter to Adela Vallejo. August 30, 1877. Vallejo Family Papers, Berkeley.

——. Letter to Platon Vallejo. March 19, 1879. Vallejo Family Papers, Berkeley.

——. *Recuerdos Historicos y Personales Tocante á la Alta California, Escritos por Mariano G. Vallejo, Commandante General que fué de la Alta California desde el año de 1836 hasta el de 1842, Historia Política del País, 1769–1849, Costumbres de Los Californios, Apuntes biográficos de Personas Notables.* Vols. 1–5. BANC MSS CD 17–21. Bancroft Library, University of California, Berkeley.

Published Books and Articles

Acevedo, Mario. *The Nymphos of Rocky Flats: A Novel.* New York: Rayo, 2006.

——. *The Undead Kama Sutra.* New York: Eos, 2008.

Acosta, Oscar. *The Revolt of the Cockroach People.* 1973. New York: Vintage Books, 1989.

Adams, Rachel. "At the Borders of American Crime Fiction." In *Shades of the Planet: American Literature as World Literature*, ed. Wai-chee Dimock and Lawrence Buell. Princeton, N.J.: Princeton University Press, 2007. 249–73.

——. *Continental Divides: Remapping the Cultures of North America.* Chicago: University of Chicago Press, 2009.

Alexander, M. Jacqui. *Pedagogies of Crossing: Meditations on Feminism, Sexual Politics, Memory, and the Sacred.* Durham, N.C.: Duke University Press, 2005.

Almaguer, Tómas. *Racial Fault Lines: The Historical Origins of White Supremacy in California.* Berkeley: University of California Press, 1994.

Alurista: A Chicano Poet. Dir. Joe Torres. Television. Prod. Tony Brun. 1976.

Ammons, Elizabeth. *Conflicting Stories: American Women Writers at the Turn into the Twentieth Century*. New York: Oxford University Press, 1992.

Amoore, Louis, Stephen Marmura, and Mark B. Salter. "Editorial: Smart Borders and Mobilities: Spaces, Zones, Enclosures." *Surveillance & Society* 5.2 (2008): 96–101.

Anaya, Rudolfo, and Francisco Lomeli. *Aztlán: Essays on the Chicano Homeland*. 1989. Albuquerque: University of New Mexico Press, 1993.

Anzaldúa, Gloria. *Borderlands/La Frontera*. San Francisco: Spinsters/Aunt Lute, 1987.

Appadurai, Arjun. *Modernity at Large: Cultural Dimensions of Globalization*. Minneapolis: University of Minnesota Press, 1996.

Archibold, Randal C. "Budget Cut for Fence on U.S.-Mexico Border." *New York Times*, March 16, 2010, http://www.nytimes.com.

Ardao, Arturo. "Panamericanismo y Latinoamericanismo." In *America Latina en Sus Ideas*, ed. Leopoldo Zea. México, D.F.: Siglo XXI Editores, 1986. 157–71.

Asbury, Herbert. *The Barbary Coast: An Informal History of the San Francisco Underworld*. 1933. New York: Thunder's Mouth Press, 2002.

Bal, Mieke. *Narratology: Introduction to the Theory of Narrative*. Toronto: University of Toronto Press, 1985.

Balibar, Étienne. "Racism and Nationalism." In *Race, Nation, Class: Ambiguous Identities*. Ed. Étienne Balibar and Immanuel Wallerstein. New York: Verso, 1991.

Bancroft, Hubert Howe. *California Pastoral, 1769–1848*. Vol. 34 of *The Works of Hubert Bancroft*. San Francisco: The History Company, 1888.

———. *History of California, Volumes I–VII*. Vols. 18–24 of *The Works of Hubert Bancroft*. San Francisco: A. L. Bancroft and Company, 1884–90.

———. *Literary Industries: A Memoir*. San Francisco: The History Company, 1890.

———. *Popular Tribunals*. Vols. 31–32 of *The Works of Hubert Bancroft*. San Francisco: The History Company, 1887.

Bauer, Ralph. "The Hemispheric Genealogies of 'Race': Creolization and the Cultural Geography of Colonial Difference Across the Eighteenth-Century Americas." In *Hemispheric American Studies*, ed. Caroline Levander and Robert Levine. New Brunswick, N.J.: Rutgers University Press, 2008. 36–56.

———. "Hemispheric Studies." *PMLA* 124.1 (2009): 234–50.

Bolívar, Simón. "The Jamaica Letter: Response from a South American to a Gentleman from This Island." September 6, 1815. Trans. Frederick H. Fornoff. In *El Libertador: Writings of Simón Bolívar*, ed. David Bushnell. Oxford: Oxford University Press, 2003. 12–30.

Brady, Mary Pat. *Extinct Lands, Temporal Geographies: Chicana Literature and the Urgency of Space*. Durham, N.C.: Duke University Press, 2002.

Brickhouse, Anna. *Transamerican Literary Relations and the Nineteenth-Century Public Sphere.* New York: Cambridge University Press, 2004.

Brintrup, Lilianet. *Viaje y Escritura: Viajeros Romanticos Chilenos.* New York: Peter Lang, 1992.

Bushnell, David. Introduction to *El Libertador: Writings of Simón Bolívar.* Ed. David Bushnell. Oxford: Oxford University Press, 2003. xxvii–lii.

Cabeza de Vaca, Alvar Núñez. *The Narrative of Cabeza De Vaca.* Trans. Rolena Adorno and Patrick Charles Pautz. Lincoln: University of Nebraska Press, 2003.

Camp, Jennie. "The Guardians." *Rocky Mountain News,* August 24, 2007, sec. Spotlight: 36.

"Capuchin." *Encyclopaedia Britannica Online.* June 16, 2009. http://www.search.eb.com/eb/article-9020196.

Castillo, Ana. "Extraordinarily Woman." In *Goddess of the Americas: Writings on the Virgin of Guadalupe,* ed. Ana Castillo. New York: Riverhead Books, 1997. 72–80.

———. *The Guardians.* New York: Random House, 2007.

———. *Massacre of the Dreamers: Essays on Xicanisma.* Albuquerque: University of New Mexico Press, 1994.

———. *Peel My Love Like an Onion: A Novel.* New York: Anchor Books, 2000.

———. *Sapogonia: An Anti-Romance in 3/8 Meter.* 1990. New York: Anchor Books, 1994.

———. *So Far from God: A Novel.* New York: W. W. Norton, 1993.

Caughey, John Walton. *Hubert Howe Bancroft: Historian of the West.* Berkeley: University of California Press, 1946.

Cerruti, Henry. *Ramblings in California: The Adventures of Henry Cerruti.* Ed. Margaret Mollins and Virginia E. Thickens. Berkeley, Calif.: Friends of the Bancroft Library, 1954.

Chai, Caymar, Guillermo Verdecchia, and Marcus Youssef. *The Adventures of Ali and Ali and the Axes of Evil.* Vancouver: Talon Books, 2005.

Chandler, Raymond. *The Big Sleep.* New York: Alfred A. Knopf, 1939.

Charlesworth, James. *The Good and Evil Serpent: How a Universal Symbol Became Christianized.* New Haven, Conn.: Yale University Press, 2009.

Ciolkowski, Laura. "'Guardians' Challenges the U.S.-Mexico Divide." *Boston Globe,* October 4, 2007, sec. Style and Arts: 8C.

Comstock, Esther J. *A True Story of Early California: Vallejo and the Four Flags.* Grass Valley, Calif.: Comstock Bonanza Press, 1979.

Cook, Robert. *Civil War America: Making a Nation.* New York: Longman, 2004.

Cooper Alarcón, Daniel. *The Aztec Palimpsest: Mexico in the Modern Imagination.* Tucson: University of Arizona Press, 1997.

Cotera, María Eugenia. "Hombres Necios: A Critical Epilogue." In González and Raleigh, *Caballero.* 339–46.

———. "Native Speakers: A Comparative Analysis of the Ethnographic and

Literary Writing of Ella Cara Deloria and Jovita González." Ph.D. diss., Stanford University, 2000.

———. *Native Speakers: Ella Deloria, Zora Neale Hurston, Jovita González, and the Poetics of Culture.* Austin: University of Texas Press, 2008.

Cros Sandoval, Mercedes. *Worldview, the Orichas, and Santería: Africa to Cuba and Beyond.* Gainesville: University Press of Florida, 2006.

Crowley, Frances. *Domingo Faustino Sarmiento.* Twayne's World Authors Series. Vol. 156. New York: Twayne, 1972.

Darío, Rubén. "Modernismo." Trans. Greg Simon, Andrew Hurley, and Steven F. White. In *Rubén Darío: Selected Writings*, ed. Ilan Stavans. New York: Penguin Group, 2005. 369–74.

Dary, David. *The Oregon Trail: An American Saga.* Oxford: Oxford University Press, 2004.

de Lint, Willem. "The Security Double Take: The Political, Simulation and the Border." *Surveillance & Society* 5.2 (2008): 166–87.

Delpar, Helen. *The Enormous Vogue of Things Mexican: Cultural Relations Between the United States and Mexico, 1920–1935.* Tuscaloosa: University of Alabama Press, 1992.

Dorn, Georgette Massey. "Sarmiento, the United States, and Public Education." In *Sarmiento and His Argentina*, ed. Joseph T. Criscenti. Boulder, Colo.: Lynne Rienner Publishers, 1993. 77–89.

Empáran, Madie Brown. *The Vallejos of California.* San Francisco: Gleeson Library Associates, 1968.

Engs, Ruth C. *Clean Living Movements: American Cycles of Health Reform.* Westport, Conn.: Praeger, 2000.

Fabian, Johannes. *Time and the Other: How Anthropology Makes Its Object.* New York: Columbia University Press, 1983.

Faugsted, George Edward. *The Chilenos in the California Gold Rush.* San Francisco: R and E Research Associates, 1973.

Fernandez, Raul A., and Gilbert G. Gonzalez. *A Century of Chicano History: Empire, Nations, and Migration.* New York: Routledge, 2003.

Fischer-Hornung, Dorothea, and Monika Mueller, eds. *Sleuthing Ethnicity: The Detective in Multiethnic Crime Fiction.* London: Associated University Press, 2003.

Flores Magón, Ricardo, Charles Bufe, and Mitchell Cowen Verter. *Dreams of Freedom: A Ricardo Flores Magón Reader.* Oakland, Calif.: AK Press, 2005.

Fregoso, Rosa Linda. "'We Want Them Alive!': The Politics and Culture of Human Rights." *Social Identities* 12.2 (2006): 109–38.

García, Alma M, ed. *Chicana Feminist Thought: The Basic Historical Writings.* New York: Routledge, 1997.

García Márquez, Gabriel. *Cien Años De Soledad.* Buenos Aires: Editorial Sudamericana, 1967.

Garza-Falcón, Leticia. *Gente Decente: A Borderlands Response to the Rhetoric of Dominance.* Austin: University of Texas Press, 1998.

Gaspar de Alba, Alicia. *Desert Blood: The Juárez Murders*. Houston: Arte Público Press, 2005.

———. "The Maquiladora Murders, 1993–2003." *Aztlán* 28.2 (2003): 1–17.

Gellner, Ernest. *Nationalism*. London: Weidenfeld and Nicolson, 1997.

Giacobbi, Steve. *Chile and Her Argonauts in the Gold Rush, 1848–1856*. Saratoga, Calif.: R and E Research Associates, 1974.

Godlewska, Anne. "The Idea of the Map." In *Ten Geographic Ideas That Changed the World*, ed. Susan Hanson. New Brunswick, N.J.: Rutgers University Press, 1997. 15–39.

Gómez-Peña, Guillermo. *ethno-techno: writings on performance, activism, and pedagogy*. Ed. Elaine Peña. New York: Routledge, 2005.

———. "The New Barbarians: A Declaration of Poetic Disobedience from the New Border." Prognoses on Movement, October 25, 2007. http://www.prognosen-ueber-bewegungen.de/en/the-project (accessed May 4, 2009).

Gonzales, Patricia, and Roberto Rodriguez. "The Story of Maps: Mesoamerica in North America." 2004. http://www.chavez.ucla.edu/Aztlanahuac/About%20the%20Aztlanahuac%20exhibit.htm (accessed April 28, 2009).

González, Jovita, and Eve Raleigh. *Caballero: A Historical Novel*. College Station: Texas A&M University Press, 1996.

———. *Dew on the Thorn*. Ed. José Eduardo Limón. Houston: Arte Público Press, 1997.

———. *Life Along the Border: A Landmark Tejana Thesis*. Ed. María Eugenia Cotera. College Station: Texas A&M University Press, 2006.

Goodchild, Michael F. "Geographic Information Systems." In *Ten Geographic Ideas That Changed the World*, ed. Susan Hanson. New Brunswick, N.J.: Rutgers University Press, 1997. 60–86.

Gordon, Joan, and Veronica Hollinger. *Blood Read: The Vampire as Metaphor in Contemporary Culture*. Philadelphia: University of Pennsylvania Press, 1997.

Grant, Madison. *The Passing of the Great Race, or, The Racial Basis of European History*. New York: C. Scribner, 1916.

Gruesz, Kirsten Silva. *Ambassadors of Culture: The Transamerican Origins of Latino Writing*. Princeton, N.J.: Princeton University Press, 2002.

Halberstam, Judith. *In a Queer Time and Place: Transgender Bodies, Subcultural Lives*. New York: New York University Press, 2005.

Hammett, Dashiell. *The Maltese Falcon*. New York: A. A. Knopf, 1930.

Harvey, David. *Social Justice and the City*. London: Edward Arnold, 1973.

Henson, Margaret Sweet. *Lorenzo de Zavala: The Pragmatic Idealist*. Fort Worth: Texas Christian University Press, 1996.

Hernández, Ellie D. *Postnationalism in Chicana/o Literature and Culture*. Austin: University of Texas Press, 2009.

The Historical Works of Hubert Howe Bancroft in Their Relation to the Progress and Destiny of the Pacific States. San Francisco, 1886.

Hubbard, Phil, Rob Kitchin, and Gill Valentine. *Key Thinkers on Space and Place*. Thousand Oaks, Calif.: Sage Publications, 2004.

Humboldt, Alexander von, and Aimé Bonpland. *Personal Narrative of Travels to the Equinoctial Regions of America, During the Years 1799–1804*. Trans. Thomasina Ross. Bohn's Scientific Library. 3 vols. London: G. Bell, 1889.

Jameson, Fredric. "The Dialectics of Disaster." *South Atlantic Quarterly* 101.2 (2002): 297–304.

Jefferson, Thomas. *Notes on the State of Virginia: With Related Documents*. Ed. David Waldstreicher. Boston: Bedford/St. Martins, 2002.

Juárez, Nicandro F. "José Vasconcelos and La Raza Cósmica." *Aztlán* 3.1 (1973): 51–82.

Junta de Fomento de Californias. *Coleccion de Los Principales Trabajos en Que se ha Ocupado La Junta Nombrada para Meditar y Proponer al Supremo Gobierno Los Medios Mas Necesarios para Promover el Progreso de La Cultura y Civilizacion de Los Territorios De La Alta Y de La Baja California*. Mexico: Galvan, 1827.

Kanellos, Nicolás. "El Clamor Público: Resisting the American Empire." *California Historical Society Quarterly* 84.2 (2007): 10–18.

———. "*Cronistas* and Satire in Early Twentieth Century Hispanic Newspapers." *MELUS* 23.1 (1988): 3–25.

———. Introducción to *Las Aventuras de Don Chipote, O, Cuando Los Pericos Mamen*. Houston: Arte Público Press, 1998. v–xvi.

———. Introduction to *The Adventures of Don Chipote, or, When Parrots Breast-Feed*. Houston: Arte Público Press, 2000. 1–17.

———. "Recovering and Re-Constructing Early Twentieth-Century Hispanic Immigrant Print Culture in the U.S." *American Literary History* 19 (2007): 438–55.

Kant, Immanuel. "To Perpetual Peace: A Philosophical Sketch." Trans. Ted Humphrey. In *Perpetual Peace and Other Essays*. 1795. Ed. Ted Humphrey. Indianapolis: Hackett Publishing Company, 1983. 107–44.

Kaplan, Amy, and Donald E. Pease, eds. *Cultures of United States Imperialism*. New Americanists. Durham, N.C.: Duke University Press, 1993.

Katra, William H. *The Argentine Generation of 1837: Echeverría, Alberdi, Sarmiento, Mitre*. Madison, N.J.: Fairleigh Dickinson University Press, 1996.

Kaye, Jeffrey. "Obama's Deportations: A Reflection of America's Fickle Welcome Mat." *Huffington Post,* March 23, 2010. http://www.huffingtonpost.com/.

Kemble, John Haskell. "The Panama Route to the Pacific Coast, 1848–1869." *Pacific Historical Review* 7.1 (1938): 1–13.

Keniston, Ann, and Jeanne Quinn, eds. *Literature After 9/11*. New York: Routledge, 2008.

Kennedy, Liam. "Black Noir: Race and Urban Space in Walter Mosely's Detective Fiction." In *Diversity and Detective Fiction*, ed. Kathleen Gregory Klein. Bowling Green: Bowling Green State University Press, 1999. 224–39.

Kreneck, Thomas H. "Recovering the 'Lost' Manuscripts of Jovita González: The Production of South Texas Mexican-American Literature." *Texas Library Journal* 74 (1998): 76–79.

Lamothe, Daphne Mary. *Inventing the New Negro: Narrative, Culture, and Ethnography.* Philadelphia: University of Pennsylvania Press, 2008.

Lefebvre, Henri. *The Production of Space.* 1974. Trans. Donald Nicholson-Smith. Oxford: Blackwell, 1991.

Lefebvre, Henri, et al. *Henri Lefebvre: Key Writings.* New York: Continuum, 2003.

Limón, José Eduardo. "Border Literary Histories, Globalization, and Critical Regionalism." *American Literary History* 20.1–2 (2008): 160–82.

———. *Dancing with the Devil: Society and Cultural Poetics in Mexican-American South Texas.* Madison: University of Wisconsin Press, 1994.

———. Introduction to González and Raleigh, *Caballero.* xii–xxvi.

Limón, Martin. *The Door to Bitterness.* New York: Soho, 2005.

———. *Jade Lady Burning.* New York: Soho, 1992.

López, Miguel R. *Chicano Timespace: The Poetry and Politics of Ricardo Sánchez.* College Station: Texas A&M University Press, 2001.

López, Tiffany Ana. "María Cristina Mena: Turn-of-the-Century La Malinche, and Other Tales of Cultural (Re)Construction." In *Tricksterism in Turn-of-the-Century American Literature: A Multicultural Perspective*, ed. Elizabeth Ammons and Annette White Parks. Hanover, N.H.: University Press of New England, 1994. 21–45.

Loveman, Brian. Introduction to *Times Gone By: Memoirs of a Man of Action.* Oxford: Oxford University Press, 2003. xvii–xxxii.

Ludmer, Josefina. *El Genero Gauchesco: Un Tratado Sobre La Patria.* Buenos Aires: Editorial Sudamericana, 1988.

Lukács, György. *The Theory of the Novel: A Historico-Philosophical Essay on the Forms of Great Epic Literature.* 1920. Cambridge, Mass.: MIT Press, 1971.

Marentes, Luis A. *José Vasconcelos and the Writing of the Mexican Revolution.* New York: Twayne, 2000.

Marquez, Benjamin. *LULAC: The Evolution of a Mexican American Political Organization.* Austin: University of Texas Press, 1993.

Martí, José. "Our America." Trans. Esther Allen. In *José Martí: Selected Writings.* 1891. Ed. Esther Allen. New York: Penguin Group, 2002. 288–96.

Martín-Rodríguez, Manuel M. *Life in Search of Readers: Reading (in) Chicano/a Literature.* Albuquerque: University of New Mexico Press, 2003.

McCaffery, John. *The Friar of San Giovanni: Tales of Padre Pío.* London: Darton, Longman and Todd, 1980.

McCann, Sean. *Gumshoe America: Hard-Boiled Crime Fiction and the Rise and Fall of New Deal Liberalism.* Durham, N.C.: Duke University Press, 2000.

McKeon, Michael, ed. *Theory of the Novel: A Historical Approach*. Baltimore: Johns Hopkins University Press, 2000.

Melosi, Martin V. *The Sanitary City: Environmental Services in Urban America from Colonial Times to the Present*. Pittsburgh: University of Pittsburgh Press, 2008.

Mena, María Cristina. *The Collected Stories of María Cristina Mena*. Ed. Amy Doherty. Houston: Arte Público Press, 1997.

Menchaca, Martha. *Recovering History, Constructing Race: The Indian, Black, and White Roots of Mexican Americans*. Austin: University of Texas Press, 2001.

Mexal, Stephen J. "The Logic of Liberalism: Lorenzo de Zavala's Transcultural Politics." *MELUS* 32.2 (2007): 79–106.

Mignolo, Walter. "Citizenship, Knowledge, and the Limits of Humanity." *American Literary History* 18.2 (2006): 312–31.

———. *The Idea of Latin America*. Blackwell Manifestos. Oxford: Blackwell, 2005.

Milligan, Bryce. "An Interview with Ana Castillo." *South Central Review: The Journal of the South Central Modern Language Association* 16.1 (1999): 19–29.

Mitchell, W. J. T. "911: Criticism and Crisis." *Critical Inquiry* 28 (2002): 567–72.

Montejano, David. *Anglos and Mexicans in the Making of Texas, 1836–1986*. Austin: University of Texas Press, 1987.

Moreno, Julio. *Yankee Don't Go Home!: Mexican Nationalism, American Business Culture, and the Shaping of Modern Mexico, 1920–1950*. Chapel Hill: University of North Carolina Press, 2003.

Moya, Paula M. L., and Ramón Saldívar. "Fictions of the Trans-American Imaginary." *Modern Fiction Studies* 59.1 (2003): 1–18.

Nakano Glenn, Evelyn. *Unequal Freedom: How Race and Gender Shaped American Citizenship and Labor*. Cambridge, Mass.: Harvard University Press, 2002.

Novick, Peter. *That Noble Dream: The "Objectivity Question" and the American Historical Profession*. Cambridge: Cambridge University Press, 1988.

Oak, Henry L. *"Literary Industries" in a New Light: A Statement of the Authorship of Bancroft's Native Races and History of the Pacific States, With Comments on Those Works and the System by Which They Were Written; and the Labors Of Assistants. The Whole Being a Reply to Statements and Claims in the Literary Industries*. San Francisco: Bacon Printing Company, 1893.

Obama, Barack. "Barack Obama's Speech on Race." *New York Times*, March 18, 2008. http://www.nytimes.com/.

Omi, Michael, and Howard Winant. *Racial Formation in the United States: From the 1960s to the 1990s*. 1986. New York: Routledge. 1994.

Ong, Aihwa. "Experiments with Freedom: Milieus of the Human." *American Literary History* 18.2 (2006): 229–44.

———. *Neoliberalism as Exception: Mutations in Citizenship and Sovereignty.* Durham, N.C.: Duke University Press, 2006.

Overstreet, Deborah. *Not Your Mother's Vampire: Vampires in Young Adult Fiction.* Lanham, Md.: Scarecrow Press, 2006.

Padilla, Genaro. *My History, Not Yours: The Formation of Mexican American Autobiography.* Madison: University of Wisconsin Press, 1993.

Paredes, Américo. *"With His Pistol in His Hand": A Border Ballad and Its Hero.* 1958. Austin: University of Texas Press, 1994.

Paredes, Raymund A. "The Evolution of Chicano Literature." *MELUS* 5.2 (1978): 71–110.

Pepper, Andrew. *The Contemporary American Crime Novel: Race, Ethnicity, Gender, Class.* Edinburgh: Edinburgh University Press, 2000.

Peréz Rosales, Vicente. *Recuerdos del Pasado.* 1882. Havana, Cuba: Casa de las Américas, 1972.

———. *Times Gone By: Memoirs of a Man of Action.* 1882. Trans. John Polt. New York: Oxford University Press, 2003.

Pérez-Torres, Rafael. *Mestizaje: Critical Uses of Race in Chicano Culture.* Minneapolis: University of Minnesota Press, 2006.

Pitt, Leonard. *The Decline of the Californios.* 1966. Berkeley: University of California Press, 1996.

"El Plan Espiritual De Aztlán." In *Aztlán: Essays on the Chicano Homeland,* ed. Francisco Lomelí and Rudolfo Anaya. Albuquerque: University of New Mexico Press, 1991. 1–5.

La Pocha Nostra. "The Chica-Iranian Project: Orientalism Gone Wrong in Aztlán." *Gómez-Peña's La Pocha Nostra,* May 4, 2009. http://www.pochanostra.com/.

———. "Manifesto: In Permanent Progress." *Gómez-Peña's La Pocha Nostra,* May 4, 2009. http://www.pochanostra.com/.

Poovey, Mary. *Making a Social Body: British Cultural Formation, 1830–1864.* Chicago: University of Chicago Press, 1995.

Pratt, Mary Louise. *Imperial Eyes: Travel Writing and Transculturation.* New York: Routledge, 1992.

Radway, Janice. "What's in a Name?" *American Quarterly* 51.1 (1999): 1–32.

Ramos, Julio. *Divergent Modernities: Culture and Politics in Nineteenth-Century Latin America.* Trans. John D. Blanco. Durham, N.C.: Duke University Press, 2001.

Ramos, Manuel. "The Mario Acevedo Interview." Denver 2006. La Bloga. July 2, 2008. http://labloga.blogspot.com/2006/01/mario-acevedo-interview-and-justo.html.

Reddy, Maureen T. *Traces, Codes, and Clues: Reading Race in Crime Fiction.* New Brunswick, N.J.: Rutgers University Press, 2003.

Rivera, John-Michael. *The Emergence of Mexican America: Recovering Stories of Mexican Peoplehood in U.S. Culture.* New York: New York University Press, 2006.

Rockland, Michael Aaron. Introduction to *Travels in the United States in 1847*. Princeton, N.J.: Princeton University Press, 1970. 1–106.

Rodó, José Enrique. *Ariel*. 1900. Trans. Margaret Sayeres Peden. Austin: University of Texas Press, 1988.

Rodriguez, Ralph E. *Brown Gumshoes: Detective Fiction and the Search for Chicana/o Identity*. Austin: University of Texas Press, 2005.

Rosenus, Alan. *General Vallejo and the Advent of the Americans*. Berkeley, Calif.: Heyday Books. 1995.

Ruffinelli, Jorge. "Alurista: Una Larga Marcha Hacia Aztlán." *La Palabra y el Hombre: Revista de la Universidad Veracruzana* 17 (1976): 30–41.

Ruiz de Burton, María Amparo. *The Squatter and the Don*. 1885. Ed. Rosaura Sánchez and Beatrice Pita. Houston: Arte Público Press, 1992.

Saldívar, José David. *Border Matters: Remapping American Cultural Studies*. Berkeley: University of California Press, 1997.

Saldívar, Ramón. *The Borderlands of Culture: Américo Paredes and the Transnational Imaginary*. New Americanists. Durham, N.C.: Duke University Press, 2006.

Sánchez, Rosaura. *Telling Identities: The Californio Testimonios*. Berkeley: University of California Press, 1995.

Sarmiento, Domingo Faustino. *Facundo: Civilization and Barbarism: The First Complete English Translation*. 1845. Trans. Kathleen Ross. Berkeley: University of California Press, 2003.

———. *Travels in the United States in 1847*. Trans. Michael Aaron Rockland. Princeton, N.J.: Princeton University Press, 1970.

———. *Viajes por Europa, Africa, i América, 1845–1847*. Vol. 5 of *Obras de D. F. Sarmiento*. Ed. Luis Montt and Augusto Belin Sarmiento. Santiago de Chile: Imprenta Gutenberg, 1885.

Schmidt Camacho, Alicia R. *Migrant Imaginaries: Latino Cultural Politics in the U.S.-Mexico Borderlands*. New York: New York University Press, 2008.

Seaman, Donna. "Dividing Lines: Ana Castillo's Characters Struggle with National Boundaries as Well as Human Ones." *Chicago Tribune*, August 11, 2007, sec. Books: 4.

Sherrow, Victoria. *For Appearance's Sake: The Historical Encyclopedia of Good Looks, Beauty, and Grooming*. Westport, Conn.: Greenwood, 2001.

Shumway, Nicolas. *The Invention of Argentina*. Berkeley: University of California Press, 1991.

Skirius, John. "Vasconcelos and *México De Afuera*." *Aztlán* 7.3 (1978): 479–97.

Sleep Dealer. Dir. Alex Rivera. Perf. Luis Fernandez Peña, Luz Martinez, and Jacob Vargas. Maya Entertainment, 2008.

Sobchack, Vivian Carol. *Carnal Thoughts: Embodiment and Moving Image Culture*. Berkeley: University of California Press, 2004.

Society of California Pioneers. *Misrepresentations of Early California History Corrected: Proceedings of the Society of California Pioneers in Regard to Cer-*

tain *Misrepresentations of Men And Events in Early California History Made in the Works Of Hubert Howe Bancroft and Commonly Known as Bancroft's Histories.* San Francisco: Sterett Printing Company, 1894.

Soja, Edward W. *Postmodern Geographies: The Reassertion of Space in Critical Social Theory.* London: Verso, 1989.

———. *Thirdspace: Journeys to Los Angeles and Other Real-and-Imagined Places.* Cambridge, Mass.: Blackwell, 1996.

"St. Pedro De San José Betancur (1626–1667)." Podcast. June 2008. http://www.americancatholic.org/Features/SaintOfDay/default.asp?id=1357.

Stepan, Nancy. *The Hour of Eugenics: Race, Gender, and Nation in Latin America.* Ithaca, N.Y.: Cornell University Press, 1991.

Stephens, Michelle Ann. *Black Empire: The Masculine Global Imaginary of Caribbean Intellectuals in the United States, 1914–1962.* Durham, N.C.: Duke University Press, 2005.

Stern, Alexandra. *Eugenic Nation: Faults and Frontiers of Better Breeding in Modern America.* Berkeley: University of California Press, 2005.

Stoddard, Lothrop. *The Rising Tide of Color Against White World-Supremacy.* New York: Scribner, 1920.

Stoker, Bram. *Dracula.* Ed. Glennis Byron. 1897. Orchard Park, N.Y.: Broadview Press, 1998.

Tani, Stefano. *The Doomed Detective: The Contribution of the Detective Novel to Postmodern American and Italian Fiction.* Literary Structures. Carbondale: Southern Illinois University Press, 1984.

Tays, George. "Mariano Guadalupe Vallejo and Sonoma: A Biography and a History." *California Historical Society Quarterly* 27.3 (1938): 219–43.

Terris, Milton. "The Changing Relationships of Epidemiology and Society: The Robert Cruickshank Lecture." *Journal of Public Health Policy* 22.4 (2001): 441–63.

Thompson, Ginger. "Report on Mexican 'Dirty War' Details Abuse by Military." *New York Times,* February 26, 2006. http://www.nytimes.com/2006/02/27/international/americas/27mexico.html.

Torpey, John C. *The Invention of the Passport: Surveillance, Citizenship, and the State.* Cambridge: Cambridge University Press, 2000.

Torres, Hector Avalos. *Conversations with Contemporary Chicana and Chicano Writers.* Albuquerque: University of New Mexico Press, 2007.

Tuan, Yi-fu. *Space and Place: The Perspective of Experience.* Minneapolis: University of Minnesota Press, 1977.

Turner, John Kenneth. *Barbarous Mexico.* 1911. Austin: University of Texas Press, 1969.

Valdez, Diana Washington. *The Killing Fields: Harvest of Women: The Truth About Mexico's Bloody Border Legacy.* Los Angeles: Peace at the Border, 2006.

Vallejo, Mariano Guadalupe. "History of California—Letter from General

Vallejo—Historical Labors—He Places His Manuscripts at the Disposal of Hubert H. Bancroft." *Sonoma Democrat*, November 27, 1875, p. 1.

Vallejo, Platon Mariano Guadalupe. *Memoirs of the Vallejos: New Light on the History, Before and After the "Gringos" Came, Based on Original Documents and Recollections of Dr. Platon M. G. Vallejo.* 1914. Fairfield, Calif.: James D. Stevenson, 1994.

Vasconcelos, José. "Bolivarism y monroísmo." In *Obras Completas.* 1934. Vol. 2. México, D.F.: Libreros Mexicanos Unidos, 1958. 1305–1439.

———. *Breve historia de México.* México: Botas, 1937.

———. *The Cosmic Race/La Raza Cosmica.* 1925. Trans. Didier T. Jaén. Baltimore: Johns Hopkins University Press, 1997.

———. *Estudios indostánicos.* 1920. Madrid: Editorial Calleja, 1923.

Venegas, Daniel. *The Adventures of Don Chipote, or, When Parrots Breast-Feed.* Trans. Ethriam Cash Brammer. Houston: Arte Público Press, 2000.

———. *Las Aventuras de Don Chipote, O, Cuando Los Pericos Mamen.* Houston: Arte Público Press, 1998.

Ventura, Gabriela Baeza. *La Imagen de La Mujer en La Crónica del "México De Afuera."* Ciudad Juárez: Universidad Autónoma de Ciudad Juárez, 2006.

Verdecchia, Guillermo. *Fronteras Americanas: (American Borders).* Toronto: Coach House Press, 1993.

Verter, Mitchell Cowen. "Biographical Sketch." *Dreams of Freedom: A Ricardo Flores Magón Reader.* Oakland, Calif.: AK Press, 2005. 8–105.

Villa, Raúl. *Barrio-Logos: Space and Place in Urban Chicano Literature and Culture.* Austin: University of Texas Press, 2000.

Willis, Damien. "Anthony, N.M., Author Ana Castillo Talks About Life, Happiness, and Her New Book." *Las Cruces Sun-News*, September 25, 2008, sec. Sunlife.

Zavala, Lorenzo de. *Journey to the United States of North America/Viaje a Los Estados Unidos del Norte de America.* Trans. Wallace Woolsey. 1834. Houston: Arte Público Press, 2005.

Index

About the Author

Marissa K. López is Assistant Professor of English at the University of California, Los Angeles.